At the Borderline of Armageddon

How American Presidents Managed the Atom Bomb

James E. Goodby

ROWMAN & LITTLEFIELD PUBLISHERS, INC.
Lanham • Boulder • New York • Toronto • Oxford

ROWMAN & LITTLEFIELD PUBLISHERS, INC.

Published in the United States of America
by Rowman & Littlefield Publishers, Inc.
A wholly owned subsidiary of The Rowman & Littlefield Publishing Group, Inc.
4501 Forbes Boulevard, Suite 200, Lanham, Maryland 20706
www.rowmanlittlefield.com

PO Box 317
Oxford
OX2 9RU, UK

British Library Cataloguing in Publication Information Available

Library of Congress Cataloging-in-Publication Data

Goodby, James E.
  At the borderline of Armageddon : how American presidents managed the atom
bomb / James E. Goodby.
      p. cm.
  Includes bibliographical references and index.
  ISBN-13: 978-0-7425-5075-9 (cloth : alk. paper)
  ISBN-10: 0-7425-5075-3 (cloth : alk. paper)
  ISBN-13: 978-0-7425-5076-6 (pbk. : alk. paper)
  ISBN-10: 0-7425-5076-1 (pbk. : alk. paper)
  1. Nuclear weapons—United States. 2. United States—Military policy. 3. United
States—Politics and government—1945–1989. 4. United States—Politics and
government—1989– I. Title.
  UA23.G7258 2006
  355.02'170973—dc22   2005034609

Printed in the United States of America

∞™ The paper used in this publication meets the minimum requirements of
American National Standard for Information Sciences—Permanence of Paper for
Printed Library Materials, ANSI/NISO Z39.48-1992.

This book is dedicated to all those
unsung heroes who helped presidents do the right thing.

Contents

~

Preface

Presidents have many powers in the American system of government, but none is more consequential than their responsibilities regarding nuclear weapons. The choices they make can change the course of human history and affect the lives of billions of people. Consciously or not, American presidents have carried this burden as trustees not only of the American people but, in a real sense, as trustees for civilization.

In more prosaic ways also, presidents are not free agents. Laws and customs frame their responsibilities. Circumstances within and outside the United States determine the issues presidents must confront. Political, military, and technical advisers define presidential options. Congress and public opinion exercise powerful influences. Still, in the final analysis, no one in the American system has anything like the authority and the range of responsibilities for nuclear weapons that are vested in the president.

- They are commanders in chief and can send U.S. armed forces into actions that could invoke the question of nuclear weapons use.
- They are responsible for foreign policy and for upholding security commitments to other countries that may entail the use of nuclear weapons or the deployment of nuclear weapons.
- They carry the final authority for releasing nuclear weapons for use in combat. This has created requirements for command and control that are unique for nuclear weapons.

- They provide guidance for strategic doctrine and for nuclear targeting policy, which generates requirements for targets to be held at risk and the numbers and types of nuclear weapons that will be needed.
- They are the chief stewards of the U.S. nuclear weapons stockpile. They decide what goes into it and what can be retired.
- They initiate budget requests for nuclear weapons and nuclear delivery systems, including support for weapons laboratories and production facilities.
- They are the chief negotiators with other nations regarding controls on nuclear weapons, and they advocate with the Senate for ratification of treaties.
- They appoint all the top officials and senior military commanders who advise them and who carry out national policies regarding nuclear weapons.
- They are the primary educators of the American people on issues of nuclear policy. No one else has the authority and the audience comparable to what a president can muster. No one is in a better position to rally the public to particular points of view.

American presidents sometimes focus on hardware issues and sometimes on international negotiations. More recently their concern is terrorist ambitions to acquire nuclear weapons. Often, presidents delegate to others, especially on the more technical issues. But always the ultimate responsibility rests with them.

The history of the nuclear age is a vast subject and I have chosen to write about it from a particular point of view: issues that U.S. presidents have faced and how they dealt with them. In a course I taught at Georgetown University in 1986–1987, I used case studies to help my students relive the problems that presidents had to confront. Later, I revised and expanded the original set of case studies to bring the discussion up to the present time.

This book does not itemize every issue that crossed the desks of presidents of the nuclear age. Some issues that have been hotly debated elsewhere will be given short shrift here. But I have included some lesser-known decisions and actions that I think will show how presidents thought about these issues. This story is skewed from another angle: in cases where I was directly and personally involved, I have included details that are not generally known or available elsewhere.

I have had the advantage of considerable continuity in observing and interpreting events. Except for the first nine years of the nuclear era, I have been closely in touch with one or another aspect of nuclear policy at the national level throughout the sixty years since the Trinity test at Alamogordo,

New Mexico, and the bombing of Hiroshima and Nagasaki. A few of the scientists who worked on the Manhattan Project are still active, as are some of my colleagues from the State Department of long ago. So I will not claim the record for longevity, but there is a long record of involvement.

I became a member of the staff of the U.S. Atomic Energy Commission in July 1954 and was assigned to work with British representatives on procurement of uranium ore from foreign sources. This arrangement was created by U.S. President Franklin D. Roosevelt and British Prime Minister Winston Churchill on June 13, 1944. Soon, I gravitated to other issues: the establishment of the International Atomic Energy Agency; a U.N. study on the effects of ionizing radiation; the London disarmament talks; the Geneva surprise attack talks; the nuclear test ban negotiations. During this time I was briefly an assistant to John von Neumann, one of the most creative scientists of the twentieth century.

In 1960 I returned to the State Department, where I had started my Washington career in 1952. By 1961 I was working full-time on the comprehensive test ban treaty, as officer in charge of test ban negotiations. In 1963 a treaty was concluded that banned all tests except those conducted underground. I then moved to the secretary of state's Policy Planning Council, where I continued to work on nuclear issues, mainly of a military character. I was the first State Department representative on the National Security Council's Net Evaluation Subcommittee where, among other things, I helped with a study on the management and termination of nuclear war.

Assigned to the U.S. Mission to the European Communities in Brussels in 1967, I helped broker a compromise with the European Atomic Energy Agency over monitoring of European nuclear facilities to support the nuclear nonproliferation treaty, which was then being negotiated. For the next few years I was involved in NATO affairs, first in the State Department, then at the U.S. Mission to NATO in Brussels, as Donald Rumsfeld's political counselor. Some of my work included participation in the newly formed NATO Nuclear Planning Group, a device for involving the allies in nuclear defense planning. All aspects of consultations with the NATO allies on nuclear issues, such as SALT I, became part of my oversight responsibilities. As a very temporary chargé d'affaires at the U.S. Mission to NATO, I greeted President Richard M. Nixon at the airport in Brussels on his last trip to Europe as president just before he resigned in August 1974.

I served in two assignments as deputy assistant secretary of state in the Ford and Carter administrations, again dealing with nuclear arms control and deployment of nuclear weapons in Europe. I was there at NATO headquarters in December 1979 in the meeting where NATO foreign and defense ministers approved the deployment of U.S. intermediate-range missiles in Europe.

President Jimmy Carter appointed me ambassador to Finland in 1980, and there I encountered one of the first political results of the NATO decision, questions about cruise missile over-flights of Finland and the perennial issue of a Nordic nuclear-free zone. And that was also a time of crisis with the Soviet Union because of its invasion of Afghanistan.

My next job was vice chair of the U.S. delegation charged by President Ronald Reagan with negotiating strategic nuclear arms reductions with the Soviet Union. My two years in that post were spent searching for a common ground, which did not emerge until later in the 1980s. President Reagan appointed me head of the U.S. delegation to the conference on disarmament in Europe in Stockholm in 1983. It was the only arms control negotiation still in business after the Soviet Union withdrew from the nuclear negotiations for more than a year to protest deployment of new U.S. missiles in Europe. In this job I met several times in the Oval Office with the president, visits arranged by Secretary of State George Shultz. My assignment was only indirectly related to nuclear weapons at that point, but it was natural that we should occasionally discuss nuclear weapons—and we did.

In 1985 I took up a position as diplomat in residence at Georgetown University, where this book was started. I also taught at Stanford University during that time, in a course on nuclear negotiations. In 1989, I took up full-time teaching, including giving courses on nuclear issues, at Carnegie Mellon University.

The Clinton administration called me back to government service in 1993 to negotiate with Russia, Belarus, Kazakhstan, and Ukraine. The purpose was to create the legal and programmatic basis for implementing legislation sponsored by Senators Sam Nunn and Richard Lugar, the Marshall Plan of nonproliferation. I left office after a year in which our delegation negotiated some thirty agreements. Not long afterward, I was called back again to see whether a nuclear warhead dismantlement agreement could be worked out with Russia. The two countries had never done that before, and after a year of trying, I concluded that it could not be done at that point.

My final job in the Clinton administration was as deputy to the former chairman of the Joint Chiefs of Staff, General John Shalikashvili, who had become a special adviser to the president and the secretary of state. Our task was to explore with members of the U.S. Senate what could be done to change their attitude toward the Comprehensive Nuclear Test Ban Treaty. Regrettably, the Senate had refused to give its assent to this treaty, which the Clinton administration regarded as a valuable nonproliferation tool. General

Shalikashvili and I met with about one-third of the Senate. The general prepared a report which we presented to President Bill Clinton in the White House on January 5, 2001. Under different circumstances, I think that report could have formed the basis for another look at the treaty. But as things turned out, that was my last job in the U.S. government. I left with a sense of having come full circle, back to the test ban treaty which had formed so large a part of my first years in Washington.

The title of this book is drawn from one of Henry Kissinger's memoirs. The full quotation sums up why I wanted to write this history: *No previous generation of statesmen has had to conduct policy in so unknown an environment at the border line of Armageddon.* I thought this was a story that succeeding generations should take to heart. Were presidential decisions invariably wise and skillfully executed? No, but nuclear weapons were never exploded over any city anywhere in the world after August 1945. That was a major achievement. Things could have turned out far differently. That they did not, we should be thankful and should take pride in the statecraft that, so far, has avoided Armageddon.

~

Acknowledgments

This book began with courses I offered at Georgetown University in 1986–1987. Ambassador David Newsom, then director of the Institute for the Study of Diplomacy in the School of Foreign Service at Georgetown, had invited me to become a research professor in the institute, an appointment I accepted with pleasure. My sincere thanks for their support go to David and to other colleagues at Georgetown, to several research assistants, and to my students. Without their criticisms and advice, this book never would have come to be.

Nearly twenty years later, I was able to complete the manuscript because of the generous support of the Massachusetts Institute of Technology and, in particular, Professor Theodore Postol, who encouraged me to take up again a project I had put aside because of the pressure of competing demands on my time. I am very grateful to M.I.T. and to Professor Postol.

To my editors at Rowman & Littlefield, Laura Gottlieb, Andrew Boney, and Lynn Weber, who believed that the manuscript conveyed a message and offered lessons for coming generations, I give my heartfelt thanks.

Over the years, many people read parts of my manuscript. I will not list them all, but two of my colleagues at the Brookings Institution, Strobe Talbott and Raymond Garthoff, have written invaluable histories of the nuclear age. They have my gratitude for their long-ago help to a new author. I also include Stanford University professors Sidney Drell and Alexander George, mentors and friends, in my pantheon of good and wise men who inspired me to try to cross the finish line. I have also benefited from the advice of another good friend, John Newhouse, author of important books on the nuclear era.

Finally, I had hoped that on the title page these words would appear: "With Priscilla Staples Goodby." My wife demurred, so I will express my gratitude here. Thank you, Priscilla.

PART I

THE LOGIC OF WAR, 1941–1952

Churchill, Roosevelt, and Truman

The atom bomb was born out of the desperate struggle in World War II between the Axis Powers and the Western democracies. For British Prime Minister Winston Churchill and U.S. President Franklin D. Roosevelt, who were close partners in this all-out effort, the logic of wartime requirements dictated policy. Developing the bomb before Germany could was the overriding consideration. Even so, Roosevelt and Churchill thought about postwar arrangements. They concluded, over some objections from their advisers, that an American-British monopoly would best serve world peace.

Vice President Harry Truman first learned of the bomb project when he became president following Roosevelt's death on April 12, 1945. By the time Germany surrendered in May and it was revealed that Hitler had not tried to build an atom bomb on the advice of his experts, the U.S. program in Los Alamos, New Mexico, was far advanced. The first secret test—"Trinity"—took place in the New Mexico desert on July 16, 1945. The first bomb was used against Hiroshima, Japan, on August 6; the second was used against Nagasaki on August 9. Japan surrendered on August 15.

The exigencies of war continued to dominate decision-making during the Truman administration. Less than three years after the end of World War II, the Soviet Union and the West were engaged in the Cold War. The Soviets' first atom bomb was tested in 1949. The Korean War began in June 1950 and continued through the rest of Truman's term of office. McCarthyism, a form of paranoia that insisted "Reds" had penetrated every institution, rattled American society. As this period was ending, the Americans and Soviets developed and tested thermonuclear weapons—a thousand times more powerful than atom bombs. Truman authorized a nuclear production base that led to a flood of nuclear weapons in subsequent administrations. The stage was set, many thought, for World War III.

CHAPTER ONE

~

At the Beginning:
Churchill, Roosevelt, and Truman

The atom bomb was an international enterprise from the beginning. Albert Einstein, in a letter dated August 2, 1939, warned U.S. President Franklin D. Roosevelt that a nuclear chain reaction in a large mass of uranium would lead to the construction of extremely powerful bombs. Many of the scientific discoveries that made the bomb possible came from European centers of scholarly research and from European-born scientists who had fled to America to escape Fascism and the Nazi horrors. Before Roosevelt authorized a full-scale attempt to create an atom bomb, the British government already had a clear picture of how the job should be done, based on extensive research and engineering studies. But of all the influences that affected American policy toward the bomb, the wartime collaboration between Roosevelt and British Prime Minister Winston Churchill was the most important. Churchill was instrumental in shaping the policies of F.D.R., the president who started it all. But Churchill encountered major resistance to the kind of hand-in-glove cooperation that he wanted. Some of the top American managers of the bomb project were wary of British intentions. Roosevelt, however, was ready to overrule his advisers and open the doors to cooperation with Britain and its scientists. Roosevelt and Churchill became true partners in overseeing the birth of the bomb.

Actions taken during the period when Churchill and Roosevelt dominated nuclear policy persisted for many years. When I entered the U.S. Atomic Energy Commission in 1954, I was assigned to work with the Combined Development Agency, a joint U.S.-British organization that managed

3

contracts for uranium ore procurement from foreign sources. The Combined Development Agency had been created as the Combined Development Trust on June 13, 1944, by Roosevelt and Churchill, essentially to obtain exclusive long-term rights to uranium ore from countries with which the two governments had good relations. By the time I arrived on the scene, almost exactly a decade after its founding, the agency was managing contracts with the Belgian Congo, South Africa, Australia, Portugal, and others. Although it was something of a relic by that time, the British attached importance to it and maintained a two-man team in Washington to conduct the day to day business.

The story of Roosevelt's handling of the atom bomb project has been told many times.[1] This chapter focuses on the struggle between competition and cooperation in international affairs, and between expansion and restraint in building nuclear weapons. These have been constant themes through all the decades of the nuclear era.

The British had been instrumental in encouraging Washington to develop the atomic bomb. In July 1941, a committee of British scientists (code-named MAUD) recommended that a uranium 235 bomb should be built, using the gaseous diffusion method to produce the enriched uranium. This galvanized the U.S. effort, which had been proceeding rather cautiously up to this point. Roosevelt authorized preliminary work to develop a bomb on October 9, 1941, two months before Pearl Harbor. This later became the Manhattan Project, headed by Major General Leslie Groves, the secret and massive complex of laboratories and engineering centers that ultimately built the first atom bombs.

Roosevelt's decision included a determination that the United States and Britain should work closely together, and that intention was transmitted to Churchill by Roosevelt. Churchill's first meeting with Roosevelt on atomic energy took place at Hyde Park, Roosevelt's family home in New York, on June 20, 1942. Churchill had in mind a thoroughly integrated effort on atomic energy, which was quite a bit more than Roosevelt's advisers were ready to accept. From then on, it was a struggle for Roosevelt's mind. Excessive British expectations foundered on the rocks of American suspicions at levels below Roosevelt. Not until July 1943 was Churchill able to move the president back to the cooperative stance that Roosevelt's instincts seem to have favored all along.

First Rules of Behavior

Churchill thought that a compact between himself and Roosevelt might overcome the disputes that had arisen. He raised this idea on July 22, 1943, with Secretary of War Henry Stimson and Roosevelt's chief science adviser, Vannevar Bush, chair of the Office of Scientific Research and Development, who were visiting London. And so it happened that the first international effort to establish rules about the atom bomb was launched by Winston Churchill in a set of propositions, later formally accepted by Roosevelt at their next meeting. This took place in Quebec on August 19, 1943. There, Roosevelt and Churchill signed the "Articles of Agreement Governing Collaboration between the Authorities of the U.S.A. and the U.K. in the Matter of Tube Alloys," usually referred to as the Quebec Agreement.[2] "Tube Alloys" was the British code word for the atom bomb project.

The Quebec Agreement became the first major political document to shape the nuclear age, and its effect was felt in ways that still persist. To Churchill goes the main credit. The text is as follows:

Articles of Agreement Governing Collaboration between the Authorities of The U.S.A. and the U.K. in the Matter of Tube Alloys; and Whereas it is vital to our common safety in the present War to bring the Tube Alloys project to fruition at the earliest moment; and Whereas this may be more speedily achieved if all available British and American brains and resources are pooled; and Whereas owing to war conditions it would be an improvident use of war resources to duplicate plants on a large scale on both sides of the Atlantic and therefore a far greater expense has fallen upon the United States;

It is agreed between us

First, that we will never use this agency against each other.

Secondly, that we will not use it against third parties without each other's consent.

Thirdly, that we will not either of us communicate any information about Tube Alloys to third parties except by mutual consent.

Fourthly, that in view of the heavy burden of production falling upon the United States as the result of a wise division of war effort, the British Government recognize that any postwar advantages of an industrial or commercial character shall be dealt with as between the United States and Great Britain on terms to be specified by the President of the United States to the Prime Minister of Great Britain. The Prime Minister expressly disclaims any interest in these industrial and commercial aspects beyond what may be considered by the President of the United States to be fair and just and in harmony with the economic welfare of the world.

And fifthly, that the following arrangements shall be made to ensure full and effective collaboration between the two countries in bringing the project to fruition:

(a) There shall be set up in Washington a Combined Policy Committee composed of

The Secretary of War. (United States)

Dr. Vannevar Bush. (United States)

Dr. James B. Conant. (United States)

Field-Marshal Sir John Dill, G.C.B., C.M.G., D.S.O. (United Kingdom)

Colonel the Right Hon. J. J. Llewellin, C.B.E.1 M-O., M.P. (United Kingdom)

The Honourable C. D. Howe. (Canada)

The functions of this Committee, subject to the control of the respective Governments, will be:

To agree from time to time upon the programme of work to be carried out in the two countries.

To keep all sections of the project under constant review.

To allocate materials, apparatus and plant, in limited supply, in accordance with the requirements of the programme agreed by the Committee.

To settle any questions which may arise on the interpretation or application of this Agreement.

(b) There shall be complete interchange of information and ideas on all sections of the project between members of the Policy Committee and their immediate technical advisers.

(c) In the field of scientific research and development there shall be full and effective interchange of information and ideas between those in the two countries engaged in the same sections of the field.

(d) In the field of design, construction and operation of large-scale plants, interchange of information and ideas shall be regulated by such ad hoc arrangements as may, in each section of the field, appear to be necessary or desirable if the project is to be brought to fruition at the earliest moment. Such ad hoc arrangements shall be subject to the approval of the Policy Committee.

Approved

AUG. 19 1943

FRANKLIN D. ROOSEVELT

WINSTON S. CHURCHILL

Postwar Control of Atomic Energy

Sir John Anderson, the British War Cabinet member responsible for the atomic program, was thinking about postwar control of atomic energy as early as 1942. Anderson's boss, Winston Churchill, intent on a U.S.-U.K.

monopoly, gave his ideas little attention. Scientists working on the Manhattan Project in the United States had similar thoughts about international controls and began to advocate them as the tide of war turned to favor the Allies. Vannevar Bush and James Conant, president of Harvard and Bush's alter ego in the bomb project, were thinking seriously about the postwar world. Bush and Conant understood it was short-sighted to think that the secrets of the bomb could be kept indefinitely. Any nation with high-quality scientific resources—which certainly included the Soviet Union—could develop an atomic bomb in a few years. In September 1944 they wrote to Secretary of War Stimson about their fears of a nuclear arms race and proposed "an international commission acting under an association of nations and having the authority to inspect."[3] The letter was essentially ignored throughout what was left of Roosevelt's presidency, except for one brief discussion with the president a month before he died.

Niels Bohr, the great Danish physicist, warned Roosevelt and Churchill that a postwar atomic arms race would endanger humanity. He hoped that informing Stalin of the project—but not of the production details—before Stalin learned of it through other means might encourage some degree of postwar cooperation. In fact, Stalin already had a fairly clear picture of what was happening from his agents in the United States. Soviet scientists already were working on the early stages of an atomic energy program. Bohr met with Churchill on May 16, 1944, and the results were exactly the opposite of what Bohr had hoped for. Churchill was put off by Bohr's style, and the case Bohr was trying to make ran head on into Churchill's firm intention to make the bomb a U.S.-U.K. monopoly. The idea of mentioning to Stalin that the Manhattan Project even existed seemed treasonous to Churchill. Bohr finally met with Roosevelt on August 26, 1944. Roosevelt's famous charm and affability led Bohr to believe that the president was interested in his thinking and would try to convince Churchill. But again Bohr's hopes were dashed.

In September 1944, Roosevelt and Churchill met at Hyde Park. Roosevelt's fourth term as U.S. president was about to be confirmed by the voters in the November election but he had only half a year to live. Churchill's hard-line views completely carried the day. The two men signed an Aide Memoire on September 19 that looked with disfavor both on international control and Niels Bohr. The document was so closely held that Roosevelt's colleagues did not learn of it until after his death. The text is as follows:

1. The suggestion that the world should be informed regarding tube alloys, with a view to an international agreement regarding its control and use, is not accepted. The matter should continue to be regarded as of the utmost

secrecy, but when a "bomb" is finally available, it might perhaps, after mature consideration, be used against the Japanese, who should be warned that this bombardment will be repeated until they surrender.

2. Full collaboration between the United States and the British government in developing tube alloys for military and commercial purposes should continue after the defeat of Japan unless and until terminated by joint agreement.

3. Enquiries should be made regarding the activities of Professor Bohr and steps taken to ensure that he is responsible for no leakage of information particularly to the Russians.[4]

Roosevelt had become convinced that U.S.-U.K. cooperation in all phases of atomic energy should continue after the war, to the exclusion of other considerations. By this time he had become aware of Britain's profound economic weakness resulting from the costs of the war. In Roosevelt's initial thinking about postwar order, Britain, China, the Soviet Union, and the United States would be the four "global policemen." This idea was one of the origins of the U.N. Security Council. Roosevelt realized that Britain would need considerable military strength if it were to play the "policeman's" role that Roosevelt envisaged. The atom bomb would provide this. Although U.S.-U.K. collaboration was not necessarily incompatible with some form of international control of atomic energy, Roosevelt and Churchill concluded otherwise, given their growing suspicions about Stalin's intentions.

The last occasion for a decision in the Roosevelt administration was on March 15, 1945, when Stimson met with Roosevelt over lunch for a discussion of atomic energy issues. Stimson told the president that he would have to decide on what to say when the first atom bomb was used. He told the president that the two options being discussed were (1) an attempt to maintain U.S.-U.K. control over the bomb versus (2) international control based on free exchange of scientific information linked to access to all scientific facilities. Roosevelt agreed that he would have to decide on a policy and have a public statement ready for use when the first bomb was detonated. Stimson knew that the first U.S. atomic bomb would likely be tested before August 1, 1945. But he and the president postponed making a decision about postwar policy. Did Roosevelt think he had already made the decision in the Hyde Park Aide Memoire? Perhaps, but there is no way of knowing. Roosevelt died at Warm Springs, Georgia, on April 12, 1945.

The Fallacy of Unilateral Advantage

From the very beginning of the nuclear age, the atom bomb was seen as special, requiring special treatment in its control and use. Scientists and politicians had different ideas about what this meant, but they all agreed that this was not just another weapon. Churchill adamantly opposed sharing scientific information about atomic energy with any other nation, and Roosevelt concurred, if the Hyde Park Aide Memoire is accepted as his last word on the issue. The corollary of this was that mechanisms for international control of atomic energy were not necessary. Both leaders, of course, recognized the enormous potential impact of atomic energy on international relations. They tended to think that atom bombs in their hands would be a force for good. And they entertained exaggerated expectations about how long this happy situation could last.

Although the scientists saw opportunities for international cooperation and thought that was the only way to head off catastrophe, the political leadership saw trouble brewing with Stalin's Soviet Union and were wary of giving away a trump card. That was why proposals for opening a dialogue with Stalin's government seemed unnatural to them. Almost certainly, it would have been impossible to block Stalin from acquiring a nuclear weapon even if they had been more inclined toward cooperation. But it is possible that the Cold War confrontations might have been a little less risky had they made the effort.

The issues confronted by Roosevelt and Churchill persisted throughout the nuclear age. They did not solve them, but they did identify them. Believing that the number of states possessing atomic weapons should be kept to a minimum, they began the process of blocking development by others. Churchill and Roosevelt—and certainly their main advisers—knew that atomic weapons were more than just another method of destruction. They understood that use of the nuclear weapon must be subject to special consideration and oversight. And that was before Hiroshima and Nagasaki. Their most fundamental insights were the need for top-level control and the advisability of preventing the spread of atomic weapons. These became the lodestars of policy for succeeding U.S. administrations. Churchill and Roosevelt, however, overestimated the difficulties of acquiring atomic weapons, and they were too hopeful in their expectations that unilateral advantages could be sustained for a long period of time.

Truman's Defense Doctrine

When Harry Truman became president on April 12, 1945, the atom bomb was almost ready for a test. Truman was now in the business of setting rules for the future of the nuclear age. In this, the British had little influence. The days of the Roosevelt-Churchill partnership were over.

The first atomic bomb was tested at Alamogordo, New Mexico, on July 16, 1945. On July 17 Truman and Churchill began meeting with Stalin in Potsdam, Germany, in a conference to discuss peace settlements in Europe. Truman was advised to speak to Stalin about a powerful new weapon without describing what it was. He did so on July 24. Stalin's response was a cool encouragement to make "good use of it against the Japanese." It was thought at the time that Stalin had not understood the import of what he had been told. Undoubtedly he did, for his intelligence was quite good on this subject.

Many studies have been written about the decision to drop atomic bombs on Hiroshima on August 6 and on Nagasaki on August 9, 1945. The most convincing explanation is that it was a "nondecision." It was expected by all the upper echelons of U.S. officials that, once developed, the bomb would be used. Roosevelt's Hyde Park Aide Memoire seemed to assume that also. Truman never regretted the use of these weapons to end World War II, but he was prudent about their use thereafter.

The Truman administration's National Security Council adopted a statement of objectives, NSC 68, drafted in 1950 mainly by Paul Nitze. By this time, the Soviet Union had conducted its first nuclear test explosion, on August 29, 1949. The debris from the explosion was collected in the atmosphere outside Soviet territory by American aircraft. The Soviets did not announce the test but Truman did, albeit with some private disbelief, on September 23, 1949. Most experts assumed that the Soviet Union wanted to avoid war with the United States but that it would seek to expand its empire through proxies and at a level of conflict that would not provoke general war. The U.S.S.R. was seen to be an expansionist state with a potentially dangerous nuclear capability. Its sponsorship of a coup in Czechoslovakia in 1948, which delivered that country to the Soviet bloc, and its support for the North Korean attack on South Korea in 1950 provided ample evidence of its hostile intentions.

Soviet expert George Kennan, a policy planner at the State Department, had recommended a policy of "containment" to deal with this threat. Containment was a pragmatic mix of policies designed to constrain Soviet expansionism while allowing time for changes within the Soviet Union that would favor long-term peace. Recipes for the mix varied according to the instincts of the principal policymakers, but Truman's national security policy was rooted in that general concept. In 1991 Kennan's prophesy would prove correct: the Soviet empire collapsed.

Presidential administrations have oscillated between a defense policy that emphasizes (1) a long-term threat, requiring a patient, long-term response, and (2) a near-term threat, with time running out, requiring an immediate and intense U.S. response. Truman took the latter view after the North Koreans attacked South Korea. And so NSC 68 included a warning—for planning purposes—that a time of peril lay ahead for the United States as the Soviet nuclear arsenal grew in strength. Nitze, who had a taste for quantitative analysis, wrote that the year when the Soviet Union could deliver 100 atomic bombs on targets in the United States would be a "critical date." That date was expected to be 1954.

Precedents for the Future

Harry Truman set precedents for the future that hardened into rules of behavior in subsequent administrations. The rhetoric changed, of course, as each president imprinted his own views and personality on nuclear policy issues. But Truman's precedents held up surprisingly well. One precedent that Truman was loathe to establish was the deployment of nuclear weapons with units of the military, but Truman was not in a position to do this anyway, because few weapons existed during his presidency. In other respects, presidents have remained within the boundaries that Truman laid out. Truman's rules are these:

Civilian control of atomic energy. It was not a given in 1945 that the U.S. atomic energy program would be under civilian rather than military control. The Manhattan Project had been launched as a military enterprise to build a bomb. Many of the scientists in the project, however, were worried about the direction of the scientific effort in the postwar period and lobbied for a governmental organization to manage atomic energy under civilian control. They succeeded in convincing Congress that this was important. Senator Brien McMahon (D-CT) took the lead in promoting this. The result was the U.S. Atomic Energy Commission, a five-person commission named by the president and confirmed by the Senate. The first chair was David Lilienthal, the chair of the Tennessee Valley Authority (TVA). The TVA had supplied the electricity needed to operate the Oak Ridge, Tennessee, laboratory that produced the uranium for the atomic bomb dropped on Hiroshima.

Nonuse of nuclear weapons. Truman was a wartime president, in office during World War II and the Korean War. The Korean War resulted in 37,000 American fatalities, and the American public might have understood if Truman had authorized the use of a nuclear weapon to end the war, as he had to end World War II. But he did not, despite appeals from the American commander in Korea, General Douglas MacArthur.

Truman was not deterred by Soviet nuclear weapons. The United States still had a monopoly at that time, despite the first Soviet nuclear test in 1949.

But Truman's military advisers did not see targets in Korea against which it made sense to use nuclear weapons, which were still in short supply. They did not think that the war should be expanded by attacking China or the Soviet Union. They thought that would bring on "the wrong war in the wrong place at the wrong time." Another consideration was the attitude of America's European allies, and here the British did continue to wield influence. Europe was seen by the Truman administration as the focus of the struggle with Stalinist ambitions. When Truman spoke too loosely on one occasion about using all the weapons at his disposal, British Prime Minister Clement Atlee rushed to Washington to make sure Britain would be consulted before the U.S. military was authorized to use nuclear weapons.

Truman's own attitude toward the devastation that nuclear weapons could cause probably was a factor, too, in his unwillingness to use them. Once he realized, from the experience with Hiroshima and Nagasaki, how different these weapons were, that they were not just bigger conventional bombs, he understood very well that special rules must govern nuclear weapons.

Presidential control of nuclear weapons. In Truman's thinking, nuclear weapons were something like the chemical weapons that had been used in his war—World War I. They had to be handled with care, perhaps sequestered so that they would not be seen as readily available for use in some future conflict. In fact, there seemed to be some doubt in his mind in the early years of his administration about the place of these weapons in the arsenals of the future. Faced with a series of crises in Europe and Asia and with pressures from Congress, Truman acceded to the need to build a powerful stockpile of nuclear weapons. But the need for presidential control was never in doubt in his mind, and he never agreed to deploy these weapons with the troops.

Weapons of deterrence, not weapons of choice in war. Truman's attitude toward nuclear weapons meant that he would reserve the use of those weapons for the most decisive moments in warfare. In practice, this meant that the weapons would be reserved for strategic purposes, defined as a major threat to the United States or its allies. Research on tactical nuclear weapons, that is, weapons of relatively small explosive power, was being conducted during the Truman administration. It was not until the Eisenhower administration that serious thought had to be given to how they would be used in combat. And so, for Truman, nuclear weapons were not battlefield weapons but weapons to be used against the war potential of a major adversary. At that time, of course, and for years to come, the Soviet Union was the main enemy.

As U.S. nuclear capabilities expanded, the Air Force's Strategic Air Command developed the means and the tactics for persuading Soviet leaders that nuclear weapons would be used against them if war should come. The main task of strategic nuclear warfare was to deter the Soviet Union from any assault on American interests by promising quick and certain retaliation. For a deterrent force to be effective, it must be credible, and that was the concern of countless commanders. Endless practice was devoted to carrying out simulated bomber attacks on the Soviet Union. Those were dangerous times, but the intent was to deter, and Soviet leaders operated under that assumption too.

Rejection of preventive war. Most scholars and scientists reinforced the idea that the atom bomb was a weapon of deterrence, "the ultimate weapon," as Bernard Brodie, one of the first writers on nuclear warfare, described it. By the end of the Truman administration, the public and Congress presumed that superiority in nuclear weaponry would deter the Soviet Union from attacking the United States. They did not presume that American leaders would start a nuclear war to prevent Moscow from acquiring the bomb. "Preventive war" was discussed in Truman's day, as in the administration of George W. Bush. The discussion in Truman's time always came back to deterrence. American planners and strategists believed in the first use of nuclear weapons by the United States, if necessary. But the idea of beginning a nuclear war to prevent a nuclear attack was rejected. Preemption—an attack to blunt a nuclear attack under way or about to begin—was another matter. Fortunately, matters never reached that stage.

Alternatives to nuclear weapons. The Truman administration believed that "balanced" military forces, meaning a strong conventional defense, were necessary both to deter the use of Soviet military force and to deal with a variety of other situations. American military capabilities should permit "congruency," that is, a military response sufficient to achieve U.S. objectives without escalating to an all-out war. The Truman administration assumed that the U.S.S.R. in time would build a formidable nuclear arsenal of its own, a correct prediction, so "balance" required strong conventional forces.

Preventing the spread of nuclear weapons. Cooperation with the British on nuclear weapons not only during but also after World War II was thought by Roosevelt to be the best way to achieve and sustain peace. Britain would be able to carry a heavier load in the postwar world if it were a full partner with the United States in nuclear weaponry. But the U.S. Congress thought otherwise. Like many others, even today, Senator Brien McMahon, the most influential politician on nuclear weapons issues, thought that American technology would produce U.S. superiority in the decisive weapon of the day. He spoke for many politicians in saying it should not be shared with anyone. His solution was to legislate against any atomic cooperation with any other country, including Britain. The British felt betrayed when Churchill's hard-won agreements with Roosevelt on nuclear sharing were largely overturned, but Truman reluctantly obeyed. This restriction was relaxed in later administrations, but it set a pattern for future U.S. nonproliferation policies.

International control over atomic energy. Truman did what Roosevelt did not live long enough to do. He appointed a high-level group led by Dean Acheson, then the under secretary of state, and David Lillienthal to recommend a policy that would bring atomic energy under international control. Robert Oppenheimer, chief scientific director of the Manhattan Project, was a senior adviser, and he brought to the table the views that many scientists shared: if the atomic bomb became widely available, a catastrophic nuclear war would ensue. The nations, including the United States, must renounce the bomb and give an international agency control over all the peaceful uses of atomic energy.

This view was logical but it would be hard to sell to Stalin, who distrusted the West at least as much as it distrusted him. Nevertheless, a plan for international control of atomic energy was recommended by Acheson and Lillienthal and accepted by President Truman. Bernard Baruch, a financier who had occupied senior government positions in both world wars, was appointed to negotiate the agreement. He added more supranational elements to the proposal, which made it still more impractical.

Baruch did his best to dramatize the issue, not that it really needed it, by declaring in his opening remarks at the U.N. in 1946 that "we are here to make a choice between the quick and the dead." Nothing he or his successors did moved the Soviet government to accept the plan. Yet a pattern was set, which most presidents followed, of trying to control nuclear weapons through international agreements. The essence of the Baruch Plan remained a part of the formal U.S. position on disarmament until 1955.

Adversarial cooperation in the midst of an arms race. Truman's decision to pursue talks in international forums with a nation that by 1948 had become America's major adversary set another precedent. Although the discussions were formalistic and arid, the idea had been planted that adversaries had a shared interest in cooperation in order to prevent mutual annihilation. Over time, U.S.-Soviet talks about nuclear weaponry became a kind of feedback loop, meaning that some degree of cooperative management, however ineptly it was done, was introduced into the nuclear arms race.

The dynamic of new technology. Truman set the nation on the path to becoming a nuclear weapons superpower, reckoning that American superiority in nuclear weapons would convince any future enemy that an attack on the United States would be a fatal misjudgment. Unchallengeable U.S. military power would keep the peace. He had bought into Churchill's reasoning.

By that time, of course, the Soviet Union had tested its first atom bomb, years ahead of the time many U.S. experts thought it might happen, and it was clear that a Cold War with the Soviets was in store. Ideas about controlling the atom had become more theoretical than real. This reasoning, plus political instincts, led Truman by 1950 to approve the building of the "super"—the hydrogen or fusion or thermonuclear bomb, as it is variously called—after a bitter debate among his scientific advisers. Many of the scientists who had created the atomic bomb, including Oppenheimer, opposed the "super," aware of the destruction that an H-bomb could inflict on humanity. But Truman had no hesitation about the correct way to proceed. It was another nondecision.

Humanity had entered an era of destructive potential that could threaten the existence of civilization and perhaps the human race. Atom bombs, like those used against Hiroshima and Nagasaki, were measured in kilotons (thousands of tons of TNT) of destructive force. Each of those bombs was less than 20 kilotons in yield. Hydrogen bombs are measured in megatons (millions of tons of TNT). A 20 megaton fusion weapon would be the equivalent of more than a thousand Hiroshima or Nagasaki bombs concentrated in a package of about the same size as the first, primitive bombs that leveled two cities.

The H-bomb decision pointed to the path that lay ahead. Technology became a prime driver of the arms race. American presidents would be under great pressure to embrace new technologies whenever they became advanced enough to build new weapons systems. And presidents nearly always would decide to build new weapons if the technology justified it. Just as Truman was lobbied to build the hydrogen bomb by powerful groups of scientists allied with politicians, so succeeding American presidents were lobbied to build the new weapon of their day. It was a dynamic driven by internal U.S. considerations, but reinforced by the existence of a highly capable external enemy, the U.S.S.R., which had its own military-industrial-technological complex.

Expanding the Production Base

President Truman set another precedent that had a major impact on his successors. This decision was not debated at all, yet it had profound consequences. He decided to expand the production base for enriched uranium and plutonium and so create the means to build very large numbers of nuclear weapons. Truman met with his advisers on this issue on January 16, 1952. A further expansion of production capacity was necessary, Secretary of Defense Robert Lovett explained to the president, because the Joint Chiefs of Staff requested a bigger stockpile of nuclear weapons than they had previously considered necessary, and said they needed it at the earliest possible date, preferably by 1960. Lovett explained that the urgency was based on the growth of the Soviet nuclear weapons stockpile to a level that soon would become very dangerous. Secretary Lovett spoke of new technology that would give the Army nuclear weapons for its use on future battlefields. This new technology, said Lovett, also would make possible the selective, rather than indiscriminate, bombing of major enemy targets.

The Air Force chief of staff, General Hoyt Vandenberg, estimated that in the event of war with the Soviet Union, 5,000–6,000 Soviet targets would have to be destroyed in order to eliminate the war-making potential of that country. He agreed with the Army that it was important for the United States to be the first nation to have tactical, or battlefield, nuclear weapons. A time would come, he predicted, when the United States and the Soviet Union would each possess so many nuclear weapons capable of striking the other's homeland that each country's nuclear strike forces would be neutralized. When that time came, the crucial advantage would lie with the country that could make the better tactical use of nuclear weapons. The danger point would come in 1955, he thought, when the Soviet Union would be in a position to use nuclear weapons for tactical purposes.

Truman's approval of the expansion is perhaps the least well-known of his major decisions. It was urged on him by Senator McMahon and many others who believed that U.S. security depended on superiority in the numbers of nuclear weapons. "Atomic plenty" was the term they used to describe the day when enough uranium and plutonium would be available for all imaginable military uses. New gaseous diffusion plants were built, as well as plutonium production reactors. The new plants provided the materials for a massive nuclear weapons building program that made it possible for the U.S. nuclear stockpile to grow from about 1,000 nuclear weapons in 1952 to over 20,000 in 1960, to almost 32,000 in 1966 (according to data from the Natural Resources Defense Council). The foundation for the era of atomic plenty was laid by Harry Truman in an act of faith in his advisers and under pressure from Congress. It would have been difficult during the Korean War for Truman to have done otherwise, but the decision, like so many others, was very easily made.

The State Department, with Paul Nitze in the lead, had strongly supported NSC 68's call for a rapid increase in nuclear capability, as well as a conventional buildup. But in the interagency debate that led later to the decision to expand nuclear production facilities, General Herbert Loper, representing the Defense Department, had thought that 200 nuclear weapons should suffice. Reflecting a view about deterrence he was to hold for many years, Paul Nitze, the lead author of NSC 68, told me that his computations showed that 10,000 nuclear weapons would be more like it, and this was what he advised. Much later, he told me that he really believed nuclear weapons should never be used, not even in retaliation; in fact, *especially* not in retaliation.

Expanding the atomic capability of the United States led to an era of atomic plenty, as was intended. And when that happened, it became an exercise in ingenuity to devise ways in which the new weapons could be integrated into the force structures of the three armed services. No service wanted to be without them. Almost inevitably, the services became heavily dependent on nuclear weapons.

It was and is typical in nuclear matters for decisions considered rather technical to be made without much debate. Truman's decision to build the infrastructure that would multiply by several times the U.S. nuclear weapons stockpile was not seriously debated at the senior levels of his administration. Truman was not presented with much dissent, although some doubts existed in the Atomic Energy Commission. Atomic energy decisions of this type typically were the province of small numbers of like-minded individuals, with little or no public debate.

This precedent ruled out a minimum deterrent, that is, a few hundred nuclear weapons to deter other nations by threatening all of their major cities. This is what Herbert Loper was talking about, but that concept would not guide the future structure of the U.S. and Soviet nuclear stockpiles. The numbers that became possible, especially as accuracy of delivery improved, gave rise to ideas about protracted strategic nuclear war, a far cry from Truman's early thinking about the atomic bomb.

Notes

1. A summary of the main events involving Roosevelt is available in a case study that I wrote with Ian Gambles, a British colleague, at Georgetown University in 1988. The case study was published as "British Decision-making, the Bomb, and the Man in the Middle, 1940–1945," Case 343 in the Pew Case Studies in International Affairs. One of the best histories of which I am aware is the account in Richard G. Hewlett and Oscar E. Anderson Jr., *The New World, 1939–46, Vol. 1, A History of the United States Atomic Energy Commission* (University Park: Pennsylvania State University Press, 1962). Another classic and more recently published history is Richard Rhodes, *The Making of the Atomic Bomb* (New York: Simon and Schuster, 1986). I drew on these accounts in my own case study. The same story is told from the vantage point of Major General Leslie Groves, the military director of the Manhattan

Project, in a still more recent and very fine book by Robert S. Norris, *Racing for the Bomb* (South Royalton, VT: Steerforth Press, 2002). Other excellent books that cover this period authoritatively and in detail are McGeorge Bundy, *Danger and Survival* (New York: Random House, 1988); Margaret Gowing, *Britain and Atomic Energy, 1939–1945* (New York: St. Martin's Press, 1964); David Holloway, *Stalin and the Bomb* (New Haven: Yale University Press, 1994); John Newhouse, *War and Peace in the Nuclear Age* (New York: Alfred A. Knopf, 1989); and Martin J. Sherwin, *A World Destroyed* (New York: Vintage Books, 1977).

2. See www.atomicarchive.com.

3. See www.doug-long.com/stimson4.htm.

4. See www.atomicarchive.com.

PART II

SETTING THE RULES FOR THE LONG HAUL, 1953–1968

Eisenhower, Kennedy, and Johnson

Wars and rumors of war formed the backdrop for presidential decision-making during the Eisenhower, Kennedy, and Johnson administrations. France and China joined the United States, the Soviet Union, and Britain as nuclear-weapon states. Dwight Eisenhower was the first president since the earliest years of the Republic to confront an adversary who could inflict massive damage on American cities. He confronted a dual crisis in 1956 when the Hungarians revolted against Soviet domination and the British and French, in coordination with Israel, tried to seize the Suez Canal. Multiple crises with China raised the question of whether to use nuclear weapons.

John F. Kennedy and Soviet leader Nikita Khrushchev faced off over Berlin, and a full-scale nuclear war was a real possibility during the Cuban Missile Crisis. Kennedy took the first steps toward what became the Vietnam War. Lyndon Johnson escalated the war while trying to persuade one of communist North Vietnam's patrons, the Soviet Union, that it should cooperate with Washington in limiting offensive and defensive nuclear weaponry. He inaugurated the first U.S. defense system against ballistic missiles.

Despite, or more likely because of the ominous challenges they faced, all three of the presidents worked hard to imprint international order on the development and deployment of nuclear weapons. Eisenhower tried for a total ban on nuclear weapons testing, and Kennedy succeeded in getting a limited test ban treaty. Johnson signed the nuclear nonproliferation treaty, one of the principal means, even today, of controlling the spread of nuclear weaponry.

At the end of these regime-creating years, the basic structure of U.S. nuclear forces had been put in place. It has not changed much in the passing years. Many of the rules of thinking about nuclear weapons also had been put in place. America's protagonist and only real rival in nuclear weaponry, the Soviet Union, accepted many of these norms and rules: centralized control, avoidance of situations that would call for the use of nuclear weapons, a prohibition on actions that would encourage the proliferation of nuclear weapons, and a ban on testing nuclear weapons in the earth's atmosphere.

CHAPTER TWO

~

Nuclear Deterrence or Preventive War: Eisenhower's Choice

The atom bomb was not an issue that American politicians felt very comfortable discussing in the first years of the nuclear age. The Joint Committee on Atomic Energy of the U.S. Congress controlled nuclear policies in Congress, with the help of the U.S. Atomic Energy Commission. It was an unusual executive branch and congressional mechanism that dominated policymaking, like any special interest. But the quickening pace of nuclear arming was evident in the first test of a nuclear device by the United Kingdom on October 3, 1952. The United States tested the first thermonuclear device on November 1, 1952, just before the election that brought the Republican Party to power for the first time in twenty years. The Soviet Union quickly caught up in that field, too. It was obvious that nuclear issues would be close to the center of U.S. national security policy debate in the coming years. Eisenhower himself, former supreme commander in Europe in World War II, was caught up in those debates and started some of them.

Eisenhower guided the nation safely through a very dangerous transition period. He knew that the United States, during his administration, would be entering a new stage in its modern history: for the first time, the United States would become vulnerable to devastating attack. He was optimistic enough to believe that time was on the side of the United States, and time has proved him right.

Reaffirming Containment

Eisenhower's great strength in building consensus was his insistence that his team think through with him the basic strategic guidelines of his administration. The organizational device he used was the National Security Council (NSC), an inner cabinet which Eisenhower met with frequently throughout his administration. Eisenhower approved the outline for a study on U.S. security policy toward the Soviet Union on May 9, 1953. The findings of the study, code-named "Project Solarium," were presented to the National Security Council on July 16, 1953, and discussed again in the NSC on July 30.[1] Eisenhower used Project Solarium to signal to his administration that he was no fan of "roll-back" or of "line-drawing," two alternatives to containment. Speaking of "line-drawing" in an NSC meeting on December 21, 1954, Eisenhower said he had always rejected this concept because it automatically gave the initiative to the enemy to seize whatever falls short of the defensive line. Eisenhower added that every place in the world is a source of irritation if you are dealing with Communists and that there would be no chance whatever of removing irritations unless we were prepared to get off the earth. This view was a far cry from the basic assumption of the "roll-back" study, too. According to the chair of that task force, the United States could not live with the Soviet Union if the latter's strength continued to increase; hence, that strength must be reduced.

When Project Solarium was reviewed at the NSC meeting of July 16, 1953, Eisenhower spoke about his views of international security in terms that bear repeating today: nuclear war was not a policy option he would ever court. In the future the only thing worse than losing a global war, he said, would be winning one. There would be no individual freedom after a nuclear war. The confrontation with the Soviet Union would be lengthy; the willingness of the American people to sustain a defense effort over an indefinite period of time must be based on their freely given acknowledgment that it was necessary. Otherwise, we would sacrifice the liberties we were trying to save. Americans, he said, had shown that they had little interest in achieving their objectives by occupying conquered territory. What would we do with Russia if we should win a global war? Eisenhower made it clear that he was against unilateral American actions. Allies, the president said, are essential, and their understanding for American objectives must be gained by persuasion.

The Primacy of Nuclear Deterrence

Eisenhower's revision of the Truman administration's national security policy proceeded with Solarium firmly in view. The Eisenhower "Statement of Policy," NSC 162/2, was adopted by the National Security Council on October 29, 1953.[2] It recognized that "as general war becomes more devastating for both sides the threat to resort to it becomes less available as a sanction against local aggression" (paragraph 6c). General war—meaning war with the Soviet Union—was regarded as unlikely and, "in view of U.S. commitments or intentions," a Soviet attack on NATO countries also was seen as unlikely (paragraph 6a). A "stalemate" between the United States and the Soviet Union was thought to be the likely result of a situation where each had the " probable capacity to inflict critical damage on the other, but is not likely to be able to prevent major atomic retaliations" (paragraph 6b). This view of deterrence assumed a rational and prudent adversary, was dismissive of the possibility of defense against nuclear attack, and disregarded the idea of preventive war.

Eisenhower was a disciple of Clausewitz, the great Prussian analyst of strategy, in the sense that he thought actions should be subordinated to a supreme strategic idea.[3] His habit was to filter out secondary matters as he analyzed problems and to pursue the main point with single-minded determination. His passionate defense of nuclear deterrence and his frequent public and private reminders of the horrors of nuclear war underscored the evident fact that his own supreme idea was to prevent war and to do so by promising that unimaginable devastation would be the almost automatic result of any major war.

Understanding Eisenhower's strategy demands an acceptance of his judgment that nuclear deterrence would prevent war with any major power. To do that, war had to be seen as an apocalyptic, history-ending event. He was deeply aware that in trying to prevent war, he was faced with a series of bad choices. The least bad was a policy requiring the first use of nuclear weapons by the United States if war was ever forced upon the nation. Eisenhower always emphasized the *deterrence of war* by nuclear weapons and never talked lightly about their use, which he described as "self-defeating." He was convinced that free American institutions would not survive a nuclear war, no matter how it ended.

The military component of the Eisenhower strategy was officially approved by him in December 1953, in the form of a paper which had been worked out by the Joint Chiefs of Staff.[4] It had already become known as the "New Look," and was further popularized in a speech to the Council on Foreign Relations on January 12, 1954, by Secretary of State John Foster Dulles. Eisenhower's policies overturned Truman's intention to increase conventional military strength to the point where it could respond in kind to Soviet probes. "Congruent" force, as Truman's NSC 68 called it, was an expensive luxury, as Eisenhower saw it. Furthermore, Eisenhower preferred to "demilitarize" the confrontation with communism in the developing world.[5] Thus, in opposition to much establishment wisdom, despite growing criticism from civilian defense experts, and over the strong case made to the contrary by U.S. Army leadership, especially General Maxwell Taylor, Eisenhower put in place a nuclear-oriented strategy and maintained it throughout the eight years of his administration. For a president who was criticized for spending too little time on the job, this was quite an achievement.

The Great Equation

An issue on today's agenda is the level of defense spending in relation to other national requirements. It was on Eisenhower's agenda, too. He called this "the great equation." The great equation was given heavy emphasis in NSC 162/2. The idea that Americans must maintain a strong defense over "the long pull," to which Truman's basic policy had also referred, was specifically endorsed. The state of the U.S. economy was seen as the prime consideration affecting staying power (paragraph 9b). The Eisenhower policy document sternly warned that "expenditures for national security, in fact all federal, state and local governmental expenditures, must be carefully scrutinized with a view to measuring their impact on the national economy" (paragraph 19).

Eisenhower, the retired general, became the butt of criticism for his efforts to hold down government spending, including defense spending. He spoke many times of his fear that excessive spending on defense could result in the United States becoming a "garrison state." Eisenhower understood that "massive retaliation" was not directly relevant to "political aggression," but he did not think that American conventional military force was the answer for that or for localized conflicts in the Third World. His solution was a deterrent strategy based on the threat of strategic and tactical nuclear weapons, coupled with economic and military assistance programs for American allies. He also relied on the CIA's covert action capabilities under the management of Allen Dulles, brother of Secretary of State John Foster Dulles.

The "First Use" Doctrine

Many of Eisenhower's discussions with his National Security Council during the first years of his administration were devoted to defining the doctrine of "first use" of nuclear weapons, the doctrine inherent in U.S. defense policy even today. The doctrine that the United States would initiate the use of nu-

clear weapons in any conflict in which it was engaged was codified in Eisenhower's national security policy document, NSC 162/2. Eisenhower's thinking about defense required that a document that would be read by so many
people, authorized or not, could show no hesitations about the use of nuclear
weapons. And it did not: "In the event of hostilities the United States will
consider nuclear weapons to be as available for use as other munitions" (paragraph 39b).

Extended Deterrence

Absolute certainty that war in Europe would be a nuclear war was one of the
basic tenets of Eisenhower's deterrence strategy. NSC 162/2 stated that "the
major deterrent to aggression against Western Europe is the manifest determination of the United States to use its atomic capability and massive retaliatory striking power if the area is attacked" (paragraph 15b). As early as
1951–1952, American military commanders in NATO had begun planning
for the use of nuclear weapons in the European theater. General Lauris
Norstad, USAF, a supreme commander of NATO forces, said that Eisenhower,
when NATO's first supreme commander, had personally approved Allied
planning for the use of several nuclear weapons, each theoretically to be of a
yield equivalent to the Hiroshima bomb.[6] The operative word is "planning."

Eisenhower had close connections with European leaders, dating from his
World War II service as supreme commander of allied forces in Europe. Thus,
he carried into his peacetime relationships the same insistence on cooperation with America's allies that had distinguished his service as supreme allied
commander in World War II and as the first NATO commander. With the
full support of the European allies, he moved the American nuclear umbrella
firmly over their heads. The idea of "extended nuclear deterrence" had its
heyday during the Eisenhower era. A Soviet attack on Western Europe would
amount to general war and would call forth the use of American nuclear
weapons against the Soviet Union.

In Europe, Eisenhower's nuclear deterrent doctrine penetrated very
deeply, but Europeans already had encouraged this strategy. Marshal of the
Royal Air Force John Slessor had advocated a nuclear deterrent strategy
while Eisenhower was at NATO headquarters; Eisenhower was familiar with
Slessor's thinking before becoming president. Slessor's book *Strategy for the
West*, published in 1954, could have been the basic treatise on Eisenhower's
strategy.[7]

Eisenhower's remarks sometimes echoed notions that Slessor had advocated and tried to popularize. In an NSC meeting on December 3, 1954, for

example, Eisenhower remarked that there were some who believed that modern warfare imposes its own limitations.[8] Slessor had written that "war has abolished itself because the atomic and the hydrogen bombs have found their way into the armories of the world."[9]

First Use in Practice: The Korea Case

Eisenhower explained his thinking about using nuclear weapons in Korea in his memoirs. He wrote that if a major U.N. command offensive were to be undertaken there, the United States would have to use nuclear weapons. The Joint Chiefs of Staff, he recalled, held the view that tactical use of nuclear weapons in Korea would not be very effective because the allies faced extensive underground fortifications. A more effective use would be against strategic targets in North Korea, Manchuria, and on the Chinese coast. Eisenhower believed that an American decision to use nuclear weapons at that time would have been extremely disruptive of alliance relationships, in particular with the British. This was the same conclusion Truman had reached. Eisenhower also worried that if the Soviet Union should enter the war, Japanese cities would be vulnerable to Soviet nuclear attack. This is the hostage problem, which still persists and which has to be an inhibiting factor in any alliance. Despite these concerns, Eisenhower wrote, he allowed word to be passed to the Chinese early in 1953 that in the absence of satisfactory progress in armistice talks, the United States would no longer be inhibited in its use of weapons nor would it be responsible for confining hostilities to the Korean peninsula.[10]

Stalin's death at about this same time probably had a major effect on Soviet and Chinese decisions to bring the war to an end that summer. Eisenhower was quite willing to settle for an armistice at the 38th parallel. He was prepared to bring pressure on President Rhee, of South Korea, to accept the armistice and did so in no uncertain terms.

General Maxwell Taylor, former Eighth Army commander in Korea, wrote revealingly of the reasons for not using nuclear weapons earlier in the war. He also wrote of his impressions of the state of mind in the Eisenhower administration early in 1953:

> The cost of attempting a breakthrough of the heavily fortified front facing the Eighth Army was clearly beyond anything the new Eisenhower Administration would or should pay simply to move the line somewhat farther north into Korea. At one time I estimated that to breach that front would require about eight additional U.S. divisions and a readiness to use tactical nuclear weapons.

. . . I had no hesitancy in assuring President Eisenhower, Secretary of Defense Wilson, and other senior officials in Washington, who probed my views before my departure, that I was quite prepared to live with a defensive strategy and not kick against the pricks.[11]

Nuclear Weapons and Force Levels

How far could Eisenhower's "New Look" in defense policy be pushed to substitute nuclear firepower for conventional forces, especially Army troops? This was hotly debated in the fall of 1953. The Korean armistice had been signed on July 27, 1953, and in the fall of that year Eisenhower was anxious to reduce his defense budget. He was being told by the joint chiefs, however, that they could not recommend cuts in force levels unless they were clear that they could use nuclear weapons in future conflicts. Dulles, Humphrey, and Wilson had more than one day in court with the president on this issue, but the decisive meeting was on November 11, 1953. They met in relative privacy, and without Admiral Radford, chairman of the Joint Chiefs of Staff. The compromise they reached was to order a limited withdrawal of troops based overseas on the theory that this would provide a rationale for cutting the budget, without granting the chiefs explicit authority to use nuclear weapons. The plan was to withdraw some ground troops from Korea and to thin out support units in Europe. On this basis, the Army's request for a force level of 1.5 million men could be rejected and the defense budget for fiscal year 1955 could be reduced.

This was not the end of the argument about whether nuclear weapons really would be available for use as readily as conventional weapons. It was only a temporary truce. In the election year of 1956, still caught between the conflicting views of Radford and Army Chief of Staff Maxwell Taylor, Eisenhower finally agreed, for the record, that the first use of nuclear weapons would be authorized in situations short of general war, that is, outside of Europe, when required by military considerations. General Andrew Goodpaster, who was Eisenhower's special assistant, had a ring-side seat at these debates, and his view was that Eisenhower never left any doubt that he retained the full power of decision regarding use of nuclear weapons. Goodpaster's comments were conveyed to me in a letter dated February 7, 1997:

I would draw a distinction, I believe, between what Eisenhower approved for defense budgets, preparations and operational plans and concepts on the one hand, and how he envisaged his actions in directing and conducting military activity (including nuclear) should conflict actually occur, on the other. Dealing with the first set of issues was a continuing largely bureaucratic struggle. On the second, he had no doubt and left no doubt that he would be actively in charge, and retained the full power of decision for himself. The efforts we often saw to force his hand on the first by tying him down on the second just as often got nowhere with him. Nor did he allow on-going foreign policy judgments and decisions to be forced by such considerations. He was willing to allow the premises for budgets and the like to be argued over, but without by any means losing his freedom of decision on current international issues or—prospectively—conduct of military affairs.

Authorizing Use of Nuclear Weapons

The doctrine of first use of nuclear weapons, as debated in the Eisenhower administration, raised the question of who would really authorize the use of a nuclear weapon in combat. Eisenhower wanted it to be believed without question that nuclear weapons would be used if the United States was attacked. Because of this policy and because he was concerned about a surprise attack—a Soviet first strike—he dispersed nuclear weapons to major military commanders and gave limited authority to military commanders to use nuclear weapons in certain circumstances if the United States was attacked.

Eisenhower insisted on tight control over an initial U.S. strategic nuclear retaliatory attack. After that, he seemed to expect nothing but chaos. In the record of a meeting between Eisenhower and his senior military advisers on August 11, 1960, Eisenhower said that the initial operations of the future would impose a requirement for greater rigidity in planning than in the past. He wanted to be very clear on this point: "for the first strike there must be rigid planning, and it must be obeyed to the letter."[12]

Military commanders accepted that the president, as commander in chief, was the ultimate authority for the use of nuclear weapons. Since surprise attack was considered a possible Soviet option, however, commanders were worried about delays in securing authorization from the president to use nuclear weapons, and Eisenhower authorized their use in certain emergency situations.

When Kennedy became president, he insisted on tightening up command and control procedures, and he imposed new demands on communications and new thinking about the role of the president in wartime.

Rejection of "Preventive War"

Eisenhower considered a surprise Soviet attack unlikely, but recognizing that it was a possibility, he sponsored the U-2 spy plane and satellite reconnaissance. He also wondered whether the American people over the long haul would maintain the forces and the readiness for instant retaliation. Small wonder that in such a novel and wholly unpredictable situation, and facing a growing nuclear threat in the depths of the Cold War, the logic of "preventive war" was considered. Preventive war meant an attack on the Soviet Union before the Soviets acquired the capability to inflict massive damage on the United States. But Eisenhower always rejected that logic. He believed that the U.S.-Soviet confrontation was going to last a long time and that it had to be dealt with pragmatically as a series of practical issues, not as a geopolitical problem that had a clear black and white answer.

Eisenhower had rejected the idea of a "critical date," a key element of NSC 68, Truman's basic document on policy toward the Soviet Union. The idea was used in NSC 68 to emphasize the need for urgency in building military forces. It had other connotations, however. Many Americans, including some of Eisenhower's top military advisers, believed that the Soviet Union would move aggressively against Western interests once a condition of mutual nuclear deterrence had been achieved. The Joint Chiefs of Staff thought that immediate operational consequences should flow from a realization that the Soviet Union could inflict severe damage on the U.S. homeland at some point in the future. This was the 1950s analogue of the phenomenon that President George W. Bush later called "a gathering threat." And the fear in the 1950s also was that the threat might not be deterrable.

The joint chiefs repeatedly drew to Eisenhower's attention a policy statement contained in NSC 162/2, paragraph 45: "In the face of the developing Soviet threat, the broad aim of U.S. security policies must be to create, prior to the achievement of mutual atomic plenty, conditions under which the United States and the free world coalition are prepared to meet the Soviet-Communist threat with resolution and to negotiate for its alleviation under proper safeguards."

In the spring of 1954, the Planning Board of the NSC began the preparation of a paper on "guidelines to implement NSC 162/2" for use during fiscal year 1956 (NSC 5422). The Joint Chiefs of Staff contributed a study to the paper which was forwarded to the Planning Board on May 25, 1954.[13] In the study, the joint chiefs explained the problem they envisaged when both the United States and the Soviet Union entered the era of atomic plenty during fiscal years 1956–59:

> With respect to general war, the attainment of atomic plenty by both the United States and the U.S.S.R. could create a condition of mutual deterrence in which both sides would be strongly inhibited from initiating general war.

Under such circumstances, the Soviets might well elect to pursue their ultimate objective of world domination through a succession of local aggressions, either overt or covert, all of which could not be successfully opposed by the Allies through localized counteraction, without unacceptable commitment of resources. The Free World would then be confronted with a situation in which the only alternative to acquiescence in progressive accretions of territory, manpower, and other resources by the Soviet Bloc would be a deliberate decision to react with military force against the real source of the aggression. This situation serves to emphasize the time limitation, as recognized in paragraph 45 of NSC 162/2, within which conditions must be created by the United States and the Free World coalition such as to permit the Soviet-Communist threat to be met with resolution, to the end that satisfactory and enduring arrangements for co-existence can be established.

The chairman of the Joint Chiefs of Staff, Admiral Radford, spoke to this issue in an NSC meeting on November 24, 1954. Radford noted that the joint chiefs had expressed more than once their view that once the Soviet Union had attained a position of nuclear balance with the United States, the Russians might initiate a general war. In other words, Moscow would no longer be deterred.

Emphasizing the need for action in the time remaining before the Soviets achieved a significant capacity for damaging the United States, Radford said, "assuming that the objectives of Soviet Communism were unchanged, the Joint Chiefs of Staff believed that some time or other the Soviet Union will elect to force the issue. Accordingly, the Joint Chiefs had concluded that the United States has only a limited period of time with which to reach an accommodation with the Communists."

The joint chiefs also made it clear to the president that they took a dim view of negotiations as a means of reaching an "accommodation" with the Soviet Union. NSC 5440, of December 14, 1954, a draft "Summary Statement of Existing Basic National Security Policy," explained the joint chiefs' views: "the U.S. must realize it will be not only fruitless, but perhaps even hazardous, to continue its efforts to arrive at solutions to world problems through the normal processes of negotiation with the U.S.S.R."

The joint chiefs never were clear in the records about what they wanted Eisenhower to do, but they called for a more aggressive stance and a higher degree of risk-taking in relations with the Soviet Union. Eisenhower recognized that if followed to its extreme, a more aggressive policy raised the question of preventive war. In an NSC meeting on November 24, 1954, Radford was pressed by John Foster Dulles to explain specifically how he would "forestall" Communist actions instead of "reacting" to them. Radford came up with the idea of outright support of the Arabs against the French in North Africa. This effort to apply the more "dynamic policy" advocated by the Joint Chiefs of Staff quickly sank out of sight, and no better illustration of how to be "dynamic" was advanced by Radford.

At the end of the meeting, Eisenhower remarked wearily that he was tired of abstractions. They got him down, he said.[14]

Creating the Strategic Triad

Eisenhower presided over the birth of the ballistic missile age. He assigned highest national priority to the development of intercontinental and inter-mediate-range ballistic missiles in 1955, an unusual step in peacetime, after being urged to do so by high-level scientific panels. New technological de-velopments and expectations that the Soviets were rapidly developing bal-listic missile technology combined to force the pace of the revolution in de-livering weapons to targets. Ballistic missiles made their first appearance in U.S. strategic forces in 1958 with the Atlas D intercontinental ballistic mis-sile (ICBM) and the Thor intermediate-range ballistic missile (IRBM), both liquid fueled. The submarine-launched ballistic missile (SLBM) joined the fleet soon afterward, aboard nuclear-powered submarines. The solid-fueled Polaris was first tested in January 1958, and Polaris submarines entered oper-ation in late 1960.

Technology moved so rapidly that President Eisenhower also authorized the development of the second-generation ICBM, the solid-fueled ICBM Minuteman I, the first prototype of which was launched just after the Kennedy administration came into office, in February 1961. With this, the Eisenhower administration had laid the foundations for the American strate-gic forces as they were to exist for the next quarter of a century and beyond. The "triad," as it came to be called, consisted of silo-based solid-fueled ICBMs, submarine-based solid-fueled SLBMs and long-range heavy bombers. Cruise missiles were also being developed.

When they were available, President Eisenhower offered intermediate-range ballistic missiles (IRBMs), the Thor and Jupiter, to the NATO allies. These were deployed in Britain, Turkey, and Italy, antedating by nearly a quarter of a century the deployment under President Ronald Reagan of American Pershing and ground-launched cruise missiles in the 1980s.

Eisenhower also approved programs that dramatically altered the nature of the U.S. bomber fleet. At the beginning of his term, U.S. Air Force bombers were propeller-driven B-29s and B-50s, about 800 in number. At the end of his term, there were over 1,800 bombers, including the jet-powered B-52 which, in modernized versions, were used by the George W. Bush administration in Afghanistan and Iraq.

Eisenhower's technical advisers thought the accuracy of U.S. intercontinental ballistic missiles and the efficiency of U.S. nuclear warheads meant that very large payloads were not required. American advances in reducing the weight of thermonuclear weapons meant that these smaller missiles were quite capable of delivering a thermonuclear warhead at intercontinental ranges. Furthermore—and very importantly—they could be developed more quickly than larger missiles. The disparity in size between U.S. and Soviet missiles led later to asymmetries in the load-carrying capacities, or throw-weight, of American and Soviet strategic missile forces. With larger missiles, the Soviet strategic forces could carry a greater cumulative weight. This difference in throw-weight later became a major arms control issue.

Eisenhower had been sensitive to this disparity. George Kistiakowsky, Eisenhower's science adviser, wrote in his diary for October 26, 1959:

> it is now the third time that he has referred back to the 1953–55 period when our missile program was set, and he questions the motives that led us to the selection of comparatively small ICBMs. Was it economy? Both York and I assured him that it wasn't a question of economy, but speed of development which led the von Neumann Committee to recommend the small missiles, since they were adequate for the military task.[15]

Eisenhower thought that manned bombers would be the mainstay of American strategic offensive forces for years. But he regarded the resources being devoted to missile research and development by his administration as quite adequate in light of what he knew of the Soviet programs. Eisenhower felt so strongly that Democratic charges of a missile gap were erroneous and unfair that he took a stand on it in his Farewell Address: "The 'bomber gap' of several years ago was always a fiction, and the 'missile gap' shows every sign of being the same."[16]

The Sputnik Shock: Insecurity's Political Fallout

During the first five years of Eisenhower's time in office, the American people and Congress supported the president's defense programs without much public debate. That the United States was becoming vulnerable to a Soviet nuclear attack was understood, but Eisenhower's programs seemed sufficient to deal with that problem. The appearance of the world's first earth-orbiting satellite, the Soviet *Sputnik*, on October 4, 1957, changed all that. The jolt that the Soviet satellite gave the American people, and the shock waves it imparted to American politics, was one of the major events of the post–World War II era. It was akin in some psychological ways to the shock of September 11, 2001.

Americans had become complacent about their technological prowess in 1957, considering that an American lead in technology was in the natural order of things. Suddenly, there was a Soviet "moon," and shortly thereafter came Khrushchev's claims to superiority in intercontinental missiles. This was a serious miscalculation by Khrushchev. *Sputnik* and Khrushchev's exploitation of it produced a shock to the national self-esteem that led Americans to question even their system of values, including the process of educating their youth. But it led to an American nuclear buildup, to Khrushchev's debacle in Cuba, and eventually to his ouster.

The problems Eisenhower faced in the aftermath of *Sputnik* were not so much technological and industrial questions as they were political and psychological. Despite his reputation and experience in defense affairs, he was thrown on the defensive. By the end of the year 1957, Congress was questioning Eisenhower's management of missile programs. Eisenhower, however, saw a need to resist increases in the defense budget that could not be usefully absorbed by the ballistic missile programs. In his memoirs, he quoted Dr. Detlev Bronk, then head of the National Science Foundation, who advised him four days after *Sputnik* that the Soviet success should not induce changes in the U.S. research and development program. The father of the German rocket program, Wernher von Braun, according to Eisenhower, said that "we don't need excessive amounts of extra money—we certainly don't have to double our present missile budget."[17] Eisenhower successfully managed to resist too heavy an investment in "primitive," first-generation ballistic missiles, but his judgment about the implications of the U.S.-Soviet military balance in 1957–1958 was difficult for him to sustain because of public furor over *Sputnik*, which was stimulated by misleading Soviet claims of major advances in strategic weaponry.

Ballistic Missile Defense

Research on missile defenses dated from the first operational ballistic missile, the German V-2 during World War II. Ballistic missile defense (BMD) projects were begun by the U.S. Air Force in 1946. The technology, however, was too primitive to proceed to the development phase in the late 1940s and early 1950s. In response to the first Soviet testing of an intercontinental ballistic missile in 1957, the Eisenhower administration accelerated research but never reached the point of deploying a system. President Eisenhower was not convinced of the technical feasibility of missile defense at that point and thought it was too expensive. Despite his objections, Congress appropriated more money for ballistic missile defense than Eisenhower wanted. He refused to spend it, setting the stage for a debate that has continued to the present day.

The Negotiating Option

Eisenhower's innate optimism required him to think about other options than nuclear war. He repeatedly encouraged his advisers to give him ideas on promoting disarmament negotiations. Eisenhower himself took the lead in initiatives designed to foster a dialogue with the Soviet Union. The U.S.-Soviet Summit Meetings, Open Skies, Atoms for Peace, the International Atomic Energy Agency, and the nuclear testing moratorium would not have been possible without his prodding, his support, and his stubbornness. His appointment of Harold Stassen, the former "boy wonder" governor of Minnesota, as special assistant for disarmament yielded some progress toward negotiations, but the lack of unified administration support for Stassen's efforts, and Stassen's own handling of his mandate, caused the enterprise to fail.

The most important of the negotiations was that concerning the nuclear test ban. Secretary of State Dulles's support for the nuclear test ban negotiations and associated test moratorium was of crucial importance. Opposition to that negotiation was strong within the administration and in Congress. George Kistiakowsky, Eisenhower's science adviser, and a key player on the Manhattan Project, strongly supported the effort. Spurgeon Keeny, a member of the science adviser's office, was a very positive influence. The State Department provided essential support at critical moments. But the effort in its essence was one of the more courageous acts of President Eisenhower personally. Without his backing there would have been no test ban treaty in the administration of John F. Kennedy.

When Eisenhower appointed Harold Stassen as his disarmament adviser in 1955, Stassen was still in the top ranks of Republicans at the national level. He had come close to being their nominee for president in 1948. A proposal similar to the Acheson-Lilienthal plan, formulated nearly a decade earlier, was still the U.S. position on nuclear disarmament. The United States ritualistically supported it and it had become a barrier to any attempt to impose piecemeal nuclear constraints. Reducing Soviet superiority in non-nuclear arms and military manpower through cuts in the Red Army had been added to the American disarmament program.

One of Stassen's first acts was to place a reservation on all previous U.S. disarmament proposals. His next move was to secure Eisenhower's agreement that partial, or limited, steps toward disarmament would be acceptable. In the fall of 1956, Adlai Stevenson, the Democratic candidate for president, came out in favor of a test ban. "Catastrophic nonsense," huffed Richard Nixon, Eisenhower's vice president. Stevenson lost the election, overwhelmed by Ike's continuing popularity. In 1957, under Stassen's leadership, a nuclear test suspension emerged as a separately identified element in proposals advanced in London by the U.S. delegation to the Five-Power U.N. Subcommittee on Disarmament (comprising the United States, the United Kingdom, Canada, France, and the U.S.S.R.).

The nuclear test ban idea continued to gain momentum in 1958. At that point, collaboration between the president's science adviser and some members of the U.S. scientific community, together with the Department of State, resulted in a proposal by Eisenhower for two international technical conferences, one on monitoring a test ban, the other on ways to prevent surprise attack. Hans Bethe, a great American physicist who had been connected with the Manhattan Project, had a decisive influence on this outcome. An exchange of notes between Moscow and Washington in April, May, and June 1958 finally led to the convening of a conference of experts on the test ban on July 1, 1958. It ended on August 21. The Western experts operated as a single delegation headed by James B. Fisk of Bell Labs. The delegation included British and French experts. The Eastern side was organized as separate national delegations, Soviet, Polish, Czech, and Romanian.

The other technical conference concerned surprise attack and how to prevent it. It ran from November 10 to December 18, 1958. The U.S. delegation was headed by William C. Foster, a successful Republican businessman, later first director of the U.S. Arms Control and Disarmament Agency. I was assigned as the Atomic Energy Commission representative to the conference. Although the U.S. delegation included several prominent scientists, it was impossible to escape the political nature of much of the subject matter. The conference adjourned in December without results.

The test ban conference, in contrast, really was technical, and it succeeded in recommending a system of monitoring nuclear test explosions. That system became known as the "Geneva system," and it consisted of most of the sensors that are used today for monitoring nuclear explosions: acoustic, seismic, and radio signals, and collection of radioactive debris. The report also recommended on-site inspections, and that proposal was supported by prominent Soviet scientists.

The next step in the test ban saga was even more dramatic. The test ban was not popular in the weapons laboratories or in the military. Edward Teller, known as the father of the hydrogen bomb, spoke against it. Many politicians in both parties were highly skeptical of it. Critically important to the beginning of the whole enterprise, and to its later development, was the strong support of President Eisenhower. Eisenhower agreed on August 21 to a negotiation to determine whether a comprehensive test ban treaty could be concluded. He proposed that it begin on October 31. The test ban negotiations began on that date, with James Wadsworth representing the United States, Semyon Tsarapkin, the Soviet Union, and David Ormsby-Gore, the United Kingdom. Eisenhower put into effect a moratorium on all U.S. testing of nuclear weapons for one year from the beginning of the talks. The Soviet Union followed suit. The moratorium was extended through the rest of his term of office and beyond.

All during 1959 and 1960, the negotiators in Geneva and their backstoppers in Washington struggled to solve one issue after another. Some of these were serious technical issues and required adjustments in the U.S. position. The impasse created by the technical requirement for on-site inspection and Soviet opposition to that, especially after the U.S. presentation of new seismic data in January 1959, led to moves by the Eisenhower administration, as early as 1959, to modify the scope of a ban on nuclear tests. Many of the opponents of a comprehensive test ban within the scientific community were willing to accept a ban that excluded underground testing which presented difficult monitoring issues. The Senate also might be more willing to give its consent to ratification of a treaty that permitted tests conducted underground. And the environmental damage caused by unrestricted testing in the earth's atmosphere would be minimized if only underground tests were permitted.

The years 1959–1960 were crucial for the test ban treaty. The very idea of a test ban was under attack on grounds of verifiability. Limitations of any kind on nuclear testing were labeled as dangerous to national security. The negotiations were kept alive, just barely, by the State Department disarmament team, with the help of the White House. Yet, in 1960, the United States and the Soviet Union came closer to an agreement on a comprehensive test ban treaty than at any other time during the Eisenhower and Kennedy administrations.

On April 13, 1959, Eisenhower wrote to the Soviet leader, Nikita Khrushchev, proposing a treaty that would ban atmospheric tests and would be based on the Geneva system. It would not require automatic on-site inspections. By February 11, 1960, Eisenhower's chief test ban negotiator, James Wadsworth, was instructed to propose a phased agreement that would ban tests in the atmosphere, in the ocean, and also in outer space to the extent that techniques for monitoring that environment would permit. Underground tests would be banned above an agreed threshold, and a research program would be conducted to improve detection of underground tests.

On March 19, 1960, Soviet Ambassador Tsarapkin agreed to the U.S.-U.K. proposal for an agreement that would come into effect in phases. But he insisted that a moratorium on all underground tests below the threshold should be instituted and that it would continue regardless of the results of the research program, in which he said the Soviet Union would participate. And he said that all tests in outer space should be prohibited.

President Eisenhower and British Prime Minister Macmillan issued a joint statement on March 29, 1960, which came close to accepting the Soviet offer of a phased treaty with a moratorium on underground tests below the threshold. Their proposal was for a "voluntary moratorium of agreed duration on nuclear weapons tests below that threshold, to be accomplished by unilateral declaration of each of the three powers." This, and the Soviet responses, in May and July, moved the three nations closer to a comprehensive test ban treaty than at any other time.

The momentum was interrupted on May 1, 1960, when the Soviets succeeded in downing a U.S. U-2 reconnaissance aircraft over Sverdlovsk (Ekaterinburg). Despite that ominous development, Khrushchev essentially accepted the Eisenhower-Macmillan proposal in a statement Ambassador Tsarapkin made in Geneva on May 3. He agreed that the moratorium would be announced by unilateral declarations. A fixed duration for the moratorium would be included in the declaration, but the nations should not automatically resume testing, he said, if the research program failed to find a way to make all underground tests fully detectable.

A test ban could have been materially advanced in a summit meeting involving Eisenhower, Khrushchev, and Macmillan scheduled for mid-May in Paris with French President de Gaulle chairing. But because of the U-2 incident, the summit discussions never got beyond the preliminaries, although all the participants traveled to Paris thinking that serious talks might still be possible. When Khrushchev demanded that Eisenhower apologize for the U-2 flights, Eisenhower refused and the meeting broke up. Had the U-2 incident not happened, and had Eisenhower traveled to the Soviet Union after the summit, as had been planned, it is very likely that some kind of comprehensive test ban agreement would have been worked out. The negotiators never came that close again until 1996.

The Eisenhower administration passed on to the incoming Kennedy administration an ongoing tripartite negotiation and a more than two-year

moratorium on all nuclear tests. Eisenhower also laid the conceptual and political basis for the limited test ban treaty that Kennedy secured in 1963.
Without this legacy, it would have been very difficult for Kennedy to restart
test ban negotiations, not to mention successfully negotiate an agreement
and get its ratification approved by the U.S. Senate.

Eisenhower and the Military-Industrial Complex

Eisenhower was perhaps the last president who could successfully resist the
politics of defense spending, and even he did not come away unscathed. In
1957, he was hit by a political bombshell in the form of the Gaither Report,
prepared for the Office of Defense Mobilization by a panel of distinguished
private citizens. This report warned that Soviet strategic nuclear forces were
rapidly expanding and that the United States population and strategic forces
were becoming increasingly vulnerable to large-scale Soviet attack. Various
remedies were urgently recommended, including strengthening the Air Force
Strategic Air Command and building fallout shelters. It was a call to arms,
challenging what many saw as the complacent defense policy of the Eisenhower administration.

Although highly classified, the gist soon leaked out and became the subject of partisan debate. Eisenhower was furious about the leak. Explaining his
point of view much later, Eisenhower neatly summed up his philosophy of
the president's function:

> the entire report could not be accepted as a master blueprint for action. The
> President, unlike a panel which concentrates on a single problem, must always
> strive to see the totality of the national and international situation. He must
> take into account conflicting purposes, responding to legitimate needs but as-
> signing priorities and keeping plans and costs within bounds.[18]

Adding to Eisenhower's difficulties, the Rockefeller Brothers Fund soon
published a report that offered much the same advice as the Gaither Report.
All of this, of course, was grist for the political mills, especially as 1958 was
a midterm election year. Public concern about *Sputnik* and what it implied
came on top of latent uneasiness in Congress about Eisenhower's reliance on
nuclear deterrence and what it might be doing to America's ability to deal
with limited war situations.

Eisenhower's response was to hold the line on defense spending while
seeking to reassure Congress and the public that U.S. defense programs by
and large were on the right track. His State of the Union Address of January

1958 and other speeches argued that the administration had taken the measure of the Soviet threat and had the right answers to it. Always, the need for fiscal soundness was emphasized and reemphasized. Eisenhower later summed up his attitude in his final State of the Union message in 1961:

> Since 1953, our defense policy has been based on the assumption that the international situation would require heavy defense expenditures for an indefinite period to come, probably for years. In this protracted struggle, good management dictates that we resist overspending as resolutely as we oppose underspending. Every dollar uselessly spent on military mechanisms decreases our total strength and, therefore, our security. We must not return to the "crash-program" psychology of the past when each new feint by the Communists was responded to in panic.

The experience served to confirm in Eisenhower's mind the "unwarranted influence" of "the military-industrial complex" of which he warned in his Farewell Address in 1961. Remarking on this, Andrew Goodpaster has said that the term "had he described it in full, would have been the military-industrial-Congressional complex."[19] He could have added "defense intellectuals," since policy entrepreneurs in think tanks and universities have always had an influential role in framing defense issues. On the whole, Eisenhower had his way on the nation's defense programs, but probably at the expense of the Republican Party's chances in the 1960 presidential election.

The Nuclear Paradox

While Eisenhower was making nuclear weapons the centerpiece of his defense policy, he also was making the public aware of the full dimensions of the disaster that would befall them if they were ever used. In a speech to the United Nations on December 8, 1953, he said:

> But let no one think that the expenditure of vast sums for weapons and systems of defense can guarantee absolute safety for the cities and citizens of any nation. The awful arithmetic of the atomic bomb does not permit of any such easy solution. Even against the most powerful defense, an aggressor in possession of the effective minimum number of atomic bombs for a surprise attack could probably place a sufficient number of his bombs on the chosen targets to cause hideous damage.[20]

In the later years of the Eisenhower administration, the meaning of "atomic plenty" was quantified by a team of military experts called the Net

Evaluation Subcommittee of the NSC, of which I was later to become a member. It had been formed to assess the results of a U.S.-Soviet nuclear exchange. The president recorded in his diary the results that a briefing in January 1956 had revealed to him. "Casualties were enormous," Eisenhower wrote, whether there was a month's warning or only a few hours. "It was calculated that something on the order of 65 percent of the [U.S.] population would require some kind of medical care and, in most instances, no opportunity to get it." He described the post-attack situation as "a business of digging ourselves out of ashes, starting again." As to the Soviet Union, Eisenhower wrote, "the damage inflicted by us against the Soviets was roughly three times greater. The picture of total destruction of the areas of lethal fallout, of serious fallout, and of at least some damage from fallout, was appalling."[21]

On February 10, 1956, Eisenhower met with the Joint Chiefs of Staff. The report he had heard the month before was still very much on his mind. He told the joint chiefs that the report left him with one overall question—how would we fight a war after the amount of devastation shown in that report, or even a small fraction of that amount?[22]

In a January 1959 meeting with John McCone, chair of the U.S. Atomic Energy Commission, Eisenhower complained that the Defense Department wanted enough nuclear weapons to destroy every conceivable target all over the world, plus a threefold reserve. This he compared with earlier calculations that the destruction of seventy targets would be enough to defeat the Soviet Union. Eisenhower told McCone that he was worried about the unrealistic attitude of the top military leaders. McCone, no dove himself, agreed that they talked about megaton explosions as though these were almost nothing.[23]

Later that same year, on March 11, 1959, Eisenhower was asked in a press conference about the use of nuclear weapons in the context of Khrushchev's threat to the Western presence in Berlin. He replied with one of his most pessimistic public assessments of the results of recourse to nuclear war:

> And, I must say, to use that kind of a nuclear war as a general thing looks to me a self-defeating thing for all of us. After all, with that kind of release of nuclear explosions around the world, of the numbers of hundreds, I don't know what it would do to the world and particularly the Northern Hemisphere; and I don't think anybody else does. But I know it would be quite serious.[24]

The precedent of nonuse set by Truman after August 1945 graduated to what Professor Thomas Schelling called "the tradition of nonuse" during Eisenhower's presidency. But some correctives to his policies had clearly become necessary by the time his term ended. His willingness to allow the military to plan on the use of nuclear weapons for a wide range of possible situations resulted in a bias toward the use of such weapons and an inflexibility in confronting military contingencies. The incoming Kennedy team saw this as one of its most urgent problems.

The Eisenhower story brings to mind a speech made in the British House of Commons in 1955 by Winston Churchill: "It may well be that we shall by a process of sublime irony have reached a stage in this story where safety will be the sturdy child of terror and survival the twin brother of annihilation."

Notes

1. This account of Project Solarium is based on the published record in *Foreign Relations of the United States* (FRUS), vol. 2, part 1.

2. NSC 162/2, dated October 30, 1953, is reproduced in the Senator Gravel edition of *The Pentagon Papers* (Boston, Mass.: Beacon Press, 1971), 412–428.

3. The following references to Eisenhower's study of Clausewitz bear on this point: John Gaddis, *Strategies of Containment* (Oxford: Oxford University Press, 1982), 135; Stephen E. Ambrose, *Eisenhower*, vol. 1 (New York: Simon and Schuster, 1983), 76.

4. Douglas Kinnard, *President Eisenhower and Strategy Management* (Lexington: University Press of Kentucky, 1977).

5. Andrew J. Goodpaster, recorded interview by Maclyn P. Burg, January 16, 1978, Eisenhower Library, Oral History No. 378, 107.

6. Lauris Norstad, recorded interview by Thomas Soapes, November 11, 1976, Eisenhower Library, Oral History No. 385, 40.

7. John Slessor, *Strategy for the West* (New York: William Morrow, 1954).

8. FRUS, vol. 2, part 1, 805.

9. Slessor, *Strategy for the West*, 16.

10. Dwight D. Eisenhower, *Mandate for Change 1953–1956* (Garden City, N.Y.: Doubleday, 1963), 179–181.

11. Maxwell D. Taylor, *Swords and Plowshares* (New York: W. W. Norton, 1972), 137.

12. Memorandum of conference with the president August 11, 1960, prepared by A. J. Goodpaster, memorandum dated August 13, 1960. Declassified June 10, 1980, NLE: MR Case No. 79–103, Document No. 5.

13. The following discussion is based on FRUS, 1952–54, vol. 2, part 1.

14. FRUS, 1952–54, vol. 2, part 1, 795–799.

15. George Kistiakowsky, *A Scientist at the White House* (Cambridge, Mass.: Harvard University Press, 1976), 129.

16. *Public Papers of the Presidents*, Eisenhower, 1960–1961, 919.

17. The Bronk comment is reported on p. 211 and the von Braun comment on p. 217 of Dwight D. Eisenhower, *Waging Peace, 1956–1961* (Garden City, N.Y.: Doubleday, 1965).

18. Eisenhower, *Waging Peace*, 221.

19. Andrew J. Goodpaster, recorded interview by Malcolm S. McDonald, April 10, 1982, Eisenhower Library, Oral History No. 477.

20. *Public Papers of the Presidents*, Eisenhower, 1953, 816.

21. Robert H. Ferrell, ed., *The Eisenhower Diaries* (New York: W. W. Norton, 1981), 311–312.

22. Memorandum for record, February 10, 1956, prepared by A. J. Goodpaster, Eisenhower Library, declassified April 15, 1980.

23. Memorandum of conference with the president, January 16, 1959, prepared by A. J. Goodpaster, Eisenhower Library, declassified August 22, 1979.

24. *Public Papers of the Presidents*, Eisenhower, 1959, 252.

CHAPTER THREE

~

John F. Kennedy:
From Crisis to Triumph to Tragedy

Eisenhower and Kennedy understood the same set of facts about nuclear war and came to quite different conclusions about their meaning. Eisenhower sought to dramatize the nuclear deterrent and to limit the occasion for the use of American military force. He thought little about general war contingencies beyond deterrence. But, in a way, it was the policy of an optimist. Kennedy imagined what might happen if deterrence failed and sought to arm himself against those contingencies. He assumed that sooner or later the United States would be at war, and he thought American nuclear and conventional forces could be made more congruent with situations that threatened American interests. The prevalence of "worst plausible case" analysis in his defense establishment amounted to the rationalization of an essentially pessimistic outlook.

John F. Kennedy began his campaign for the presidency by returning to the idea that was at the core of Truman's NSC 68: the Soviet threat was growing and the United States must respond to it before it would be too late. Time was not on the side of the United States. In a speech on the Senate floor on August 14, 1958, Kennedy charged that Eisenhower had wasted vital years—"the years the locusts have eaten." Kennedy had selected a sure-fire issue: safety in a dangerous world. He argued that there would be a period when America would lag behind the Soviet Union in offensive and defensive missile capabilities: "the most critical years of the gap would appear to be 1960–1964."[1] The Democratic platform of 1960 claimed: "our military position today is measured in terms of gaps—missile gap, space gap, limited-war gap."[2]

Kennedy narrowly won the election. In his Inaugural Address, he said, "man holds in his mortal hands the power to abolish . . . all forms of human life," adding, "we offer not a pledge but a request: that both sides begin anew the quest for peace, before the dark powers of destruction unleashed by science engulf all humanity in planned or accidental self-destruction."[3]

In his State of the Union message, delivered ten days after the inauguration, Kennedy rejected Eisenhower's "long pull" philosophy of defense in favor of a more urgent pace. Injecting a note of alarm and crisis to underscore the new tempo, Kennedy said: "I speak today in an hour of national peril and national opportunity. . . . Each day we draw nearer the hour of maximum danger, as weapons spread and hostile forces grow stronger . . . the tide of events has been running out and time has not been our friend."[4]

Kennedy needed no reminding of the dangers of nuclear war. But his judgment was reinforced by briefings he received in 1961 from the NSC Net Evaluation Subcommittee, of the type which had moved Eisenhower to enter gloomy thoughts in his private diary. Sorensen wrote that one such briefing confirmed for Kennedy "the harsh facts he already knew: . . . that a policy of 'pre-emptive first strike' or 'preventive war' was no longer open to either side."[5]

Kennedy is remembered today for his persistent and successful effort to achieve a nuclear test ban treaty and for his judicious handling of the Cuban Missile Crisis. These two events turned the tide in U.S.-Soviet relations and in world history. Kennedy's speech of June 10, 1963, at American University on the shared fate of humanity is far more in tune with the historical memory of the man than his apocalyptic warnings that "time has not been our friend."

The Missile Gap and the Dynamics of the Nuclear Arms Race

The missile gap controversy is one of the best available case studies of the political clout of defense issues and of their unintended consequences. It may have influenced Soviet leader Khrushchev's aggressive policies in 1961. The episode had profound consequences on the American political scene for a long time afterward. Kennedy's secretary of defense, Robert McNamara, shared his doubts about a missile gap on background with reporters on February 6, 1961. But when this good news was published, Kennedy's press secretary immediately denied the accuracy of the story. Kennedy himself, at a press conference on February 8, referred to ongoing Defense Department studies and said it was too early to reach a judgment.[6] McNamara quickly became the dominant voice in defense policy during Kennedy's time, despite his premature truthfulness. His rise was aided by his personal rapport with Kennedy and his loyalty. His success in meeting so many of Kennedy's ambitious defense goals within the brief span of the Kennedy presidency was truly remarkable.

Kennedy went no further in clarifying the missile gap situation in the spring of 1961, even though on March 13, 1961, McGeorge Bundy, Kennedy's national security adviser, had written to Theodore Sorensen, Kennedy's chief political adviser and speech writer, about the missile gap and the impending Special Message on Defense. Bundy had said: "The phrase 'missile gap' is now a genuinely misleading one, and I think the President can safely say so."[7] According to Sorensen, Kennedy had not been told about the most sensitive information available to the United States before he became president—the U-2 reconnaissance aircraft photographs of Soviet missile sites—and it took several months to reconcile conflicting estimates.[8] In the meantime, Khrushchev was allowed to think that the Americans believed his boasts about Soviet prowess in ballistic missiles.

The Kennedy administration waited until the autumn of 1961 before informing the public that no missile gap existed. By that time U.S. intelligence estimates had been harmonized and all agreed that the strength of Soviet missile forces was not so great as many had feared. The Berlin crisis of 1961 was at a fever pitch; the construction of the Berlin Wall had commenced in August 1961. And at the end of August, the Soviets broke the nuclear testing moratorium that Eisenhower had started in 1958. Their series of huge nuclear explosions raised the levels of radioactivity in the environment to record levels.

In the autumn of 1961 the Kennedy administration had strong reasons for asserting the extent of American strategic power, rather than its deficiency. Roger Hilsman, director of intelligence and research in the Department of State, wrote that the decision to reveal the truth about the missile gap was taken because if Khrushchev "were allowed to continue to assume that we still believed in the missile gap, he would probably bring the world dangerously close to war."[9] This observation underscores the obvious: to let the missile gap myth continue unchallenged for as long as it did was to assume the risk of Soviet miscalculation.

The deputy secretary of defense, Roswell Gilpatric, was selected to be the first senior Kennedy administration official to acknowledge that the United States knew it enjoyed considerable superiority over the U.S.S.R. in strategic nuclear forces. On October 21, 1961, in a speech to the Business Council, in Hot Springs, Virginia, Gilpatric summed up the situation by saying that "the destructive power which the United States could bring to bear, even after a Soviet surprise attack upon our forces, would be as great as, perhaps greater than, the total undamaged force which the enemy can threaten to launch against the United States in a first strike."[10]

Khrushchev probably knew this but was banking on American perceptions of vulnerability to yield concessions. He was probably also hoping to strengthen his own domestic positions. His policy guaranteed that the missile gap would become a political issue in the United States, with the quite foreseeable consequences of a greater-than-needed American missile-building program which later encouraged a greater-than-needed missile-building program in the Soviet Union.

The Missile Buildup

Kennedy believed in military superiority and he used his first State of the Union message to announce that he was taking immediate action to "strengthen our military tools." On March 28, 1961, Kennedy requested a supplemental defense appropriation of $650 million for fiscal year 1962. This included funds designed to raise the production level of Polaris submarines from five per year to twelve per year and to accelerate the development of the Polaris A-3 missile system so that it would be available a year earlier than previously planned. Kennedy called for doubling Minuteman production capacity and for speeding up improvements in the design of the Skybolt missile. This airborne ballistic missile, in which the British also had an interest, was to be given additional funding. Kennedy recommended increases for airborne and ground alert for the bomber forces, early warning systems and air defense, and improvement of command and control of the strategic forces.

Eisenhower had created the strategic triad: bombers, submarine-launched ballistic missiles, and land-based intercontinental ballistic missiles. Decisions made during the early months of the Kennedy administration determined size of the triad for years to come. The SALT I agreement of 1972 during the Nixon administration froze the numbers of American strategic missiles at levels programmed during the Kennedy administration. Those numbers remained the standard for U.S. force structure decisions until President Reagan called for deep reductions in strategic forces in May 1982.

The intelligence estimates available to the administration by the fall of 1961 had no effect on the size of the Kennedy strategic nuclear program. In September 1961, McNamara recommended to the president a force of 1,200 Minuteman missiles. At a Thanksgiving weekend meeting with his advisers at Hyannis Port, Kennedy endorsed that program. In this meeting, Kennedy was given the chance to revise downward the 1,200 Minuteman missiles that his defense secretary had recommended. The question was put to him by his own White House staff, but the president declined to take issue with McNamara's recommendations.[11]

In 1962 Kennedy requested a formal review of whether any changes were needed in U.S. defense or foreign policy in light of a National Intelligence Estimate which projected Soviet forces of the future. The estimate showed that the deployment of Soviet missile forces over the period 1962–1967 was likely to proceed at a slower rate than was assumed by McNamara when he made his recommendations to Kennedy. Secretary of State Dean Rusk, Secretary of Defense McNamara, Joint Chiefs of Staff Chairman Lyman Lemnitzer, and Director of Central Intelligence John McCone advised the president that no change was needed. Their assumption, of course, was that the United States should be in a position to ride out a Soviet first strike on U.S. land-based missiles.

More to the point, the superiority of U.S. strategic nuclear forces was considered an essential basis for foreign policy by the Kennedy administration, as it had been for Eisenhower. Walt Rostow, chair of Dean Rusk's Policy Planning Council, and later President Johnson's national security adviser, remarked that "when crises were tense, the favorable balance of the numbers—no matter how ambiguous their real meaning—was a comfort."[12]

Sorensen commented that he did not believe "that the President ever regretted ordering the increase in striking power."[13] The question this poses for future historians is whether the Kennedy missile buildup contributed to the Cuban Missile Crisis or made it more manageable, or both. The wisdom at the time was that local conventional superiority is what made the Soviet concessions possible, but that is arguable. Whatever the verdict, Kennedy's decisions during 1961 both enlarged and speeded up the missile programs he had inherited from Eisenhower, so that the U.S.-Soviet strategic comparison at the time of the Cuban Missile Crisis was overwhelmingly favorable to the United States.

Khrushchev insisted that the motivation for his desperate gamble in Cuba in 1962 was his determination to deter an American attack on Cuba. But he spoke of a strategic rationale, too: "In addition to protecting Cuba, our missiles would have equalized what the West like to call the 'balance of power.'"[14] Theodore Sorensen, a participant in the U.S. handling of the crisis, saw it the same way: "He [Khrushchev] had attempted a quick, easy step to catch up on the Americans in deliverable nuclear power."[15]

The Kennedy administration seemed to assume that Moscow would reconcile itself to permanent American strategic superiority. Events proved this assumption quite wrong.

Khrushchev had overplayed his hand in exaggerating Soviet strategic assets after *Sputnik* and the first Soviet test of an intercontinental ballistic missile in 1957. In so doing, Moscow had made Eisenhower's caution about deploying first-generation ballistic missiles seem short-sighted, rather than prudent, and had encouraged the belief in the United States that a missile gap existed. By the time Kennedy was elected, it was too late for the Soviets to influence the public mood in the United States, and they did not really try.

Ballistic Missile Defense: Kennedy Punts

McNamara's first instinct when he took the reins as defense secretary was to deploy a modest number of antimissile missiles, which he thought would complicate a Soviet attack.[16] But this was one of the few causes that he took on that was rejected by President Kennedy. Most of Kennedy's White House advisers, except for General Maxwell Taylor, thought that the technology was not ready for deployment. McNamara learned fast. In reporting to Congress on defense programs during fiscal year 1962, he said that "many problems remain to be resolved." He cited the ballistic missile defense system's ability to overcome countermeasures, a test of its effectiveness which had not yet been met.[17]

Even though "many problems" had not been solved, the decision was not a simple one for Kennedy to make. The Soviets had become interested in defenses against ballistic missiles at a very early date and had actively pursued a development program. A Soviet test site for these purposes was photographed by the last successful U-2 flight at the end of April 1960. During the first year of the Kennedy administration, U.S. intelligence found that an air defense system was being deployed to protect Leningrad. It was suspected of having some capability against incoming ballistic missiles, a notion that was later discredited. Another missile gap was in the making. Khrushchev and other Soviet officials again contributed to that perception with boastful and fanciful remarks.

Ballistic missile defense is a case where trust in the miracles of modern science—and the necessities of politics—has always trumped the laws of physics. The beginnings of this pattern can be seen in the Kennedy administration. Ballistic missile defenses can be overwhelmed by sheer numbers of incoming warheads and by decoys, not to mention cruise missiles, bombers, and people with suitcase bombs. But hope springs eternal. Kennedy's handling of the problem was a classic "kick the can down the road" approach. He decided to invest in research and development. Kennedy's budget message to the Congress of January 17, 1963, promised that "high levels of effort will continue on developing a defense against missiles including further testing of the Nike-Zeus anti-missile missile and initial development of the more advanced Nike-X surface-to-air missile."[18]

Kennedy also tried another approach to defenses against nuclear attack, which backfired. He suggested that Americans should build fallout shelters, a form of passive defense. By the time that fad had run its course, many an American backyard had been dug up and many a cellar stocked with canned goods. Kennedy backed away from the idea fairly quickly, realizing that he had created an incipient panic.

The Beginning of Nuclear War-Fighting Doctrines

Truman and Eisenhower thought of nuclear weapons as civilization-ending devices. Kennedy did not think differently, but he had become convinced, mainly by Albert Wohlstetter, a RAND Corporation analyst, that U.S. nuclear forces could be destroyed in a first strike by the Soviet Union. The success of a first disarming strike would depend on whether the United States had hardened or concealed its nuclear forces so that they would be invulnerable. If a substantial portion of the American forces could be saved, and an adversary understood that fact, deterrence of a first disarming strike should work. If deterrence failed, then a U.S. counterattack could be launched against the remaining Soviet nuclear offensive forces (a counterforce response) or against Soviet economic and population centers (a countervalue response). In theory, a well-protected Soviet offensive force might then respond with another attack on U.S. strategic forces or an attack on U.S. population centers. It was imagined by analysts of such exchanges that one side could emerge with enough advantages to be judged victorious. And from such analyses the idea of protracted nuclear war became a respectable concept.

The problem of U.S. vulnerability to a Soviet first strike had been discussed among national security specialists for many years, especially since the RAND Corporation, established as an Air Force think tank, had promulgated reports R-266 on "Selection and Use of Strategic Air Bases" in 1954 and R-290 on "Protecting U.S. Power to Strike Back in the 1950s and 1960s" in 1956. Albert Wohlstetter had also written an influential article entitled "The Delicate Balance of Terror," which was published in the January 1959 issue of *Foreign Affairs*, summarizing the RAND reports. Kennedy's speech to the Senate on August 14, 1958, rested on these analyses. He had accepted Wohlstetter's argument that the missile gap missed the point, that the sufficiency of strategic forces available to the United States *after* a Soviet first strike was the real problem.

In the climate of those times, this was a sensible way to preserve deterrence, which is not a static, but a dynamic concept. This also was the beginning of an assumption that nuclear weapons could be used, as other weapons, in a traditional war-fighting role, rather than as the ultimate weapon. It was a seductive argument, based on previous military experience and current needs, and it led to extravagant and unnecessary expenditures.

Changing NATO Strategy

Kennedy and McNamara concluded that much of what they thought was wrong with Eisenhower's strategy—excessive reliance on nuclear weapons, inadequate conventional capabilities, inflexible doctrines, and loose command and control over nuclear forces—was epitomized by the NATO alliance as they found it in 1961. NATO, its strategy and forces, absorbed a large part of American defense resources and energies. There was considerable suspicion, both bureaucratic and political, in NATO about the defense policies of the Kennedy administration. Because of Eisenhower's insistence that any war in Europe would be a nuclear war, nuclear weapons policies—regarding both deployment and use of nuclear arms—came to a focus in Europe more than anywhere else.

The specifics of much of the Kennedy policy toward Europe were developed in a study that Kennedy had asked Truman's secretary of state, Dean Acheson, to undertake. Kennedy accepted the main lines of Acheson's recommendations and proceeded to make them the basis for his relations with Western Europe. The administration's thinking was presented to the allies during 1961–1962. The main features were:

- A change from a NATO strategy heavily reliant on early use of nuclear weapons to one of "flexible response," where the initial response might not necessarily be nuclear.
- A force structure that would give more weight to conventional capabilities.
- Increased emphasis on allied sharing of nuclear responsibilities, in particular an alliance multilateral nuclear force (MLF), promoted by the State Department's Policy Planning Staff.
- An American strategic deterrence policy that envisaged avoiding attacks on Soviet cities while attacking Soviet military targets.
- Heavy emphasis on the need for concentration of strategic nuclear capabilities in the hands of the United States and criticism of British and French independent nuclear forces.

The president took his case directly to the senior military advisers of the Atlantic Alliance on April 10, 1961. Speaking in Washington to the Military Committee of NATO, chaired by Lord Mountbatten, Kennedy said: "there should be a reinforcement of capabilities of NATO in conventional weapons. NATO needs to be able to respond to any conventional attack with conventional resistance which will be effective at least long enough, in [NATO Supreme Commander] General Norstad's phrase, to force a pause." Kennedy bluntly emphasized to the military leaders his intense concern that the release of nuclear weapons should remain under his control at all times: "We propose to see to it, for our part, that our military forces operate at all times under continuous, responsible command and control from the highest authorities all the way downward—and we mean to see that this control is exercised before, during, and after any initiation of hostilities against our forces, and at any level of escalation."[19]

This stance reflected not only Kennedy's wish to control a nuclear war to the extent he could, but also a concern in the Kennedy administration that nuclear weapons might be fired without proper authority. An illustration of this concern was McGeorge Bundy's January 30, 1961, memorandum to the president: "a subordinate commander faced with a substantial Russian military action would start the thermonuclear holocaust on his own initiative if he could not reach you."[20]

The massive reorientation of the Atlantic Alliance proposed by Kennedy and McNamara, and later President Johnson, faced formidable difficulties. President de Gaulle was at the height of his campaign of stressing the independence and grandeur of France, and France had only recently joined the "nuclear club," having tested a nuclear device in 1960. Britain was going through an antinuclear campaign domestically and was seeking admission to the European Community. To both the British and the French, still smarting from Eisenhower's opposition to their attempt to seize the Suez Canal in 1956, their newly won nuclear status was not to be questioned. It gave them a seat at the high table and it gave them some, perhaps illusory, independence. A shift to a conventional defense strategy was, at the time, an inconvenience at best.

Khrushchev was trumpeting his strategic nuclear capabilities both verbally and with nuclear test explosions and was threatening the Western position in Berlin. The Federal Republic of Germany was going through a leadership transition and was torn between its relations with France and the United States. Eisenhower's strategic views were familiar and responsive to Western European sensibilities. European leaders did not conceive of nuclear weapons as war-fighting instruments but as the ultimate deterrent. The idea of the carefully calibrated use of nuclear weapons was not congenial to the Europeans, especially since they realized that their countries would be destroyed even in a limited nuclear engagement. Nor was the idea of making Europe safe for another conventional war appealing to them.

Europeans liked to think in terms of what they assumed would be the most likely situation, not the worst case. To them, the most probable situation was one in which the Soviet government would be deterred by its expectation of what would happen if it chose war in Europe in the face of a commitment as strong as that which the Americans had given. As the credibility of "trading New York for Hamburg" came to be questioned, the likelihood of a nuclear response gave way to uncertainty. But even uncertainty, considering the consequences of a Soviet misjudgment, was thought by the Europeans to be an adequate deterrent.

The Uses of a Summit Disaster

Kennedy and Khrushchev met for their first and only summit in Vienna on June 3–4, 1961. Khrushchev renewed a threat made earlier to change the status of Berlin. Eisenhower had met similar threats in the period after *Sputnik* but had brushed aside Khrushchev's demands and held fast to his nuclear deterrent doctrine. Kennedy reacted very differently. Soon after his return to Washington, he made a dramatic appeal to Congress for more resources for American conventional forces. He requested increases in the size of the Army from 875,000 to 1 million men, and smaller increases in the size of the Air Force and the Navy. Draft calls were to be doubled and tripled; reserve units were called to active duty. More money was to be spent on conventional equipment. These actions were meant to be seen as a sign of U.S. determination to defend its rights in Berlin, but the crisis also offered Kennedy an opportunity to do what he wanted to do anyway—create a more balanced U.S. force structure.

Kennedy hoped that the crisis would have a galvanizing effect on Europe. Vigorous efforts were made, especially by Defense Department officials, to persuade the NATO allies to improve conventional defenses. The results were forecast by the NATO commander, General Norstad, who told Kennedy in October 1961 that the president's emphasis on conventional forces only made the European allies doubt the firmness of his commitment to the nuclear deterrent.[21]

The conventional buildup ordered by Kennedy in the United States was not matched by the allies in Europe. Faced with this resistance, Kennedy authorized McNamara to try the tactic of overwhelming the allies with rational argument, challenging long-held dogma on nearly every point. In May 1962, McNamara launched a full-scale attack on the status quo with a comprehensive speech at a meeting of NATO foreign and defense ministers in Athens. The Athens speech signaled the beginning of an intense effort, mostly led by McNamara, to overcome European resistance to the defense policies of the Kennedy administration. It was a frustrating experience. Some policies of the Kennedy administration were modified or dropped within two years. Others—especially the goal of a robust allied conventional capability—were partially achieved, but it took years of nagging by successive U.S. administrations.

Refining Nuclear Options

McNamara's Athens speech not only outlined the rationale for building a "flexible response" into NATO defense plans but also addressed U.S. theories about the nature of strategic warfare. McNamara hoped that a strategy of striking military targets while avoiding cities would strengthen the credibility of the American deterrent. The idea sounded like a more plausible way to wage nuclear war than trading city for city. To accomplish this would require "unity of planning, executive authority, and central direction." Hence, weak nuclear forces operating independently—such as the U.K. and the French—were undesirable. The "no-cities" strategy evolved into "assured destruction"—which meant attacks on cities (countervalue)—and "damage limitation"—which meant attacks on military targets (counterforce).

The learning process continued. McNamara found that a counterforce doctrine generated endless requirements for nuclear weapons to match an expanding list of targets. He also found that Europeans did not believe nuclear weapons should be made more "useable," even in theory, and that they doubted the Soviets would be willing to play this game.

A Nuclear Rollback?

In February 1962, Kennedy had asked British Prime Minister Macmillan whether maintaining the British nuclear deterrent would not encourage French and German nuclear aspirations.[22] Macmillan let it pass, but the matter came to a head when, in November 1962, Kennedy accepted McNamara's recommendation to cancel the Skybolt airborne ballistic missile program. The program had been shaky for some time on cost-effectiveness grounds, but the British government had staked the future of its nuclear forces on it, so Macmillan was in serious political trouble when McNamara cancelled

Skybolt. The main topic when Macmillan and President Kennedy met for a previously scheduled conference in Nassau in December 1962 was how to maintain a British nuclear deterrent, not how to roll it back. Macmillan's personal appeal to Kennedy led to an agreement, largely fashioned by Kennedy himself, to furnish Polaris missiles to the United Kingdom under conditions which committed these forces to NATO while retaining national control in London. A similar offer was made to the French but was rejected.

In the background of this episode was something called the multilateral force (MLF). The idea was to have multinational crews operate ships carrying intermediate-range nuclear-armed missiles provided by the United States under U.S. control. It was conceived by Europeanists in the State Department as a way of providing a nuclear force to NATO and so encourage the elimination of national nuclear forces. The MLF was formally on the Kennedy administration's agenda with Europe throughout the president's time in office, but Kennedy did little to promote it. His White House staff, and others, were skeptical, although the MLF was pushed valiantly by lower-level officials, especially in the State Department's Policy Planning Staff. It enjoyed a brief comeback in Johnson's administration. But the proposal never enjoyed broad political support in the Congress or in Europe. With neither Kennedy nor Johnson totally committed to it, the MLF foundered and sank by the end of 1965.

The Negotiating Option: The Nuclear Test Ban Treaty

The limited nuclear test ban treaty of 1963 was the first major agreement affecting nuclear arms in the nuclear age. I was directly involved in the endgame and so will recount the moves and countermoves in some detail. For the Kennedy administration and for the world generally, 1961 was an "annus horribilis." The Bay of Pigs fiasco in Cuba in April was followed by the disastrous summit meeting with Soviet leader Nikita Khrushchev in June in Vienna. The Berlin Wall was built in August. The test ban negotiations reflected the general mood.

On March 21, 1961, the negotiations resumed after a brief policy review by the new administration. Kennedy's team decided that Ike had been on the right track and sent Arthur Dean, a New York lawyer, to Geneva with proposals designed to meet some Soviet objections to the U.S.-U.K. proposals. But he retained Eisenhower's proposal for twenty on-site inspections annually in Soviet territory to monitor a comprehensive test ban treaty.

On April 18, 1961, the U.S. and U.K. delegations introduced a new treaty draft. The key obligation regarding test explosions covered "all nuclear weapon test explosions except those underground explosions which are recorded as seismic events of less than magnitude 4.75." This treaty, and a proposed moratorium on underground tests, could have been the basis for real negotiations. But Khrushchev had decided to pressure Kennedy rather than negotiate with him. Internal politics in Moscow, the growing split with China, and military interests in testing had convinced Khrushchev that he should abandon the test ban negotiations.

To do this, Khrushchev relinked the test ban with general disarmament, an arrangement that the United States had also advocated in the days of the Baruch Plan. He proposed a "troika," a Control Commission consisting of the Warsaw Pact, NATO, and the neutral/nonaligned countries, each bloc to have a veto over operations of the commission. The talks that had begun hopefully in 1958 under Eisenhower, Macmillan, and Khrushchev seemed about to sputter out. The Soviet negotiators stonewalled and blustered, retreating from positions they once had accepted, and proposing unreal alternatives—all this at a time when Kennedy and Macmillan had hoped to move rapidly to conclude a test ban treaty.

The Sino-Soviet split had become quite serious by that time, and Khrushchev may have thought that he needed a stable East Germany on his western flank. In any case, he pressed very hard for a settlement that would ratify East Germany's existence as an independent state with Berlin as its capital. The atmosphere in U.S.-Soviet relations became highly charged. Khrushchev's desperate moves to exploit the perceived Soviet advantage in rocketry to settle the German question on Soviet terms were matched by Kennedy's moves to overcome that perception and preserve U.S. rights in Berlin.

Kennedy persisted, despite Khrushchev's about-face. The negotiations resumed in Geneva in late August, and I was there at the table on August 28, 1961, as a member of the U.S. delegation with Ambassador Arthur Dean, Charles Stelle, and David Mark, two top-flight Foreign Service officers. Dean offered to accept a comprehensive ban on nuclear weapons tests at once, if the control system could be improved. If that proved impossible, the United States would accept a treaty exempting only underground tests below 4.75 seismic magnitude, but a three-year moratorium would be imposed even on those tests. Tsarapkin's dusty reply was that the Soviet Union would accept a ban on tests only as a consequence of a treaty on general and complete disarmament. The handwriting was on the wall.

Despite the obvious implication of Tsarapkin's behavior, the U.S. and U.K. delegations continued on the course that Eisenhower had set and Kennedy had accepted. On August 30, we introduced new treaty language to ensure that the administrator of the inspection system would operate impartially and that nationals of nonaligned nations would be assigned to inspection teams, as the Soviets had demanded. Tsarapkin followed his orders. The idea that a test ban treaty could be accepted prior to general and complete disarmament was out of the question. The climax of this charade came the next day, in Moscow, when the Soviet Union announced the resumption of nuclear testing in the atmosphere. The Soviet test series began on September 1 and continued until November 4. The drama of that occasion was underscored by the effects of the largest H-bomb ever tested—57 megatons—that generated a huge amount of dangerous radiation around the world for many years. Adding to the gloom that fall was the almost simultaneous death in a mysterious airplane crash in Africa of U.N. Secretary General Dag Hammarskjold.

Probably all of the Americans at the table for the next session on September 4—Stelle, Mark, and myself—doubted privately that we would ever return to the talks. I certainly did. Arthur Dean had been recalled to Washington. Stelle read into the record a joint statement of Kennedy and Macmillan which they had issued on September 3. Kennedy and Macmillan had proposed an immediate agreement with the Soviet Union "not to conduct nuclear tests which take place in the atmosphere and produce radioactive fallout." They urged Khrushchev "to cable his immediate acceptance of this offer and his cessation of further atmospheric tests." Most importantly, for the future of the test ban negotiations, they dropped any requirement for international controls over atmospheric tests. They stated that they were "prepared to rely upon existing means of detection, which they believe to be adequate, and are not suggesting additional controls." The statement "urged that their representatives at Geneva meet not later than 9 September to record this agreement and report it to the United Nations." Tsarapkin read into the record the Soviet government's long statement of August 31 announcing "the decision to carry out experimental nuclear weapon explosions."

The Soviet statement said that Soviet tests were necessary because the NATO allies were fanning the arms race and the United States was just waiting for a pretext to end the moratorium. In addition to military objectives, Khrushchev's motivations certainly included the aim of enhancing the Soviet position in Berlin and Germany. The statement was full of anti-German invective. The Kennedy administration's missile buildup may have reinforced Khrushchev's determination to resume testing, and must have influenced the Soviet military, but Khrushchev had clearly decided very early in 1961, and most likely in 1960, to make that move.

The negotiators met again on September 9, the day by which Kennedy and Macmillan had asked for a response to their offer of an atmospheric test ban. Tsarapkin read into the record a statement by Khrushchev released earlier that day in Moscow. In a very long diatribe that attacked the West and argued for general and complete disarmament, Khrushchev rejected an atmospheric test ban, noting that the proposal was similar to a proposal the United States and United Kingdom had made in 1959. Stelle answered with a brief rebuttal and proposed that the conference recess pending the completion of U.N. General Assembly debate on a test ban treaty. Tsarapkin proposed that the communique should say that "the Conference then ceased its work," but was persuaded to settle for a recess. On September 15, the United States resumed testing underground.

The U.N. General Assembly adopted a resolution on November 8, asking that negotiations be resumed. In response, the United States formally proposed to Moscow that the negotiators should restart their talks in Geneva. Moscow responded favorably and the negotiators met again on November 28. On the first day, Tsarapkin picked up the Kennedy-Macmillan proposal for a ban on tests in the atmosphere, which required no international inspection, but reverted to earlier Soviet positions that extended the uninspected ban to other environments. He submitted a four-article draft treaty that required the parties "not to conduct tests of any kind of nuclear or thermonuclear weapons in the atmosphere, in outer space or under water." Article 3 of the treaty obliged the parties not to test underground while a control system was being set up as part of an agreement on general and complete disarmament.

The elements of a limited test ban treaty had emerged in the Soviet proposal, but two major issues stood in the way. The Soviets insisted on banning underground tests indefinitely without any control system in place. And Ambassador Dean stated, on behalf of the United States, that "the atmospheric, under-water and outer-space environments demand adequate international treaty control and an appropriately coordinated international effort just as much as does the underground environment." He pointed out that the September 3 Kennedy-Macmillan offer referred only to atmospheric tests. The international situation was not conducive to a limited test ban treaty negotiation at that time, and these irreconcilable positions led to another impasse. The negotiators recessed on December 21, 1961.

The impasse, in fact, had become so severe that the United States and the United Kingdom returned to Geneva on January 16, 1962, determined to bring matters to a head. Stelle said that if the Soviets were not prepared to negotiate a treaty with international controls, the conference should adjourn. The issue of the test ban could be referred to the Eighteen-Nation

Disarmament Committee (ENDC) which was considering general disarmament. Agreement was not possible even on this. On January 29, Michael Wright, the British negotiator, as chair for the day, declared the conference adjourned.

Kennedy and Macmillan made another effort to jump-start negotiations in a letter to Khrushchev on February 7, 1962. In it, they proposed that their foreign ministers begin negotiations, hoping that they could "overcome this recent setback" in the test ban talks. Khrushchev responded with a proposal for negotiations at the heads of government level. And so another initiative went nowhere.

Finally, on March 2, 1962, Kennedy announced that the United States would resume testing in the atmosphere at the Pacific testing grounds in late April. The previous U.S. test series had been conducted underground. But Kennedy also said that if the Soviet Union was willing to accept the U.S.-U.K. comprehensive test ban treaty before late April, the United States would not conduct its planned nuclear test series. Khrushchev angrily rejected the offer the next day.

The test ban negotiations were not dead, despite all this, but they were living through the last days in their original construct. After this, things would change. The U.S. idea to transfer the talks to the Eighteen-Nation Disarmament Committee was accepted by Moscow and a U.S.-U.K.-U.S.S.R. subcommittee on nuclear testing was established within the ENDC. The subcommittee began its deliberations on March 21 but remained stymied by the Soviet refusal to accept international controls and the U.S.-U.K. opinion that some form of control was essential. Some neutral and nonaligned nations supported a moratorium on all tests as long as the conference was in session. The Soviet delegation accepted the idea but Washington objected. And so the month of April was taken up by posturing and maneuvering. The U.S. atmospheric test series began on April 26. On July 21, Moscow announced that it would conduct another series of tests. Tests in the atmosphere began during the first week in August 1962. The test of August 5 was a 30 megaton explosion. And so things stood until August 27. The deadlock seemed absolute, the prospects for any agreement practically nil, the atmosphere rancorous.

Here, it is time to emphasize the crucial role that Prime Minister Macmillan played in the final success of the test ban negotiations. Kennedy's determination to press on with test ban negotiations had always been egged on by his British partner in the enterprise. Harold Macmillan, Tory prime minister, was an aristocrat of the old school. To him, living forever under a nuclear sword of Damocles was a fate that humanity should not have to bear. He also had worked closely with Eisenhower in pushing forward the negotiations.

Macmillan and Kennedy discussed the test ban issue frequently, with Macmillan always urging Kennedy to consider new ways of moving the negotiations to a successful conclusion. He supported the idea of a quota of on-site inspections, for example, when an idea was needed to prevent the Soviet Union from rejecting on-site inspections out of hand.

The British embassy in Washington was almost a part of the U.S. back-stopping team in Washington. As closely allied negotiating partners, it was natural and correct that the staffs should coordinate the details of the joint British-American approach to the talks. I frequently used that channel to try out tactics and substantive ideas. Occasionally, Macmillan would pick up an idea floated at the staff level in Washington and send it back to Kennedy under his imprimatur. This channel was an important, I would say essential, key to the success of the test ban negotiations.

Macmillan also spurred on the talks by appealing to Kennedy's competitive spirit. On one occasion, Under Secretary of State George Ball invited Jacob Beam, assistant director of the Arms Control and Disarmament Agency (ACDA), and myself to his office to listen to a tape he had made of a telephone conversation between himself and President Kennedy. In it, Kennedy was quoting Macmillan as saying that Ike was a wonderful fellow but that he was poor at follow-through. Kennedy told Ball that he never wanted that criticism to be made of him. The atmosphere the Kennedy-Macmillan connection created was one of optimism about what could be done with enough imagination and perseverance.

Another factor that was decisive in producing a test ban treaty in 1963 was the interagency process that Kennedy had set up. For backstopping the U.S. delegation in Geneva, it was simple in the extreme, and this facilitated rapid tactical shifts, when necessary, in the negotiations. The clearance process for tactical instructions consisted of my clearing a telegram with my counterpart in the International Security Affairs section of the Office of the Secretary of Defense. My counterpart's name was Captain Elmo "Bud" Zumwalt, USN, later chief of naval operations. He had been ordered by the assistant secretary of defense, John McNaughton, a wonderful man later killed in a plane crash, to cooperate with me in moving the negotiations along. It helped that there was complete support for a comprehensive test ban treaty in the civilian leadership of the Kennedy administration. I have never worked in a more unified administration.

The Joint Chiefs of Staff assumed that this negotiation would be as unproductive as all other post–World War II negotiations with the U.S.S.R. and paid little attention to it, at first. Within the Arms Control and Disarmament Agency and the State Department, there were not many required clearances, so instructions frequently went out with only three or four names attached to them. The small NSC staff, directed by McGeorge Bundy, usu-ally was not involved in the daily clearance process. The White House Sci-ence Adviser's Office was always highly supportive. The senior staff member there was Spurgeon Keeny, who made many contributions to the whole process. In later administrations, as arms control moved to center stage, the clearance process became rigid and cumbersome, sometimes paralyzed.

Developing broad policy lines for the test ban negotiations was a different matter altogether. A Committee of Principals, usually deputy heads of agen-cies or senior assistant secretaries, met to debate and recommend policy pa-pers. This was a fairly elaborate process; it took weeks to approve papers.

In 1962, as the talks seemed to founder, this policy-making machinery was working full tilt. This was the most important decision-making period during the Kennedy administration. Some of the senior officials in the administration favored a system based on mutual inspection by the three major adherents to a test ban treaty. They argued that this would be simpler and more effective than an international inspection organization. It would also answer Soviet criticism of international inspection systems. And so a system described as "adversarial" inspection was worked out and approved by the president.

The Committee of Principals reaffirmed the quota approach to on-site in-spections, and the numbers discussed were in the double digits, based on an estimate of the numbers of unexplained seismic events that might occur an-nually in Soviet territory. The quota was really a political number, however, based on guesses about what it would take to gain the Senate's consent to rat-ification.

Another issue that was revisited in 1962 was unmanned seismic stations. British scientists during the Eisenhower administration had suggested that sealed, tamper-proof seismographs could be placed in the territories of Britain, the United States, and the Soviet Union. This close-in monitoring system, it was thought, would improve the capacity to detect and identify low-yield or decoupled underground explosions. The idea was to place the unmanned seismic stations in earthquake-prone regions of the U.S.S.R., where the Soviets might try to pass off a nuclear test as an earthquake. And so, led by ACDA deputy director Adrian "Butch" Fisher, several of us were involved in what Fisher called "the great earthquake hunt," to determine where unmanned seismic stations should be located.

But from my negotiator's point of view, the most important task of the Committee of Principals that summer was to approve language for two treaties that we could bring to the table in Geneva. Supported by Arms Control and Disarmament Agency Director William Foster and Assistant Director Jacob Beam, those of us in the negotiating team in ACDA advocated proposing two treaties simultaneously. The first would be a treaty banning tests in all environments. I had little expectation that it would ever be accepted by Moscow, although it took up a lot of the committee's time. I was more attached to the second initiative, a simple treaty banning nuclear tests in the atmosphere, outer space, and underwater that would permit underground tests. It would be monitored by sensors deployed by each participant, but no formal inspection system would be required. It built, of course, on ideas already introduced by both sides during earlier phases of the negotiation.

The negotiating concept behind all this was that we would tell the Soviets that the United States and the United Kingdom preferred the comprehensive treaty, but if Moscow could not accept the inspection system that a comprehensive ban on testing would require, the United States would reluctantly settle for a three-environment ban.

I had favored a limited test ban treaty since my days at the Atomic Energy Commission. The hurdles involved in a comprehensive ban included getting the Soviets to accept on-site inspection and the U.S. Senate to accept what would probably turn out to be fairly limited inspection rights in Soviet territory. I continued to think it was important to start a nuclear restraint regime with the Soviet Union, even if it was not ideal. And I wanted more than ever to stop poisoning the environment with radioactivity.

Most of the attention of the Committee of Principals and their senior staff was directed to the comprehensive test ban treaty. It had been the U.S. goal since 1958 and it would clearly be a more powerful arms control tool than a treaty that permitted underground testing. Besides, it was a more complex legal document, requiring a lot of detailed attention. The limited test ban treaty was drafted by three people: Tom Pickering, then my assistant, Alan Neidle, an ACDA attorney, and myself. Of course, many others ultimately were involved, but we created the basic structure and most of the language.

One of the big issues we wrestled with was how to define a violation of the ban against tests in the atmosphere. We realized, of course, that radioactive gasses often were vented into the atmosphere when an underground nuclear explosion took place. We wanted to discourage that from happening, but at the same time, we did not think that minor venting should be construed as a violation. Our solution was to stipulate that a violation would have occurred "if such explosion causes radioactive debris to be present outside the territorial limits of the State under whose jurisdiction or control such explosion is conducted." Unfortunately, this clause became a source of repeated disputes between the United States and the Soviet Union. One reason for this was the lack of any extensive interchange between U.S. and Soviet experts about the meaning of the terms in the limited test ban treaty prior to the signing of the treaty in July 1963. The 1962 draft treaty also contained a provision allowing nuclear explosions for peaceful purposes to bring the Atomic Energy Commission on board. It had no support elsewhere and did not make it into the final treaty in 1963. We coordinated the language of the limited treaty very closely with the British through the British embassy in Washington.

After considerable debate about the comprehensive treaty and very little debate about the limited test ban treaty, both documents were approved by the Committee of Principals. Both documents were introduced simultaneously in the Geneva negotiations on August 27, 1962. Kennedy and Macmillan issued a statement to bring public attention to the two treaties. Following our tactical line, they said that a comprehensive treaty would be best, but a limited treaty, without the need for on-site inspections, also would be beneficial.

Ambassador V. V. Kuznetsov, Soviet representative in Genera, on August 29 rejected the two treaties. His argument was simple: the comprehensive treaty still required obligatory on-site inspection and the limited treaty would legitimize continued nuclear testing. He complained that other nations could legitimately develop nuclear weapons by testing underground. Krushchev, in letters to Kennedy, reiterated that Moscow would accept a ban on underground testing that would be provisional. He suggested a five-year moratorium but refused to accepted a limited test ban without a moratorium on underground testing. This dusty discourse was broken off by the Cuban Missile Crisis.

In October 1962, the U.N. General Assembly was to take up the test ban issue, as usual, in its annual disarmament debate. I was sent there to advise Adlai Stevenson, the U.S. ambassador to the U.N. On October 22, he asked the senior members of the delegation to meet him in his office that evening. The purpose, as we learned only when we arrived, was to watch President Kennedy on television announce the presence of Soviet missiles in Cuba and the U.S. determination to see them removed. Kennedy's speech included a warning that caught my attention: "It shall be the policy of this nation to regard any nuclear missile launched from Cuba against any nation in the Western Hemisphere as an attack by the Soviet Union on the United States, requiring a full retaliatory response upon the Soviet Union." I asked Stevenson whether there were nuclear warheads in Cuba. He had no information on that, he said, but we learned much later that there had been, and that the Soviet commander, for a time, had authority to use them.

The next days at the United Nations were tense, as they were everywhere else. The only difference was that we were in daily contact with Soviet diplomats. They were telling us that there was no chance that Soviet ships bound for Cuba would turn around. But the ships did turn around, and the crisis receded. Khrushchev's attempt to gain a nuclear advantage over the United States had failed.

The prospects for a test ban treaty, either comprehensive or limited, did not seem very bright after the settlement of the Cuban Missile Crisis in October 1962. Today, it is commonly supposed that after looking into the nuclear abyss, Kennedy and Khrushchev saw immediately that they had to do something about the test ban treaty. That was not at all the way it looked to me in November and December 1962. By December 1962 I had become so discouraged that I recommended President Kennedy take unilateral action to limit test explosions, similar to the Kennedy-Macmillan proposal for an atmospheric test ban in September 1961. I drafted a memorandum for ACDA Director Foster to send to National Security Adviser McGeorge Bundy. The gist of the memorandum, which Foster sent to Bundy on December 7, was that the United States would refrain from testing in the atmosphere, outer space, or underwater for a period of time to be determined by the president. If the Soviet Union conducted a "massive test series" during that time, the United States might be obliged to resume testing in those environments earlier than anticipated. If, on the other hand, the Soviet Union did not conduct a "massive test series" during that time, this would be taken into account in determining the need for future U.S. testing. The idea was to try to entice Moscow into an extendable moratorium. Attached to the memorandum was a proposed statement for Kennedy to issue to the public at an appropriate time. Butch Fisher and others in ACDA began consultations with Congress shortly afterward. But this initiative was soon interrupted by a letter from Khrushchev which, ironically, resulted only in another setback for the negotiations.

According to Khrushchev, he had been led to believe by Ambassador Arthur Dean, the chief U.S. test ban negotiator, that the United States would be willing to settle for three or four on-site inspections annually. Writing to Kennedy on December 19, 1962, Khrushchev proposed a framework for a comprehensive test ban treaty based on two or three on-site inspections and unmanned seismic stations. His idea, evidently, was that this should be enough to nail down the deal, and a treaty could quickly be negotiated and ratified by the Senate.

Kennedy replied on December 28, disabusing Khrushchev of his idea that the United States would settle for two to four on-site inspections. Ambassador Dean, he said, had mentioned a number between eight and ten. Kennedy had hoped this lower number, as compared with the twelve to twenty on-site inspections previously proposed, would encourage

Khrushchev to increase his offer. There were other difficulties, as well, regarding where on-site inspections might take place and where unmanned seismic stations might be located. Nonetheless, Kennedy proposed a private meeting in the United States between ACDA Director Foster and a Soviet representative to try to bridge the differences.

Khrushchev wrote again to Kennedy on January 7, 1963, showing some flexibility on where on-site inspections could take place and where seismic stations could be located. But he was absolutely adamant on two to three inspections. He agreed to the meeting with Foster, which was probably a mistake, given the serious misunderstanding that had occurred about on-site inspections, and subsequent events.

Foster met bilaterally, in deep secrecy, with Soviet representatives at the Soviet Mission to the United Nations on January 14, 1963. Bill Foster led the U.S. side. Charlie Stelle, Alex Akalovsky, and I were his advisers. The chief Soviet representatives were the Soviet U.N. ambassador, N. T. Federenko, and Ambassador S. K. Tsarapkin, the chief Soviet test ban negotiator in Geneva.

It was clear from the beginning that the on-site inspection quota was going to be a problem. Starting with a quota of twenty on-site inspections annually, the United States was now willing to accept seven or eight annually. Lowering that to three would risk losing a two-thirds favorable vote in the Senate, and Kennedy was not willing to do that.

My own opinion was that the Senate would not give its consent to a treaty that allowed only three on-site inspections annually. To maximize the prospects for Senate consent to a single-digit figure, perhaps seven, or even five, annually, I advised Foster to concentrate on the qualitative aspects of the inspection process. If we could argue to the Senate that each on-site inspection would have a high probability of proving or disproving a violation of the treaty, the quota of inspections could be a lower number.

Foster tried out this idea on Federenko and Tsarapkin in the first session of the secret talks. The Soviets saw this as a technical approach to an essentially political issue and would have nothing to do with it. It became apparent almost immediately that Tsarapkin was the real negotiator and that he was there to nail down three on-site inspections and to do nothing else.

The talks had been considered so sensitive that the British had not been invited. They soon got wind of what was happening. On the second day of the talks, we were joined by David Ormsby-Gore, the British ambassador in Washington and former U.K. chief test ban negotiator in Geneva. The tripartite talks quickly bogged down in the face of Tsarapkin's obstinate unwillingness to discuss anything but the number of on-site inspections, and his number at that.

We tried to talk about unmanned seismic stations, but that went nowhere. Out of the "great earthquake hunt" had come a *National Geographic* map of the Soviet Union with several X's inked in to identify the proposed locations for unmanned seismic stations. They were located in the seismic zones of the Soviet Union. I asked for authority to give it to the Soviets in hopes of at least triggering some intellectual curiosity on their part. Foster agreed, and I unfurled the *National Geographic* map before a Soviet delegation member and explained how the unmanned seismic stations so positioned could give us a better monitoring system. But the Soviets were so focused on the inspection quota that the "great earthquake hunt" came to naught. Tsarapkin broke off the talks on January 31. And so by the end of January 1963, we seemed to be back where we started.

My opinion, then and now, is that we had a fighting chance in the New York talks of getting beyond the rote repetition of ritual formulas and into a real negotiation of a framework for a comprehensive test ban. But that would have required the Soviet partner to have some flexibility and that, apparently, was out of the question. Khrushchev had worked hard to get his hardline Politburo colleagues to agree to two or three on-site inspections and he had no give in that position. Other things could have been discussed, but Tsarapkin refused.

Khrushchev still had bitter memories of our efforts in the New York talks when he wrote to Kennedy on June 8: "if in December of last year we agreed to the conducting of a certain minimum number of inspections on the cessation of underground tests, we did so only and exclusively out of political considerations, with a view to making easier for you, Mr. President, the ratification of a treaty on the cessation of tests by the Senate of the USA." He said that the January experience "cannot be called anything other than painful" and that the talks "left nothing but disillusionment behind them." Kennedy suggested in one of his letters that a discussion of how inspections would be conducted was related to the number required. But Khrushchev failed to understand or accept this point.

In the spring of 1963, with the test ban negotiations again in the doldrums, I raised with the British embassy the possibility of a special mission to Moscow. The idea was to make a final appeal directly to Khrushchev to resume serious negotiations. Khrushchev had invested some of his diminishing political capital in accepting the principle of inspections on Soviet territory for the first time in the history of the U.S.S.R. and had lost his bet.

Khrushchev was increasingly engaged in a power struggle in the Kremlin and, simultaneously, in a struggle with Mao Zedong for supremacy of the Communist movement. His time and energies were taken up with China and with fending off internal challenges to his rule. I thought that a high-level emissary who could talk directly with him was the only way to revive the talks.

The British embassy liked the idea of trying to rise above the recalcitrant Soviet bureaucracy by sending a mission directly to Khrushchev and reported it to London. Macmillan refers to the message from his embassy in Washington in his book *At the End of the Day, 1961–1963* (1973). A message from Macmillan soon reached President Kennedy with the proposal that a joint U.S.-U.K. mission to Moscow be offered to Khrushchev.

Ambassador Jacob Beam and I, of course, favored a positive reply from Kennedy. But when we discussed this with the top State Department expert on the Soviet Union, Ambassador Tommy Thompson, he counseled against it. I was surprised, since I had assumed that the administration would be united in going the extra mile to overcome Soviet resistance to a test ban treaty. So far as I know, Thompson's argument against a special mission was not based on opposition to a test ban. His judgment was that Khrushchev was preoccupied with preparations for a showdown with Mao and that a special mission would be a distraction. He counseled deferring the proposal.

ACDA Director Foster, fortunately, agreed with Jake Beam and me that the president should respond favorably to the Macmillan initiative. So did the White House, and on April 15, 1963, the joint U.S.-U.K. proposal was sent to Khrushchev from Kennedy and Macmillan. It took over a week for American Ambassador Foy Kohler to get to Khrushchev, but he finally did on April 24. Khrushchev replied on May 8 with a long polemic, but in the midst of it, he accepted the idea of receiving emissaries in Moscow. In another letter on May 31, he agreed to receive the U.S.-U.K. emissaries on July 15. This letter was a response to another letter from Kennedy and Macmillan that raised all the issues that troubled Khrushchev. It was a letter which was not necessary and which might have disrupted the proceedings, as may have been intended by opponents of the treaty, but fortunately it did not.

What happened next is in dispute among observers of the scene in Moscow. It is clear that at some point in the spring or summer of 1963, perhaps in the last two weeks of June, Khrushchev began to see a limited test ban treaty, even without a moratorium on underground tests, as a serious option. He was still speaking critically of it as late as the middle of June 1963. But by July 2, he had accepted the idea. What happened?

My theory has been that Khrushchev realized after 1962 that he could not bluff Kennedy. So he needed an accommodation with the West, because he could not afford to be engaged in a two-front struggle. That probably was his position in the last years of the Eisenhower administration, too. After his disastrous fling with atomic diplomacy in 1961–1962, he returned to a policy of accommodation with the West. I believe that the China dispute must have been important in shifting Khrushchev's thinking toward a limited test ban. But others, including those who were close to Khrushchev at the time, including former Soviet diplomats, have told me they believe that the Cuban Missile Crisis was the dominant reason for his switch.

Whatever the explanation, there now began a period of public diplomacy that set the stage for the conclusion in July of the limited test ban treaty. At the American University in Washington, D.C., on June 10, 1963, Kennedy gave one of his greatest speeches. Ted Sorenson, Kennedy's close adviser and speech writer, says he used bits and pieces of prose from previously written material, as well as new material. Historian Arthur Schlesinger describes the same process, saying that staff papers available in the White House were used as sources. Bill Foster's recommendation of December 7, 1962, which had been held in abeyance after Khrushchev's letter of December 19 was received, was one of those available.

The relevant points for test ban purposes in the June 10 speech were two: first, the United States would refrain from testing nuclear weapons in the atmosphere so long as the Soviet Union did likewise; second, the Soviet government had accepted the U.S.-UK proposal for a special mission to Moscow. The idea that Bill Foster had sent to National Security Adviser McGeorge Bundy in December 1962 and the special mission idea that I had floated with the British embassy in the spring of 1963 had both ripened to the point where they paved the way for the decisive meeting in Moscow in July 1963.

In response to Kennedy's speech, Khrushchev delivered a landmark speech in Berlin on July 2, 1963. This made it clear that a limited test ban treaty was now acceptable to Moscow. It was certain that Khrushchev had crossed the Rubicon when he omitted the usual Soviet call for a moratorium on underground tests linked to the treaty banning tests in the atmosphere, outer space, and underwater. The Soviet leader announced that Moscow favored "an agreement on the cessation of all nuclear tests in the atmosphere, in outer space, and under-water." He added that "the road is open to a solution of this problem." Khrushchev also proposed the simultaneous conclusion of a nonaggression pact between NATO and the Warsaw Pact. To me, this was a signal that he had written off the Chinese and wanted to do business with the West. Now it was clear that an agreement on a limited test ban treaty was at hand, as proved to be the case not many days later. The meeting was set for July 15. The chief U.S. representative was the very senior and distinguished statesman Averill Harriman. The British representative was Lord Hailsham.

To ensure that there would be no misunderstanding this time, Kennedy wrote a letter, dated July 12, 1963, which Harriman handed to Khrushchev when he met with him in Moscow on July 15. The following extract makes it clear what Kennedy wanted to happen:

> I share the view which you have put forward in your important statement in Berlin that it is sensible to reach agreement where agreement is now possible, in the area of testing in the atmosphere, under water, and in outer space. Governor Harriman will explain that we continue to be in favor of such a more limited agreement and that we are encouraged by your statement in Berlin to believe that it is now possible.

If he had not already received enough assurances that he would not again be hung out to dry, Khrushchev certainly had with this letter.

In their preliminary talks with Foreign Minister Andrei Gromyko, Harriman and Hailsham made pro forma statements about the comprehensive test ban treaty, but the differences were recognized to be unbridgeable and discussions turned quickly to the limited test ban. The text they had before them was based on the treaty that Neidle, Pickering, and I had drafted in the summer of 1962. It had lain dormant for a year, but now its time had come. From the standpoint of clarity and mutual understanding, it was unfortunate that there had been almost no discussion of the treaty language in all that time. And there was very little discussion in the Moscow talks, either. Gromyko made an effort to get Harriman to agree to a NATO-Warsaw nonaggression pact, which Khrushchev had proposed, but this was politely deferred. Only modest changes were made in the text of the treaty. It was initialed on July 25, 1963, and signed by Secretary of State Rusk, Gromyko, and the British foreign secretary, Lord Home, on August 5, 1963.

On July 26, Kennedy delivered a moving speech on the test ban treaty to buttress his administration's campaign to gain the Senate's consent to ratification. Having previously sounded out key senators on the idea of a limited test ban, the administration was fairly sure it would win the necessary two-thirds majority, and it did. The administration worked very hard to build the necessary support among Republicans and Democrats alike. Despite fierce opposition from the nuclear testing lobby, the positive 80 to 19 vote on September 24 was bipartisan. Everett Dirksen (R-IL), the Senate Republican leader, spoke in favor of it and voted for it, as did many other Republicans. Southern Democrats provided more than half of the nay votes. The treaty was ratified by Kennedy and entered into force on October 10. It was especially pleasing to Kennedy in the last weeks of his life that, when he spoke at public gatherings about the test ban treaty, the audience response was enthusiastically supportive. The limited test ban treaty passed its fortieth anniversary in 2003 and is the basic global legal norm governing the conduct of nuclear test explosions.

Notes

1. U.S. Senate, *Congressional Record*, August 14, 1958, 17569-17573.

2. *Congressional Quarterly's Guide to U.S. Elections*, 2nd ed., 1985, 110.

3. Theodore C. Sorensen, *Kennedy* (New York: Harper and Row, 1965), 245–247.

4. See www.janda.org/politxts.

5. Sorensen, *Kennedy*, 513.

6. *Public Papers of the Presidents*, Kennedy, 1961, 67–68.

7. Papers of President Kennedy, National Security Files, DOD, 3/61, Box 273, Kennedy Library.

8. Sorensen, *Kennedy*, 612.

9. Roger Hilsman, *To Move a Nation: The Politics of Foreign Policy in the Administration of John F. Kennedy* (Garden City, N.Y.: Doubleday, 1967), 163.

10. Joseph A. Loftus, "Gilpatric Warns U.S. Can Destroy Atom Aggressor," *New York Times*, October 22, 1961, 1.

11. Arthur Schlesinger, *A Thousand Days* (New York: Houghton Mifflin, 1965), 499–500.

12. Walt W. Rostow, recorded interview by Richard Neustadt, April 25, 1964, John F. Kennedy Library Oral History Program, 98.

13. Theodore Sorensen, recorded interview by Carl Kaysen, March 26, 1964, John F. Kennedy Library Oral History Program, 12.

14. Nikita Khrushchev, *Khrushchev Remembers* (Boston: Little, Brown, 1970), 494.

15. Sorensen, *Kennedy*, 724.

16. Memorandum from Secretary McNamara to President Kennedy, "Program for Deployment of Nike-Zeus," September 30, 1981; Memorandum from David Bell, Director, Bureau of the Budget, National Security File, Box 275, Kennedy Library.

17. Department of Defense, *Annual Report for Fiscal Year 1962*, 13.

18. *Public Papers of the Presidents*, Kennedy, 1963, 32.

19. *Public Papers of the Presidents*, Kennedy, 1961, 254–255.

20. Papers of President Kennedy, National Security Files, Box 313, Folder NSC Meetings, 475–507.

21. Schlesinger, *A Thousand Days*, 853.

22. Schlesinger, *A Thousand Days*, 849.

CHAPTER FOUR

~

Lyndon Johnson:
The Offense-Defense Riddle

President John F. Kennedy was assassinated on November 22, 1963, in Dallas, Texas. His vice president, former Senate Majority Leader Lyndon B. Johnson, was sworn in as president the same day. Johnson, one of the most successful majority leaders the Senate had ever known, shared his predecessor's opinion that nuclear war would be a catastrophe. Perhaps even more than Kennedy, he saw the advantages of strategic nuclear arms control agreements with the Soviet Union. He worked very hard to persuade the Soviets to negotiate limitations on offensive and defensive strategic nuclear weapons. He successfully presided over the negotiation of the nuclear nonproliferation treaty, still the basic global norm against the spread of nuclear weapons.

In the Senate, he had been aligned with the southern Democrats on defense issues. Senator Richard Russell (D-GA), chair of the Senate Armed Services Committee, was a longtime friend. Although Johnson had taken the lead in strengthening the space program and had seen the political utility of the missile gap issue, he had not staked out a clear programmatic alternative to Eisenhower's nuclear policies. In fact, he had established a comfortable and cooperative relationship with President Eisenhower on foreign and defense policies.

Johnson's first year as president was an election year. His focus was mainly on domestic issues and on pushing the Congress, very successfully, to move long-stalled legislation. He assumed the presidency during one of the few brief periods of relative tranquility in U.S.-Soviet relations during the Cold

War. Pressures on Berlin had diminished. The resolution of the Cuban Missile Crisis and the conclusion of the test ban treaty had yielded a superficial calm in East-West relations. The confidence of the West had been restored. Moscow was preoccupied with China. The buildup of American strategic forces, especially the Minuteman and Polaris programs, was still under way, and the United States enjoyed a comfortable edge over the Soviet Union in strategic forces. But in Moscow, a power struggle was under way: Khrushchev would have only one more year to serve before being replaced by Leonid Brezhnev and Alexei Kosygin in October 1964. And in that same month, China would explode its first nuclear bomb.

The situation in Vietnam was not going well, but it was seen as a problem more in the Chinese than the Soviet context. Although Soviet-Chinese relations had taken an irreparable turn for the worse, American policymakers generally saw no opportunities in that; some even doubted it had happened. Encouraged by advisers held over from the Kennedy administration, Johnson gradually became entrapped in Vietnam. He won the presidency in his own right against Senator Barry Goldwater of Arizona in 1964 on what amounted to a peace platform, but within a year the United States was engaged in a full-scale war in Vietnam.

Johnson, McNamara, and Nuclear Politics

Johnson shared with Kennedy an immense admiration for Secretary of Defense Robert McNamara's intellect and ability. When he took office, Johnson had every reason to think that American defense programs were going well and that the secretary of defense, despite some problems with Congress, was a phenomenal success. Johnson trusted McNamara's judgment as well as his intellect and gave him at least as strong a hand in determining the administration's defense policy as Kennedy had. McNamara gladly accepted the responsibility, which ultimately meant that he was the lightning rod for everything that anyone disliked about the Kennedy-Johnson defense policy.

McNamara's reputation for getting the president's business done, and quickly done, led the defense secretary into an executive role that transcended that of defense. McNamara was among those "talked up" as Johnson's vice presidential running mate prior to the election campaign of 1964.[1] Johnson was ready to let McNamara run the Pentagon, but others were not. McNamara did not engage in traditional Capitol Hill logrolling as many of his predecessors had done. His strong assertion of civilian judgment and his emphasis on systems analysis in selecting new weapons systems made him a controversial figure both on the Hill and with the armed services.

Defense policy was a subject of intense partisan debate in the presidential election year of 1964. Senator Barry Goldwater, the Republican presidential candidate, was also the standard-bearer of the conservative movement within the Republican Party. McNamara became a special target for Republican attacks on Democratic defense policies. McNamara's decisions to cut back Air Force programs—the B-70 and Skybolt—came in for heavy criticism from Goldwater. The Democrats had charged the Eisenhower administration with allowing "bomber gaps" and "missile gaps" to develop. Now it was payback time. Goldwater accused McNamara of frittering away American nuclear superiority. The Republican platform of 1964 asserted: "The Administration has adopted policies which will lead to a potentially fatal parity of power with Communism instead of continued military superiority for the United States." Unfortunately for his case, during the campaign Goldwater spoke rather casually about the use of nuclear weapons, permitting Johnson to convert Goldwater's statements into a peace issue.

Johnson's landslide victory in 1964 reinforced the president's confidence in McNamara, particularly since the secretary of defense had vigorously rebuffed Goldwater's charges and attacked the Republican record on defense. McNamara's authority and his close relationship with Johnson reached a peak in 1965, which was also the year in which Johnson committed the nation to a major war in Vietnam. After that, the political climate soured both for Johnson and McNamara as the Vietnam War escalated. McNamara's relations with Congress nose-dived. Henry Trewitt, of the *Baltimore Sun*, observed in his biography of McNamara: "at the bitterest stage no less than five congressional investigations were under way into McNamara's stewardship of the Pentagon."

As a Cabinet officer with an extraordinary ability to execute presidential wishes, McNamara became very visible, to the point where he was accused of running his own show. In fact, McNamara was deeply loyal to Kennedy and Johnson. Their agenda was his agenda. If he erred, it was in encouraging them to believe they could do all the things they wanted to do. In the nuclear field, this led to overbuilding, and in Vietnam to a quagmire. But he imposed reasoned analysis on defense decisions.

How Much Is Enough?

A strategy based on nuclear deterrence has to address the question of what it takes to deter. "How much is enough?" was a much analyzed issue in the 1960s and the source of bitter political debate. The question is with us today. The Kennedy administration's recommendations to Congress, approved by

Kennedy in the fall of 1961, had called for 1,200 Minuteman ballistic missiles. This number was increased to 1,300 a year later after the cancellation of Skybolt. The number dropped back to 1,200 in the budget request sent to Congress in January 1964. Shortly after the 1964 presidential election, McNamara decided that 1,000 should be enough and President Johnson endorsed this decision in December, over the opposition of the Air Force chief of staff, General Curtis LeMay.

Grappling with the problem of "damage limitation" had impressed on McNamara the futility of counting on additional missiles to limit the devastation that an attack on the United States would cause. He was out of step with many important senators, both Democrat and Republican, who thought in more traditional terms of superiority. McNamara's decision about Minuteman reflected a more fundamental conclusion: the "nuclear stalemate" foreseen during the Truman and Eisenhower administrations was just over the horizon. McNamara thought that nothing could have prevented that outcome "short of a massive preemptive first strike in the 1950s."[2] Eisenhower had seen that, too, but had dismissed the preventive war "solution" which some had put to him.

Now, in the mid-1960s, the unimaginable damage to both countries that a nuclear war would almost certainly inflict raised questions about the meaning and effect of superiority. Some spoke about "making the rubble bounce" to suggest the idea of overkill. But the majority view in the U.S. government was that deterrence required the United States to demonstrate through its nuclear plans and deployments a confidence that it could emerge from a nuclear war in a better position than the Soviet Union. Others thought that the margin of difference was likely to be meaningless amid the ruins caused by even a small-scale nuclear war. That led some to think that a minimal deterrent force, so long as it was survivable, should suffice. The situation forced serious strategic thinkers to consider how the United States and the Soviet Union might act together to establish and maintain stability rather than compete to achieve superiority. When the pressures of Vietnam permitted him to do so, McNamara wrestled with this problem during the whole time he served President Johnson.

Planting the Seeds of Future Instability

Unintended consequences have been commonplace throughout the nuclear era. Deployment of weapons that solved one defense problem often created others. Such was the case with the multiple independently targetable reentry vehicles, or MIRVs. Politically, the MIRV was a readily available answer to critics who complained that the Soviet Union had surged ahead in ballistic missile defenses. MIRVs could overcome such defenses. The longer-term significance of the MIRV was that it had the potential to become a destabilizing influence in the U.S.-Soviet strategic relationship. A meta-stable condition is one in which a small input produces a large change, and this is what MIRVs did.

Multiplying the number of warheads each missile could carry was a way to overwhelm defenses against incoming ballistic missile warheads. The first multiple reentry vehicles (MRVs) followed a trajectory to the earth's surface that was determined by the missile's guidance system. The warheads could not be targeted independently of each other. Because of that and because accuracy had not been sufficiently developed, MRVs were not an effective way of attacking missile silos that had been "hardened," that is, built to withstand a near miss of a nuclear warhead. It was probably inevitable that after the deployment of MRVs, the next step would be to find a way to guide each one of the multiple warheads independently to its target.

In a situation where two nations have equivalent numbers of fixed, land-based missiles and each, because of MIRVing, has equivalent larger numbers of warheads, it was thought that great advantages could accrue to the nation that struck first. The ratio between warheads and silos is favorable to warheads. In theory, therefore, the nation that strikes first can expect to destroy nearly all of its opponent's silo-based missiles, while retaining some number of its own land-based missiles and warheads, in addition to whatever other forces it may have. This was a scenario that strategic planners worried about as soon as both sides acquired MIRVs. The availability of submarine-launched ballistic missiles, which are survivable through concealment, and bombers, which can be put on airborne alert, should suffice to deter disarming strikes against missile silos. But worst-case planning was the norm.

Two days before his inauguration, in January 1965, Johnson transmitted an unusual "Special Message to the Congress on the State of the Nation's Defenses." In it he alluded, without naming it, to the MIRV. Development of MIRVs had recently been authorized and obviously it was politically important to the president and to McNamara: "Major new developments in strategic weapons systems we propose to begin this year are: A new missile system, the Poseidon, . . . a series of remarkable new payloads for strategic missiles. These include: . . . *guidance and re-entry vehicle designs*, to increase many fold the effectiveness of our missiles against various kinds of targets." But of antiballistic missiles (ABMs), he said only: "we shall continue the research and development which retains the options to deploy an anti-ballistic missile system." Johnson also asserted: "it is already clear that without fallout shelter protection for our citizens, all defense weapons lose much of their effectiveness in saving lives."[3]

Three years later, in his annual budget message to the Congress on January 29, 1968, Johnson announced that he was requesting funds which would "convert our strategic missile force to the more effective Minuteman III and Poseidon; equipping those missiles with multiple, independently targeted warheads." This was eight months before the MIRV was ready for flight testing. It was also McNamara's last budget message. He became president of the World Bank that spring.

Looking back on this classic story of technology, Eisenhower's director of defense research and engineering, Herbert York, remarked: "The MIRV did eventually turn out to have enormous consequences, but didn't seem too important at the time and, besides, it was not entirely new, being derived from the MRV, which in turn had been started earlier."[4]

The consequences became quite apparent in the late 1970s, when Soviet acquisition of MIRVs combined with the Soviet Union's very large missiles and increasingly accurate guidance systems theoretically, at least, rendered all of the American fixed, land-based missiles vulnerable to destruction by only a part of the Soviet missile force. In the face of this possibility, President Reagan's Commission on Strategic Forces (the "Scowcroft Commission") recommended in 1983 that, in the future, U.S. land-based missiles should have only one warhead. The commission pointed out that an attacker could not then destroy more than one U.S. warhead with one of the attacking warheads.

The MIRV technology also made possible—and probably inevitable—a strategy predicated on fighting a protracted nuclear war, that is, a sequence of nuclear exchanges spread over days, weeks, or months. The idea brings to mind Einstein's comment that after the bomb, everything changed except man's way of thinking.

The First Ballistic Missile Defense Debate

Soviet defense programs created pressures in the United States to match and, preferably, surpass what the Soviets were doing. Now the Soviets seemed to be ahead in building an ABM system. American analysts doubted that an ABM system around Moscow would work against a large attack, and an upgraded air defense system near Leningrad was even less capable. But at the same time, Soviet missile factories were steadily cranking out new intercontinental ballistic missiles (ICBMs), "like sausages," as Khrushchev once said. National Intelligence Estimates between 1963 and 1967 consistently underestimated the pace of Soviet deployment of ICBMs. Soviet operationally deployed land-based intercontinental missiles had reached 213 in mid-1965 and 570 by mid-1967, with more sites still being built.

These numbers were still below the levels of Soviet deployments McNamara had projected early in the Kennedy administration and well below the 1,054 ICBMs the United States would have when it leveled off in 1967. McNamara's last report to Congress, in January 1968, credited the Soviets with having 750 ballistic missiles capable of striking the United States, including those launched both from land and sea. McNamara thought that the Soviets might not build a force large enough and capable enough to destroy most U.S. land-based missiles, but this seemed to many observers to be exactly what they intended.

Developing and deploying the MIRV was Johnson's and McNamara's answer to a Soviet ballistic missile defense system. But that response was not enough for those in Congress and the military who ardently believed that the Soviet Union had a head start on ballistic missile defense programs. And so another decision of the Johnson administration was to develop and deploy an antiballistic missile system. Eisenhower and Kennedy had faced pressure from Congress to deploy an ABM system, but by the time of Johnson's presidency, the ABM had become a well-known and controversial public issue, thanks to lobbies in Congress and in the private sector. There was, by then, a long history of presidential involvement in ABM decisions. Eisenhower and Kennedy thought the technology was not ready. That position had insulated them from political heat. Johnson thought the same, but ultimately he had to face the first serious debate in the United States about the pros and cons of missile defense. And he lost.

Very prominent in the background of the Johnson administration's budget review at the end of 1964 was the first Chinese nuclear test explosion on October 16, 1964, and the appearance of a large new Soviet antimissile missile, the Galosh, at the November 7 parade in Moscow honoring the Bolshevik Revolution. The budget review followed closely upon an election campaign in which Johnson and McNamara had been attacked by Goldwater for their failure to provide for an adequate level of strategic forces. Johnson, fresh from his victory, felt comfortable with McNamara's recommendation that Nike-X deployment be deferred once again, especially since he could announce other new weapons developments. But by 1966 a full-scale airing of the arguments for the ABM began when the Joint Chiefs of Staff, in the midst of the Vietnam War, publicly rejected McNamara's arguments for delaying the deployment of ABMs and supported a system to defend against a Soviet attack.

The idea gathered momentum on Capitol Hill, where Democrats controlled both houses of Congress. In April 1966, the Senate Armed Services Committee, chaired by President Johnson's longtime friend and colleague Richard Russell of Georgia, voted to add preproduction funds for Nike-X to the defense authorization bill. The full Senate supported the augmented defense bill a week later. And in May, the joint chiefs unanimously recommended production and deployment of an ABM system to defend against a Soviet missile attack. In June, the House also approved the Senate's preproduction funds for Nike-X.

And so the political climate soured for Johnson and McNamara as the Soviet Union added more missiles to its offensive forces and as the Vietnam War escalated, with no end in sight for either process. The "credibility gap" was how the media labeled the administration's explanations of the war. For McNamara, six years in a highly exposed position had earned him many enemies. It had come to the point where a wartime president would have to choose between his secretary of defense and the Joint Chiefs of Staff, who were supported by important congressional committees, including many of Johnson's closest associates.

The decisive meeting took place in Austin, Texas, on December 6, 1966. McNamara knew that another deferral of deployment could not be sustained in the face of an alliance between the joint chiefs and Congress. With the prospect of a major defense issue shaping up for the 1968 campaign that could hurt the Democrats, there was only one way the president could move—toward deployment. McNamara came prepared with a compromise: propose to the Congress, he said, a contingency fund for ABM preproduction expenditures, linked to two conditions: (1) there was no commitment to a specific deployment schedule or plan, and (2) deployment would be contingent on the results of an effort to negotiate an ABM deployment freeze with the Soviet Union. Johnson accepted the compromise. But Lyndon Johnson was in serious political trouble, and so was his secretary of defense. For McNamara, it was his last chance to use his once formidable influence with the president. He bought a year's grace, but he put the deployment decision in the hands of Moscow.

Through the first half of 1967, the American offer to negotiate on ABM deployment was scorned by the Soviet leaders, who made it clear that they were more worried about American offensive forces. The Arab-Israeli War in June 1967 created an occasion for a visit to the United Nations by Soviet Premier Alexei Kosygin. Johnson jumped at the chance to meet with Kosygin during his U.S. visit and they did so on June 23 and 25, 1967, in Glassboro, New Jersey. In his memoirs, Johnson says he told Kosygin that he "had been waiting for three months for his answer on starting talks on ABMs and ICBMs." But Kosygin preferred to talk about the Middle East. Johnson said that "each time I mentioned missiles, Kosygin talked about Arabs and Is-raelis."[5] Finally, the president arranged for McNamara to make the case for ABM limits to Kosygin while the two leaders were having lunch on June 23. In startling contrast to the later Soviet reaction to Reagan's ballistic missile defense initiative, Kosygin said that ballistic missile defense was not a threat, but that offensive weapons definitely were. Johnson wrote that "Kosygin ap-parently had come to Glassboro with a block against this subject. Time and time again, he implied that we only wanted to talk about limiting ABMs, while the Soviets felt that ABMs and offensive nuclear weapons should be linked. I reassured him repeatedly that we wanted to limit both offensive and defensive weapons, and McNamara said the same. But the point did not get across clearly—or Kosygin chose not to understand."[6]

When Kosygin returned to New York on Sunday, June 25, he made the Soviet position clear to a press conference: "the anti-missile system is not a weapon of aggression, of attack, it is a weapon of protection."[7] Thus, another opportunity to restrain the arms race was missed.

Johnson's next actions were dictated by the decision he had taken in De-cember. The Soviets seemed to have no interest in talks. Leaders of Congress, including his close friend Senator Richard Russell, were pressuring him to de-ploy a ballistic missile defense system. The Republicans were promising to make his failure to deploy defensive systems an issue in the next elections. The Vietnam War was in full swing and the joint chiefs, whose support was absolutely essential to him, had made it emphatically and unanimously clear that they wanted ballistic missile defense to offset the growing Soviet threat. Not long after Glassboro, Johnson and McNamara came to an understanding that ballistic missile defense deployment would have to be announced not later than January 1968. This was the date of the last presidential budget message before the November elections.

Defense against Limited Ballistic Missile Attacks

In their times in office, Presidents George H. W. Bush, Bill Clinton, and George W. Bush each endorsed ballistic missile defenses against limited at-tacks by "rogue states." This idea goes back at least to the Johnson presi-dency. McNamara chose to describe the defense system he was required to deploy as one intended to deal with a limited attack, and specifically a Chi-nese attack. By 1966, McNamara was intrigued with the idea of an anti-Chinese defense. A fixation with Chinese nuclear capabilities had permeated the Kennedy administration and had even prompted some discussions of a preventive "surgical strike." McNamara saw in the China rationale a way to place the ballistic missile defense deployment outside the context of the U.S.-Soviet strategic balance, where he was convinced it would lead to an intensification of the arms race. The China rationale, he hoped, would silence domestic critics while avoiding a new competition with the U.S.S.R. The Chinese helped, by detonating their first thermonuclear bomb in June 1967.

On the occasion of a scheduled speech in San Francisco on September 18, 1967, the secretary of defense unveiled the administration's decision. The plan included two types of interceptor missiles, each armed with nuclear warheads. One type of missile, Spartan, would intercept incoming reentry vehicles outside the earth's atmosphere. The other defensive missile, Sprint, would intercept incoming warheads within the earth's atmosphere. The system was designed to protect U.S. population centers against a light attack. McNamara described the system as "Chinese-oriented" and said that production would begin at the end of the year. In his January 29, 1968, budget message to Congress, President Johnson said that the Sentinel ballistic missile system, as it was named, was designed "to meet the threat posed by the emerging Chinese nuclear capability."[8]

End of the McNamara Era

McNamara's speech of September 18, 1967, was a valedictory, of sorts. Speaking of the U.S. strategic build-up decided in 1961, he said

> our current numerical superiority over the Soviet Union in reliable, accurate and effective warheads is both greater than we had originally planned and more than we require. . . . if we had had more accurate information about planned Soviet strategic forces, we simply would not have needed to build as large a nuclear arsenal as we have today.

Speaking of the pressures to build new weapons, he continued:

> There is a kind of mad momentum intrinsic to the development of all new nuclear weaponry. If a weapons system works and works well, there is a strong pressure from many directions to procure and deploy the weapons out of all proportion to the prudent level required.
>
> What is essential to understand here is that the Soviet Union and the United States mutually influence one another's strategic plans. Whatever their intentions or our intentions, actions—or even realistically potential actions—

on either side relating to the buildup of nuclear forces necessarily trigger reactions on the other side. It is precisely this action-reaction phenomenon that fuels an arms race.[9]

Lyndon Johnson and Robert McNamara had been drifting apart in their thinking about Vietnam. In November 1967, McNamara was nominated by Johnson to be president of the World Bank. McNamara left the post of secretary of defense on February 28, 1968, and was replaced by Clark Clifford, a longtime unofficial adviser to Johnson. McNamara's judgments on strategic defense issues had influenced two presidents. He had lost only one major battle, ballistic missile defense deployment, and he had helped to define the strategic nuclear policies of the Kennedy and Johnson administrations. In some ways, his instincts on defense had become much like Eisenhower's. In particular, the role of nuclear weapons as a deterrent rather than as meaningful "war-fighting" systems was a conviction that Eisenhower and McNamara held in common.

The Negotiating Option

Johnson's interest in strategic arms control was not just a device to deal with the issues of ballistic missile defense. He had decided at the outset of his administration that he would work for limitations on strategic offensive and defensive arms. In his message to the Eighteen-Nation Disarmament Committee on January 21, 1964, Johnson said:

> we must first endeavor to halt further increases in strategic armaments now. The United States, the Soviet Union and their respective Allies should agree to explore a verified freeze of the number and characteristics of strategic nuclear offensive and defensive vehicles. For our part, we are convinced that the security of all nations can be safeguarded within the scope of such an agreement and that this initial measure preventing the further expansion of the deadly and costly arms race will open the path to reductions in all types of forces from present levels.[10]

The Soviets' reaction to this proposal was scathing. It had nothing in common with disarmament, they said, and was only a propaganda ploy. Not until July 1968 was Johnson able to announce "an agreement that we have actively sought and worked for since January 1964." The agreement he referred to was simply to begin talking about limiting offensive and defensive weapons. But it was a significant advance into a highly sensitive area.

The domestic scene in the United States had changed in the year since Johnson and McNamara pleaded with Kosygin at Glassboro to begin talks on nuclear arms control. The president had announced on March 31, 1968, that he would not be a candidate for reelection. Pressured by Congress in 1966–1967 to deploy a ballistic missile defense, the administration found itself in 1968 fighting off attempts in the Senate to postpone deployment. For a variety of reasons, mainly related to Vietnam, the grip of the Senate Armed Services Committee had weakened. The mood of the Senate had become more skeptical toward defense spending. Within a year from the time when Johnson felt he was being forced to deploy a ballistic missile defense, he was being pressured *not* to deploy it.

Soviet agreement to talks on offensive and defensive strategic nuclear forces came in late June 1968, shortly after the Senate had defeated a move to postpone deployment of a ballistic missile defense. The talks Johnson had sought throughout his administration were not to begin during his time as president. He had seen the Promised Land but he was not to enter it. Johnson was supposed to announce on August 21, 1968, that he would visit Moscow in October and that the talks on nuclear weapons would begin soon thereafter. During the previous night, the Soviet Union and its Warsaw Pact allies invaded Czechoslovakia to quell the "Prague Spring," a liberalizing movement within the Communist Party of Czechoslovakia. Johnson's announcement, and the talks, were cancelled and U.S.-Soviet negotiations could not begin until after Johnson left office.

The nonproliferation treaty negotiated and signed within Johnson's presidency may be the most important arms control treaty ever negotiated. Essentially, it was a bargain between the nuclear-weapon states and the non-nuclear-weapon states. A nuclear-weapon state was defined as a state that had manufactured and exploded a nuclear weapon prior to January 1, 1967. Great Britain, the Soviet Union, and the United States signed the treaty in 1968 as nuclear-weapon states. China and France chose not to sign the treaty initially but later joined it as nuclear-weapon states. The bargain was that the non-nuclear-weapon states would give up their rights to acquire nuclear weapons and, in return, the nuclear weapon states would assist them in developing civil applications of nuclear energy and would themselves seek to work for nuclear disarmament.

An important element of the treaty was a requirement that the non-nuclear-weapon states would negotiate a safeguards agreement with the International Atomic Energy Agency (IAEA). The purpose of this IAEA monitoring, as initially conceived, was to verify that nuclear materials furnished to the non-nuclear-weapon states were not being diverted to make nuclear weapons. In the past decade, this provision has been interpreted as also allowing searches for clandestine nuclear weapons programs.

The impetus for the treaty came from a series of U.N. General Assembly resolutions aimed at discouraging transfer of nuclear materials and information by the nuclear-weapon states and at preventing acquisition of nuclear weapons by non-nuclear-weapon states. But Johnson suggested the outlines of what eventually became the nonproliferation treaty in his message to the Eighteen-Nation Disarmament Committee on January 21, 1964. The proposal had been gestating within the Arms Control and Disarmament Agency during the Kennedy administration. It had seemed to be a logical follow-on to a test ban treaty.

A U.S. draft treaty on nonproliferation was submitted to the Eighteen-Nation Disarmament Conference on August 17, 1965. There were differences with the Soviet Union, in particular over the U.S.-backed multilateral force (MLF), but the United States and the Soviet Union shared a common interest in a treaty and began to work out the details between them. Secretary of State Dean Rusk took a leading role in this with Soviet Foreign Minister Gromyko.

Much of the detailed work was done by the staff of the still new Arms Control and Disarmament Agency. George Bunn, the first general counsel of ACDA, became the chief negotiator. At the time, I was assigned to the U.S. Mission to the European Communities, responsible for working with the European Atomic Energy Community (Euratom). The nations of the European Communities refused to accept IAEA safeguards because Euratom had its own multilateral safeguards agency that was doing similar work. I collaborated with Enrico Jaccia, the head of Euratom's safeguards agency, in arranging a compromise that allowed IAEA to monitor the work of Euratom's safeguards agency. And so another problem was resolved.

The treaty was completed and approved by the U.N. General Assembly on June 12, 1968. It was opened for signature on July 1, 1968, and was signed on that day in the White House by President Lyndon Johnson. Never given to understatement, as he signed it, the president called the treaty "the most important international agreement since the beginning of the nuclear age." In his memoirs, he wrote that "if July 1, 1968, figures in the history books of the future, it will be because of what happened that morning in the East Room of the White House." Johnson had no reason to be modest. The treaty became a fundamental piece of the nuclear restraint regime built up during the Cold War. It is still an essential part of the diplomacy of the twenty-first century. His predecessor, John Kennedy, had worried in 1963 that fifteen to twenty nations might become nuclear powers within a decade. Thanks to

Johnson's treaty and the nonproliferation regime that coalesced around it, by 2005, fewer than ten countries had become nuclear weapon states.

Notes

1. Lyndon B. Johnson, *The Vantage Point* (New York: Holt, Rinehart and Winston, 1971), 98–99.

2. McNamara's speech to the United Press International Editors and Publishers, San Francisco, September 18, 1967, quoted in Robert S. McNamara, *The Essence of Security: Reflections in Office* (New York: Harper and Row, 1968), 55. Also in the *New York Times*, September 19, 1967, p. 18.

3. *Public Papers of the Presidents*, Johnson, 1965, 65–66.

4. Herbert York, *Race to Oblivion: A Participant's View of the Arms Race* (New York: Simon and Schuster, 1970), 156.

5. Johnson, *The Vantage Point*, 483.

6. Johnson, *The Vantage Point*, 484.

7. Murrey Marder, "Russia Rejects Talks on Anti-Missile Race," *Washington Post*, June 27, 1967, A1.

8. *Public Papers of the Presidents*, Johnson, 1968, vol. 1, 98.

9. From McNamara's speech of September 18, 1967, in McNamara, *The Essence of Security*, 57–59.

10. "Documents on Disarmament 1964," U.S. Arms Control and Disarmament Agency Publication 27, 8.

PART III

FACING THE PROBLEMS OF PARITY, 1969–1980

Nixon, Ford, and Carter

It was a turbulent time in American politics. Threatened with impeachment, Richard Nixon, in August 1974, became the first American president ever to resign. The Vietnam War was dividing the country. Saigon fell to the North Vietnamese in April 1975. The Soviet Union was perceived to be using its nuclear parity to gain geopolitical advantage. A growing conservative movement led first by Senator Barry Goldwater (R-AZ) and then Governor Ronald Reagan of California insisted that the United States was neglecting its defenses.

Presidents Richard Nixon, Gerald Ford, and Jimmy Carter inherited a strategic nuclear triad consisting of bombers, intercontinental ballistic missiles and submarine-launched ballistic missiles. The missile-building program started in the Kennedy and Johnson administrations had been essentially completed and a new cycle of building was being considered. While debate raged on about what kind of forces to build, the United States added to its nuclear warhead inventory multiple independently targetable reentry vehicles—the notorious MIRVs. Accuracy of delivery was greatly enhanced to deal more effectively with hardened targets—mainly Soviet land-based missiles in concrete silos. Advances in information technology made command and control of these forces more effective.

All these developments were pressed into service in the effort to derive some advantages at a time when the Soviet Union was building new missiles at a rapid rate and U.S.-Soviet strategic parity was within sight—in the rearview mirror, some thought. By the time of Ford's administration, Soviet strategic forces had surpassed those of the United States in some categories. U.S. and Soviet land-based missiles had become vulnerable, raising concerns about a disarming first strike, even though U.S. submarine-based missiles and bombers were still relatively invulnerable. Technology and the advent of something like parity in strike forces soon led to new strategic doctrines.

Nixon and his secretary of state, Henry Kissinger, inaugurated what they called an "era of negotiations" in which they attempted to link objectives in various U.S.-Soviet negotiating arenas to achieve results across a broad front. Nuclear arms began to be seen as bargaining chips. Nixon achieved the first agreement to limit U.S.-Soviet strategic arms (SALT I) and one of the most important agreements of the nuclear era—the antiballistic missile (ABM) treaty of 1972. Ford and Carter tried to build on those accords but failed, owing to a political backlash against detente, and concerns about Soviet capabilities to wage nuclear war.

~

CHAPTER FIVE

Richard Nixon: Only Connect

The Vietnam War and domestic discontent dominated the presidential election campaign of 1968. Nuclear war and nuclear weapons, issues that had damaged Goldwater's 1964 campaign beyond repair, were not high on the national agenda. The Democratic candidate was Vice President Hubert Humphrey, a former senator with a strong record of support for arms control. He was saddled with public dissatisfaction with Vietnam and stigmatized further by the disastrous image of riots at the 1968 Chicago Democratic National Convention. Richard Nixon ran a campaign based on a centrist position, emphasizing his experience, his knowledge of the world, and his ability to "bring us together."

Nixon delivered his major campaign statement on defense close to election day. The *New York Times* described his October 24 speech as "militant" and "belligerent" and contrasted it with Humphrey's emphasis on arms control. Nixon charged that the Democrats have "concluded that by marking time in our defense program, we could induce the Communists to follow our example, slacken their own defenses, and then we would have peace in our time." The result of this, he claimed, was "a gravely serious security gap." Nixon declared that "this parity concept means superiority for potential enemies" and he said that his goal would be "clear-cut" superiority.[1] This goal was consistent with the Republican Party's platform for the 1968 election, which charged that "not retention of American superiority, but parity with the Soviet Union has been made the controlling doctrine in many critical areas."[2] The timing of Nixon's speech was significant: it was delivered as President

Johnson was making a last-ditch effort to gain a breakthrough in peace talks with the North Vietnamese. An aggressive attack on the Democrats' management of defense policy would help to hold public attention on an issue where Nixon thought the Democrats were vulnerable.

The election was a close one, as it had been in 1960, but Nixon received the winning margin of votes. He was able to make the "security gap" work for him this time. Nixon's Inaugural Address emphasized the olive branch, in contrast to the arrows he had brandished in his preelection speech on defense policy. The juxtaposition of the two speeches symbolized the necessary relation between power and negotiation, Nixon's formula for a successful foreign policy. Of defense, Nixon said: "we will be as strong as we need to be for as long as we need to be." He stressed that "we are entering an era of negotiations" and asked for international cooperation "to reduce the burden of arms, to strengthen the structure of peace."[3]

Nixon had said in his campaign that he would revive and strengthen the National Security Council system of staffing decisions. In fact, he was determined to assign to the White House maximum authority for key national security decisions. By establishing a highly-qualified NSC staff under Henry Kissinger, Nixon created the bureaucratic means to dominate national security policy. In the process, he gave great authority to Kissinger, who exercised it to the hilt.

Sufficiency, Linkage, and Ballistic Missile Defense

Nixon's first press conference as president was held one week after his inauguration, and he used the occasion to begin to define his strategic policies. He conveyed the idea of connecting negotiations by saying he wanted "to see to it that we have strategic arms talks in a way and at a time that will promote, if possible, progress on outstanding political problems at the same time." Nixon also began to distance himself from the idea of strategic superiority. "Parity," as a proper description of the relationship between U.S. and Soviet strategic forces was wrong, he reasoned, because wars begin when each side believes it has a chance to win. "Therefore, parity does not necessarily assure that a war may not occur." Of "superiority," he said, in a statement worthy of McNamara, that it "may have a detrimental effect on the other side in putting it in an inferior position and, therefore, giving great impetus to its own arms race." Concluding the tutorial, he said, "I think 'sufficiency' is a better term, actually, than either 'superiority' or 'parity.' "[4]

Writing some years later, Nixon made his views even clearer: "absolute superiority in every area of armaments would have been meaningless because there is a point in arms development at which each nation has the capacity to destroy the other. Beyond that point, the most important consideration is not continued escalation of the number of arms, but maintenance of the strategic equilibrium while making it clear to the adversary that a nuclear attack, even if successful, would be suicidal."[5]

President Nixon's penchant for connecting policy objectives meant that he considered major defense decisions in the context of U.S. foreign policy goals, not simply as questions of defense capabilities and affordability. He tried to think how defense decisions would advance specific U.S. political and security objectives. When applied to strategic arms negotiations, this idea gave rise to the criticism that it was a political or "bargaining chip" approach, which in some cases was exactly what it was. The first bargaining chip was Nixon's support for ballistic missile defense.

The Nixon administration's strategic review process began, as it usually does, with a review of the defense budget. This task was assigned to Secretary of Defense Melvin Laird, a former congressman who had made a specialty of defense. Laird designated his deputy, David R. Packard, co-founder of Hewlett-Packard, to take charge of the review. The question of ballistic missile defense was one of the most important aspects of the review. Opposition to missile defenses in the Congress had been building, and Nixon was obviously concerned about having his hand forced.

The defense review was formally launched on February 6, 1969. On the same day the Defense Department announced that Laird had ordered the Army to stop acquiring new missile defense sites and to cease construction activity pending a one-month review of all major weapons systems. At that point, land had been acquired only in the Boston area, but the Army was asking for authority to acquire sites near Seattle and Chicago.[6]

Nixon was asked about the defense review and Johnson's Sentinel defense system at his second press conference as president on February 6, 1969. He said he did not accept the Johnson-McNamara rationale for missile defenses, a stance he had also taken during the presidential campaign.

I do not buy the assumption that the ABM [antiballistic missile] system, the thin Sentinel system, as it has been described, was simply for the purpose of protecting ourselves against attack from Communist China. This system, as are the systems that the Soviet Union has already deployed, adds to our overall defense capability. I would further say that, as far as the threat is concerned, we do not see any change in that threat, and we are examining, therefore, all of our defense systems and all of our defense postures to see how we can best meet them consistent with our other responsibilities.[7]

Nixon's rejection of the anti-Chinese rationale for the ballistic missile system and his conception of it as a part of the U.S.-Soviet strategic balance altered the way in which the system would be deployed. And this placed it squarely in the context of bargaining with the Soviet Union, which is where Nixon's ideas about sufficiency and linkage policy suggested it should be. It also presaged Nixon's opening to China later in his administration.

The Johnson-McNamara decision had required the Army's planned missile defense deployment to be directed at the defense of the population, an action which many had thought would be well received by the cities concerned. Air Force General Curtis LeMay's view of this was expressed in his book *America Is in Danger*, published in 1968: "Always ready with a new objection, Mr. McNamara maintained it would be political mayhem in this country to try to select the twenty-five or fifty cities for ABM protection. I have more faith in the wisdom and common sense of the American people."[8] As it turned out, it was not the losers in the competition for defense but the winners who took umbrage at the Army's choices. When the cities to be defended learned of their good fortune—which included nuclear warheads stored in their vicinity—many of their citizens organized protests against the deployment and made sure that their representatives in Congress felt the heat.

With the issue no longer in the hands of a few experts and congressional power brokers, Nixon faced a real possibility of losing one of his most important bargaining chips. His early moves away from an urban defense were essential to saving the program, but he still needed a strategic rationale for missile defense deployment, the task that Packard was taking in hand.

The Nixon Ballistic Missile Defense

Packard presented his preliminary report to the president on February 20, 1969. It included two options for population defense and one option designed to defend Minuteman intercontinental ballistic missile (ICBM) sites. The hardware was essentially the same as that designed for the Johnson-McNamara system. The president held another press conference on March 4 and announced that there would be a meeting of the National Security Council the next day, "which will be entirely devoted to an assessment of that ballistic missile defense system." Nixon added that after the NSC meeting, he planned to "make some additional studies on my own involving the Defense Department and other experts whose opinions I value. I will make a decision and announce a decision on ABM at the first of next week."[9]

Packard presented the same options to the National Security Council as he had to the president and recommended the option for the defense of Minuteman silos. Nixon's advisers generally supported that approach, and after hearing them out, Nixon said he would decide later. During the weekend of March 8–9, at Key Biscayne, Florida, Nixon decided on a defense of Minuteman sites, which had evidently been his choice all along. He thought of it as protecting a U.S. second strike capability. The next question was how to deploy the system, which was relevant both to funding and to Nixon's ability to adjust the program as necessary to link it to developments in negotiations with the U.S.S.R. His team developed a phased plan of deployment, initially to begin work on only two of the planned twelve sites. This would avoid being locked into the whole system at the outset. It might also be more palatable to Congress.

On March 14, 1969, President Nixon announced his decision personally at a news conference. Calling his proposed ballistic missile defense deployment the "Safeguard" system, Nixon said that in modifying Johnson's Sentinel system, he had decided to place "the emphasis . . . on protecting our deterrent, which is the best preventive for war." He flatly said that the program "does not provide defense for our cities, and for that reason the sites have been moved away from our major cities." He had found, he said, "that there is no way that we can adequately defend our cities without an unacceptable loss of life." Another major difference from Johnson's program, Nixon stressed, would be that Safeguard would be installed in phases, rather than on a fixed deployment schedule. The reasons for this were related to the development of the Soviet and Chinese missile threat, evolving technology, and the situation in any arms control negotiations. Accordingly, there would be an annual review of the program. Nixon also pointed out that the first site would not be completed until 1973.

Nixon's approach, of course, was conditioned by the congressional mood, as well as by the factors he mentioned in his announcement. He said as much in his March 14 press conference when he described the program as "a minimum program . . . which provides options to change in other directions," but that he expected "a very close vote." He even remarked that the decision would be so close, it might be decided by one vote—which turned out to be the case.

How to Give It Up

To justify forgoing a defense against ballistic missiles after fighting with Congress to win the right to deploy it, Nixon had to prepare public opinion. He had to convince Americans that the U.S.-Soviet strategic balance was really at or near parity and that deterrence could be maintained without U.S. superiority or a ballistic missile defense system. At his March 14 press conference, in addition to announcing his decision, Nixon presented his thinking about strategic deterrence in a prepared statement and in give and take with the press. He said that a city defense "needs to be a perfect or near perfect system to be credible." The fact that ballistic missile defense could reduce American fatalities by more than 50 percent did not impress him because the United States "would still lose 30 to 40 million." In contrast, he remarked, "it is necessary only to protect enough of the deterrent that the retaliatory second strike will be of such magnitude that the enemy would think twice before launching a first strike." He thought that protecting two Minuteman sites (the initial deployment plan) "could be decisive insofar as the enemy considering the possibility of a first strike." In his prepared statement, Nixon asserts that the only way to save lives "is to prevent war."

Nixon also made use of McNamara's "action-reaction phenomenon"; he said that he wanted to make the ballistic missile defense system "so clearly defensive in character that the Soviet Union cannot interpret this as escalating the arms race." This he had accomplished, he thought, by "moving the city defense out of it, and the possibility of that city defense growing into a thick defense."[10]

Nixon's prepared "Statement on Deployment of the Antiballistic Missile System" also ruled out an increase in the number of sea- and land-based missiles and bombers on action-reaction grounds. The statement maintained that an increase in U.S. missiles would provide only marginal improvement of the U.S. deterrent, "while it could be misinterpreted by the Soviets as an attempt to threaten their deterrent." This interaction, the statement said, "would therefore stimulate an arms race."[11]

Taken in their entirety, these decisions and the explanations offered by President Nixon paralleled the arguments that Robert McNamara had made at great personal cost to himself. These arguments had now been sanctified by the new occupant of the White House. A few direct quotations will underscore this point. Speaking to a commemorative session of NATO's North Atlantic Council in Washington on April 10, 1969, Nixon said: "Let's put it in plain words. The West does not today have the massive nuclear predominance that it once had, and any sort of broad-based arms agreement with the Soviets would codify the present balance."[12]

And in a press conference on April 18, he remarked that during the 1962 Cuban Missile Crisis, the experts "agreed that the U.S. superiority was at least 4 to 1 and maybe 5 to 1, over the Soviet Union in terms of overall nuclear capability. Now we don't have that today. That gap has been closed. We shall never have it again because it will not be necessary for us. Sufficiency, as I have indicated, is all that is necessary."[13]

Nixon won his battle with Congress in a Senate vote on August 6, 1969. The negotiations that led to the antiballistic missile (ABM) treaty in 1972 began with the arguments the Nixon administration made to Congress in 1969. Nixon privately briefed the congressional leadership on his ballistic missile defense decisions, using the bargaining chip argument. At the heart of his thinking was the instinct "that tactically we needed the ABM as a bargaining chip for negotiations with the Soviets; they already had an ABM system, so if we went into negotiations without one we might have to give up something else, perhaps something more vital. In that sense, we had to have it in order to be able to agree to forgo it."[14]

The results of Nixon's management of arms control negotiations were mixed. The first strategic arms limitation agreement (SALT I) was important because it broke the ice. A precedent was set for more important agreements later. But it did little to halt the nuclear arms race. The other result of his negotiations, the ABM treaty signed at Moscow on May 26, 1972, by Nixon and Soviet General Secretary Brezhnev, was arguably one of the two most important arms control treaties of the Cold War period, the other being the nonproliferation treaty. Nixon thought that "the ABM treaty stopped what inevitably would have become a defensive arms race, with untold billions of dollars being spent on each side for more and more ABM coverage."[15]

Even with an enormously expensive layered system of defense, it was, and is, doubtful that anything like a leak-proof shield could be built when the adversary has thousands of nuclear warheads. In his memoirs, Nixon recognized that in abandoning population defense, he was embracing "the concept of deterrence through 'mutual terror': by giving up missile defense, each side was leaving its population and territory hostage to a strategic missile attack. Each side therefore had an ultimate interest in preventing a war that could only be mutually destructive."[16] That such an unnatural and immoral condition should be changed is beyond doubt. The obvious answer is to reduce nuclear weapons to the lowest level possible and work for political change. But to most politicians, it has always seemed intuitively more reasonable to build a defense against missiles. This is the same philosophy that led to the "impregnable" Maginot Line that the German Army easily avoided in World War II.

The 1972 missile defense treaty lasted until 2002. It became the cornerstone of arms control during the Cold War, and both sides saw it that way. Almost from the beginning of its life, the treaty was attacked by lobbyists for ballistic missile defense. Finally, opponents became strong enough to bring it down, basing their argument on the premise that Russia and the United States had become friends and partners. But the treaty served a useful purpose for three decades. And next to the opening to China, it was Richard Nixon's most impressive achievement.

The MIRV Again

During the time that Nixon was fighting for ballistic missile defense, the MIRV became politically contentious. It had finally dawned on Congress, the press, and some within the administration that MIRVs were destabilizing because they gave an advantage to the attacker. The times were not propitious for making this case, partly because Nixon had to husband his political capital to get the ballistic missile defense decisions he wanted.

Secretary of Defense Laird and others worked very hard to convince Congress that the Soviet offensive buildup warranted the modest steps that the administration was asking Congress to fund. The data supporting this argument were contained in Laird's first full program and budget report to the Congress in February 1970. By then, he could report that the Soviets had "more operational ICBM launchers, over 1,100, than the United States, 1,054."[17] Of course, the United States held a commanding lead in heavy bombers and advantages in submarine-launched missiles as well.

The Nixon administration emphasized that Soviet missile forces included nearly 300 very large ICBMs, called SS-9s, which were thought to be highly accurate and to carry a 25 megaton warhead. The Soviet Union had started to flight-test the technique of multiple reentry vehicles (MRVs) late in 1968 and continued the testing in 1969 using the giant SS-9 as a launcher. The administration maintained that these warheads were rapidly rendering Minuteman silos vulnerable even though the warheads were not individually targeted. Since they were not, the probability that each one could destroy a U.S. missile was not very great. Ascribing to multiple reentry vehicles the characteristics of the MIRV was a case of polemical overkill. The rapid growth of Soviet offensive capabilities was impressive enough, even without exaggeration.

Laird pointed out quite accurately that "for some time, the Soviet forces which became operational in a given year have often exceeded the previous intelligence projections for that year."[18] Although the Soviet Union had lagged behind the United States in submarine-launched ballistic missiles, Laird reported that the Soviets could have from thirty-five to fifty modern ballistic-missile-carrying submarines by 1974–1975, in contrast to the forty-one Polaris submarines operated by the United States. Whatever one might think about Soviet first-strike capability or the Moscow ballistic missile defense system, the Soviet offensive threat was growing at a rapid rate.

The MIRV was an answer to the growing threat, so a MIRV slowdown was inconvenient from many points of view. But Nixon was being pushed from within his administration by the head of the Arms Control and Disarmament Agency, Gerard Smith, to propose a joint U.S.-Soviet moratorium on all multiple warhead testing (MRVs and MIRVs) or at least to stretch out the U.S. MIRV flight testing program. At the same time, a groundswell developed in Congress favoring a halt to MIRV testing.

The Joint Chiefs of Staff vigorously opposed any delay or limit on MIRV testing. Secretary of Defense Laird, who was important to Nixon for many reasons, not the least of them being his effective advocacy of ballistic missile defense before the Congress, favored proceeding with MIRVs. Kissinger also opposed a unilateral U.S. cessation of MIRV testing. He advised Nixon on May 23, 1969, that such a step by the United States "might create pressures to halt the Minuteman III and Poseidon programs," since MIRV warheads were developed in association with those two missiles.[19] There was little doubt how Nixon would decide. On June 19, 1969, Nixon told a press conference: "We are considering the possibility of a moratorium on tests as part of any arms control agreement. However, as far as any unilateral stopping of tests on our part, I do not think that would be in our interest. Only in the event that the Soviet Union and we could agree that a moratorium on tests could be mutually beneficial to us, would we be able to agree to do so."[20] The Soviet government was unwilling to sign up for a moratorium on MIRV testing while the United States had a lead in MIRV technology.

And so the Nixon administration proceeded with the deployment of MIRVed ballistic missiles. The first full squadron of MIRVed Minuteman III intercontinental ballistic missiles was activated in December 1970, and deployments continued throughout the Nixon administration. The submarine-launched MIRVed missile, Poseidon C3, became operational with the first patrol of the USS *James Madison* in March 1971.[21]

The MIRV program was expected to provide an offensive offset to the Soviet buildup in ICBMs and to neutralize Soviet ballistic missile defense deployments. But, as it turned out, the greater throw weight of Soviet missiles meant that the U.S.S.R. could field more MIRVs than the United States. This led to a situation that U.S. defense planners came to regard as one of America's most serious strategic problems, the vulnerability of U.S. land-based missiles.

Modernizing the Triad

After the 1972 Moscow summit and the conclusion of the SALT and ABM agreements, the Nixon administration asked for a substantial increase in the defense budget. Nixon justified this increase in his remarks at a press conference on June 29, 1972. He argued that, without the SALT agreements, he would have had to ask the Congress "to approve an increase in the defense budget for nuclear strategic weapons of at least $15 billion a year on a crash program." According to Nixon, "Mr. Brezhnev made it very clear that he intended to go forward in those categories that were not limited." As Nixon told the Congress: "we need a credible defensive position so that the Soviet Union will have an incentive to negotiate a permanent offensive freeze."[22] (SALT I was an interim agreement.)

The use of arms control to promote a larger defense budget had become standard practice by this time. The habit had begun when the joint chiefs obliged Kennedy to spend more money on nuclear-related items as a price for supporting the test ban treaty. The Nixon administration launched a series of research and development programs as the first step toward building new strategic delivery vehicles. Two of the most important programs were in support of a new ballistic missile and advanced cruise missiles.

In McNamara's fiscal year 1969 budget statement, the outgoing secretary of defense had said: "Although a new land-based ICBM does not appear to offer any particular advantage over the Minuteman III in super-hard silos, I believe we should keep that option open by starting development now of a silo which could be used for either the Minuteman III or a new ICBM."[23] Laird's budget proposals to Congress in 1970 dwelt on the problem of Minuteman vulnerability to Soviet attack. A new ICBM was not mentioned at that time.[24]

James Schlesinger, Nixon's last secretary of defense, asked for funds in the spring of 1974 for "advanced technology leading to the development of an entirely new ICBM." He said that the administration was "considering the technologies for both a new, large payload fixed-base missile which could be launched from existing Minuteman silos, and a new mobile missile, either ground or air launched." The technology Secretary Schlesinger hoped to develop, he said, "would give the new ICBM a very good capability against hard targets."[25] This request for funds led directly to the MX (missile X), later called the Peacekeeper, and the source of controversy for several presidents thereafter.

Very late in his administration, Nixon's advisers also gained his support for the revival of the strategic cruise missile, a small unmanned jet aircraft with a possible range of thousands of miles. Similar but more primitive systems had been dropped at the end of the Eisenhower administration in favor of ballistic missiles. Like other defense decisions of the Nixon administration, the rationale was not exclusively military. The main proponent of the system's development was Henry Kissinger, who saw it as an asset in negotiations with the Soviet Union. Kissinger described his role in his memoirs:

> On July 13, 1973, I wrote to Bill Clements [Deputy Secretary of Defense] insisting that we proceed with a long-range cruise missile. The Pentagon was thinking of cancelling this weapon both for budgetary reasons and to prevent its being used as an excuse to kill off the Air Force's cherished new bomber, the B-1. . . . I argued to Clements "that a long range bomber-launched cruise missile program makes sense strategically and could help our SALT position." Clements went along enthusiastically and the cruise missile program was saved.[26]

The cruise missile was an old idea, but new technology had made it a highly accurate weapon. It would be increasingly difficult to detect and shoot down, could be launched from aircraft, and would assist bombers in striking targets even through heavy air defenses. The cruise missile could also be launched from surface ships, submarines, and from the ground. The compact size of the cruise missile would make concealment relatively easy. Nixon's successor, Gerald Ford, had reason to reflect on this development, and Kissinger's role in it, since it figured in his failure to conclude a SALT agreement during his presidency.

Changing Concepts of Nuclear War

Eisenhower always chose to emphasize the *deterrence* of war, rather than the methods of waging strategic nuclear war. If deterrence failed, his plan was very simple—all U.S. strategic forces would be launched in a massive attack on the enemy's cities. He expected nothing but complete devastation thereafter. Nuclear war, to Eisenhower, was not only unwinnable but also unmanageable. Kennedy had thought in terms of *controlling* the launch of strategic nuclear forces throughout a war and had insisted on having the ability to do this at the presidential level. The technology available to him would not have accomplished all that he hoped for, but improvements in information technology and guidance systems gave subsequent presidents and military commanders many more options.

The MIRV had provided the numbers of warheads and a missile/warhead ratio favorable for targeting an array of military objectives. Accuracy of warheads was improving and seemed likely to improve still further. Satellites, computers, and improvements in communications were making flexible use of the nuclear force hypothetically easier to manage. The condition of essential equivalence in the hardware available to both sides meant that planners had to think about how to use these highly capable forces to eke out some advantage. It became possible during the 1970s to contemplate managing a strategic nuclear war in much the same manner as nineteenth-century artillery battles had been managed. The shorthand term for this type of strategy was "war-fighting."

The start of a major shift in strategic nuclear targeting policy formally began on January 17, 1974, when Nixon signed a policy directive, NSDM 242, "Planning the Employment of Nuclear Weapons." This directive authorized the Defense Department to develop the capacity for limited strategic nuclear strikes against hardened Soviet targets, in contrast to the very large attacks on which previous planning had been based. This development was made possible by MIRVs, the achievement of greater accuracy, overhead reconnaissance, and improved command and control. Now the doctrine began to catch up with the technological possibilities. The directive, the consequences of which are discussed in the next chapter, eventually led to other decisions, which gradually led to a strategy of deterrence based on a war-fighting capability and eventually to a doctrine of "protracted nuclear war."

In one guise or another, the idea of limited strategic options had been discussed at length and in many different places around the country long before Nixon approved the policy that Schlesinger began to implement in 1974. In 1963, I took part in a study of "War Management and Termination" conducted by the Net Evaluation Subcommittee of the NSC, which explored this idea. U.S. strategic attack options for many years had included the idea of less than all-out attacks. But Nixon's signature on NSDM 242 in January 1974 endorsed the idea of limited strategic options, a sound idea in principle, but one which carried with it many consequences.

Nixon authorized Schlesinger to issue guidance on "Nuclear Weapons Employment Policy," and that was done by Schlesinger in April 1974. It included the idea that a strategic nuclear war could proceed in stages, perhaps over a rather lengthy period of time. It required preplanning of a series of limited response options, and a strategic force that could be rapidly retargeted, that would have some ability to destroy hard targets, and that could accurately strike soft targets while minimizing collateral damage.[27] Here are all the ingredients, save the large numbers of warheads, for a counterforce-oriented, war-fighting nuclear force.

The shift in thinking about nuclear war at that time was inevitable, given growing Soviet nuclear capabilities and the hope that nuclear war, somehow, could be limited. Schlesinger argued that limited nuclear options were needed to enhance deterrence and that the Soviets were beginning to acquire a force with just such characteristics. This thinking lent credence to the idea that nuclear war could be conducted as previous wars had been fought: war, as Clausewitz wrote, was still politics by other means. A nuclear war might not be won, but maybe it could be managed. Perhaps this policy contributed to deterrence, but it began another age of excess, surpassing in some ways the material excesses of the 1960s. Nuclear war planning began to develop elaborate schemes for first, second, and third strikes. Reagan's reaction to these fantasies led to an abandonment of arms control as the handmaiden of strategic nuclear planning. In its place, Reagan favored another approach: nuclear weapons should be eliminated.

Notes

1. R.W. Apple Jr., "Nixon Promises Arms Superiority over the Soviets," *New York Times*, October 25, 1968, 1.

2. *Congressional Quarterly's Guide to U.S. Elections*, 2nd ed., 1985, 118.

3. *Public Papers of the Presidents*, Nixon, 1969, 3.

4. *Public Papers of the Presidents*, Nixon, 1969, 17–19.

5. Richard M. Nixon, *RN: The Memoirs of Richard Nixon* (New York: Grosset and Dunlap, 1978), 415.

6. William Beecher, "Sentinel Project Halted by Laird Pending Review," *New York Times*, February 7, 1969, 1.

7. *Public Papers of the Presidents*, Nixon, 1969, 70–71.

8. Curtis E. LeMay and Dale O. Smith, *America Is in Danger* (Mahwah, N.J.: Funk and Wagnalls, 1968), 102.

9. *Public Papers of the Presidents*, Nixon, 1969, 184.

10. *Public Papers of the Presidents*, Nixon, 1969, 210–212.

11. *Public Papers of the Presidents*, Nixon, 1969, 218.

12. *Public Papers of the Presidents*, Nixon, 1969, 274.

13. *Public Papers of the Presidents*, Nixon, 1969, 303.

14. Nixon, *RN*, 415–416.

15. Nixon, *RN*, 617.

16. Nixon, *RN*, 617–618.

17. Melvin R. Laird, *Fiscal Year 1971 Defense Program and Budget*, February 20, 1970, 35.

18. Laird, *FY1971 Defense Program and Budget*, 34.

19. Kissinger, *White House Years* (Boston: Little, Brown, 1979), 211–212.

20. *Public Papers of the Presidents*, Nixon, 1969, 473–474.

21. Thomas Cochran, William Arkin, and Milton Hoenig, *Nuclear Weapons Databook* (Cambridge, Mass.: Ballinger, 1984), 104.

22. *Public Papers of the Presidents*, Nixon, 1972, 711.

23. Robert McNamara, *The 1969 Defense Budget*, January 22, 1968, 60.

24. Laird, *FY1971 Defense Program and Budget*, 50.

25. James R. Schlesinger, *Report of the Secretary of Defense to the Congress on the FY1975 Defense Budget and the FY1975–1979 Defense Program*, 56–57.

26. Henry A. Kissinger, *Years of Upheaval* (Boston: Little, Brown, 1982), 273.

27. James R. Schlesinger, *Report to the Congress on the FY1976 and Transition Budgets*, February 5, 1975, I-13.

CHAPTER SIX

∼

Gerald Ford: A Time to Plant

On December 6, 1973, Republican Congressman Gerald Ford of Michigan became vice president of the United States after Nixon's twice-elected vice president, Spiro Agnew of Maryland, was obliged to resign when faced with charges of corruption. The Watergate crisis had been roiling American politics all that year, as well, following Nixon's landslide victory over Senator George McGovern in November 1972. On August 9, 1974, Richard Nixon became the first president in American history to resign and Gerald Ford was sworn in. President Ford reaffirmed Nixon's foreign and defense policies. He retained Nixon's national security team but soon added two important figures, Donald Rumsfeld and Richard Cheney, to the highest levels of his administration.

The Ford administration was guided by three main ideas in conducting defense policy during its brief tenure:

- The Soviets were outspending and outproducing the United States in the defense area, and the decline in U.S. defense spending had gone too far.
- The NATO nuclear posture in Europe was badly in need of repair and renovation.
- "Assured destruction" was an inadequate guide to strategic planning, and war-fighting strategies must be developed.

Ford was in office only a little over two years, but he had a major impact on nuclear policy, nonetheless. President Ford's achievement was to plant a set of ideas solidly in U.S. public policy debate. The harvest would come in later administrations.

Stalemate in Nuclear Arms Control

Henry Kissinger had become secretary of state, as well as national security adviser, in September 1973, replacing William Rogers. Kissinger used this power early in the administration of Gerald Ford to renew the effort to reach a second strategic nuclear agreement with Brezhnev. Nixon and Kissinger had not been successful in defining with the Soviet Union the parameters for a strategic arms limitation agreement, and U.S.-Soviet detente was being increasingly criticized for failing to produce results. Many felt that detente and defense were not being well synchronized. But when Ford assumed office in August 1974, a great deal of staff work on strategic limitations already had been done. The new administration was able to move out fairly rapidly with the idea of "equal aggregates," which meant that each side could have equal numbers of launchers and a subset of MIRVed missiles. The numbers selected were 2,400 for launchers and 1,320 for MIRVed missiles.

The American proposals were formally presented to General Secretary Brezhnev at a U.S.-Soviet summit meeting held in Vladivostok in November 1974. The meeting seemed wildly successful, for Brezhnev accepted Ford's plan, evidently over the objections of some of his military commanders. When they returned to Washington, as Kissinger later recounted in his memoirs, "Ford and I watched with dismay as the Vladivostok agreement dissolved before our eyes." Advocates of arms control complained that there were really no limits placed on nuclear forces because the aggregate numbers were so high. Other critics began to call for nuclear reductions.

The fatal blow was that the composition of the aggregates began to be questioned. One issue was whether to include a Soviet medium bomber, code-named "Backfire" in the aggregates or in a separate deal. The Defense Department argued that refueled Backfires could reach the United States. Another issue was Moscow's demand that U.S. sea-launched cruise missiles be included, arguing that these could strike Soviet territory. With all the criticism Ford was facing from the Reagan wing of the Republican party, he was not about to be accommodating. Neither was the new secretary of defense, Donald Rumsfeld, who had replaced James Schlesinger at the end of 1975. The obvious compromise was offered in a letter that Ford sent to Brezhnev on February 16, 1976. He proposed that the two contentious issues of Backfire and sea-launched cruise missiles be left out of the new agreement. This was rejected by Brezhnev on March 17, 1976, and that was the end of the road for nuclear negotiations in Ford's term of office.

The implementation of the Vladivostok parameters had become irretrievably bogged down when political maneuvering for the 1976 presidential elections was getting underway. The arms control account also was being overshadowed by worsening U.S.-Soviet relations and the appearance of major setbacks for U.S. standing globally. Saigon fell to the Communist North Vietnamese on April 30, 1975, and Soviet-assisted Cuban support for Angolan rebels had achieved some successes for left-wing insurgents in the same year. Ford's domestic critics charged that his administration was not reacting strongly enough to the steady buildup in Soviet strategic forces.

A Backlash on Defense Spending

The powerful momentum of the Soviet strategic buildup had been the subject of warnings since Johnson's administration. Nixon had emphasized this even as he was recommending Senate approval of SALT I and trying to negotiate the terms of SALT II. Nixon, with the approval of Congress, bequeathed to Gerald Ford a vigorous program of strengthening U.S. strategic forces. Spending on these forces was in a temporary decline, but the new weapons systems Nixon had sponsored created a bow wave that would require larger budgets in later years. Defense Secretary Schlesinger, in his report to Congress during the spring of Nixon's last year in office, underscored the massive military effort the Soviets were making. He noted, for example, that during 1973 the Soviets had started to test MIRVs. Summarizing, Schlesinger commented: "the new Soviet ICBM program represents a truly massive effort—four new missiles, new bus-type dispensing systems, new MIRVed payloads, new guidance, new-type silos, new launch techniques, and probably new warheads."[1] Ford quickly decided to make defense spending one of his key issues, as it had been when he was a member of Congress. He authorized a systematic campaign with Congress and the nation's allies to show that the Soviet drive was affecting the overall military balance.

Soviet and Cuban military support for Marxist regimes in Africa, Soviet activism in the Middle East War of 1973, as well as continuing dramatic improvements in Soviet military forces, had combined by 1974 to make it easy for critics to charge that Soviet activities in the Third World were on the upswing because America was slipping behind the U.S.S.R. in military strength. Those who held this point of view did not argue that Brezhnev was practicing nuclear diplomacy along Khrushchev's lines, but rather that the

Soviet leadership had become emboldened to take more risks because it believed the correlation of forces favored the Soviet Union and its allies. And so, U.S.-Soviet detente, and Kissinger's management of it, became a convenient target for Ford's critics, especially in the conservative wing of the Republican Party, but also among those Democrats allied with Senator Henry Jackson (D-WA). "Detente" became such a political liability to Ford that the president finally abolished the word from his lexicon. In fact, the American public mood did shift to a more pro-defense stance during 1974–1975, although not enough to support continued aid for South Vietnam.

By 1976, Ford was vulnerable not only on detente policy but also on defense, and especially on the nuclear balance. Ford found it useful to say in March of that year that "in my Presidency, I have proposed the two largest peacetime defense budgets in American history."[2] Ford's own instincts and his congressional record were strongly pro-defense. The need for a substantial and sustained defense effort was a theme that Ford had also pursued as vice president. Nixon wrote in his diary for June 1974 that "Ford is on the kick that we ought to have a huge increase in the defense budget."[3] All of the standing requests of the armed services had been approved during Nixon's administration; Ford's defense budgets, which the president took pride in personally reviewing, funded each of the strategic programs under way when he assumed office.

In February 1975, Ford declared that the decline in the defense budget had gone far enough: "As a result of Congressional actions and inflation, defense spending in 1976—measured in real terms—will be more than one-third below the peak Vietnam war level and about 20 percent below the pre-Vietnam level."[4]

Despite Ford's emphasis on defense spending, his stewardship of defense policy was being attacked from within his own party. Ronald Reagan announced his intention to run for president, informing Ford of that by telephone on November 19, 1975.[5] He and other critics contended that the United States was becoming a second-rate power. Ford responded that the United States was unsurpassed in military capability, that indeed Congress should authorize more for defense, and that his own defense budget proposals were the highest in peacetime U.S. history. In a press conference on April 2, 1976, he suggested that his critics should "look at the record of the Congress for the last six years, where the Congress has cut $32 billion out of the defense appropriation bills."[6]

The truth is that Ford was highly successful in persuading Congress to embark on a new cycle of investment in strategic weapons systems. His first full year as president was a real turning point. A Brookings Institution report describes the result:

In that year [FY 1975], apprehension about the continuing growth in Soviet military power brought about a major turning point in U.S. defense policy. . . . in 1975, policies were adopted that would expand general-purpose force levels (that is, army divisions, navy ships, and air force tactical squadrons) and would accelerate the pace at which new weapons, both general purpose and strategic, were being developed and introduced into deployed units . . . these programs turned the defense budget around, and real spending obligations began to rise rapidly.[7]

The Nixon-Ford administrations happened to be in power just as one building cycle was ending and before the next one started. New weapons systems, such as the B-1 and MX, were still in various stages of research and development. Systems developed during the Nixon-Ford administrations would be ready for production and deployment, a high-cost stage in the weapons acquisition cycle, in succeeding administrations.

Nuclear Weapons in Europe and Schlesinger's Downfall

U.S. nuclear dispositions in Europe became a source of friction between Secretary of Defense Schlesinger and Secretary of State Kissinger, adding to the tensions that already existed between them. This issue was one of those used to justify Schlesinger's dismissal. Ford wrote about this in his memoirs:

During my Presidency, he [Schlesinger] opposed outfitting with nuclear weapons-firing capability the F-15 [the aircraft was really the F-16] fighters we were sending to our NATO allies and he urged me repeatedly to withdraw significant numbers of our nuclear weapons from Western Europe. The argument could be made that they constituted an unnecessary financial drain. Kissinger and I were aware of that. But we wanted to use those weapons as bargaining chips in our discussions of SALT and the mutual reduction of forces in Europe. We wanted to get something in return from the Soviets before we took them away. Schlesinger wanted to remove them unilaterally.[8]

The nuclear issue was not the only problem Ford had with his defense secretary. Schlesinger had eloquently and persistently developed Ford's theme that America was underspending for defense. But Schlesinger's approach to Congress did not appeal to Ford. Ford recalled in his memoirs that he had strongly opposed a cut in his defense budget made in the fall of 1975 by the House Appropriations Committee, chaired by Representative George Mahon, but believed that he "could enlist some help in the Senate to restore the cuts." At this point, Secretary Schlesinger publicly denounced the cuts as "deep, savage and arbitrary." In Ford's opinion, "sounding off like that about a respected committee chairman was not the way to win friends on Capitol Hill."[9]

Secretary Schlesinger favored a modernization program for NATO's theater nuclear forces. Encouraged by influential senators, he envisaged substantial reductions in short-range, "battlefield" nuclear weapons deployed in Europe. Schlesinger's assistant for atomic energy, Donald Cotter, wrote in 1983 that "the seed of the Modernization Program was planted in 1974 when Senator Sam Nunn (D-Georgia) published a report entitled 'Policy, Troops, and the NATO Alliance.' "[10] The report led to Public Law 93-365, passed on August 5, 1974, which directed:

> the Secretary of Defense shall study the overall concept for use of tactical nuclear weapons in Europe; how the use of such weapons relate to deterrence and to a strong conventional defense; reduction in the number and type of nuclear weapons which are not essential for the defense structure for Western Europe; and the steps that can be taken to develop a rational and coordinated nuclear posture by the NATO Alliance that is consistent with proper emphasis on conventional defense forces.[11]

There were about 7,000 U.S. nuclear weapons in Europe, a number which had been more or less constant since McNamara imposed a ceiling at that level. Schlesinger supported withdrawing certain types of nuclear weapons from exposed, frontline locations in order to improve their chances of surviving a Soviet attack. This would also make their use more a matter of careful deliberation than a "use it or lose it" proposition. Kissinger saw all this as an essentially political decision of considerable consequence which, of course, it was.

Schlesinger had been directed by PL93-365 to report to Congress by April 1, 1975. His unclassified report was rather bland, mentioning relocation of nuclear weapons to enhance survivability, ducking the question of reductions in levels of nuclear weapons deployed in Europe. It foreshadowed two developments which dominated the nuclear policies of the Carter administration. One was a reference to the possibility of deploying longer-range nuclear forces in Europe. The other was a reference to reductions in collateral damage (e.g., damage to civilians and cities) which could be achieved through "special warhead effects such as enhanced radiation."[12] The developments that Schlesinger encouraged—the enhanced radiation weapon and long-range missiles for Europe—later became issues that seriously affected the presidency of Jimmy Carter.

The F-16 and related nuclear issues in Europe were matters in which I was closely involved and on which I had been reporting developments regularly to Hal Sonnenfeld, then the counselor of the Department of State. Kissinger's judgment was that withdrawal of significant numbers of nuclear weapons from the Federal Republic of Germany would leave so few deployed there that they would become an easy prey for antinuclear activists seeking to make West Germany a nuclear-free zone. This possibility made nuclear dispositions a fundamental political issue, not just a military issue. Ford agreed. On November 2, 1975, Ford asked Schlesinger for his resignation.

Donald Rumsfeld was named to succeed Schlesinger. Rumsfeld had been a Republican member of Congress from Illinois and then director of Nixon's Office of Economic Opportunity. He was appointed U.S. ambassador to NATO in 1973. He had been a friend of Ford's in Congress, promoted his appointment as vice president, and was a natural choice as Ford's chief of staff when Ford became president.

Soon after Rumsfeld took office as secretary of defense, he chaired an NSC meeting that reversed Schlesinger's F-16 decision. Henry Kissinger took part in the unusual role of an agency head, not the chair. The F-16 was made nuclear-capable, and reductions in the levels of nuclear weapons deployed in Europe were deferred.

Nuclear Restraint vs. Nuclear War-Fighting

Gerald Ford's two-year presidency accelerated a change in American thinking about the nature of strategic nuclear war that had started in Richard Nixon's administration. Most of the thinking about nuclear war up until that time was based on the idea of escalation from conventional to tactical nuclear to strategic nuclear conflict. When a war reached strategic levels, very large counterforce or countervalue attacks would come into play. No definitive or convincing theories existed as to how long such a conflict might go on, but despite Kennedy's insistence on presidential control, the general expectation was that war would be spasmlike and would end quickly, with devastating results. This nightmare drove political leaders to look for ways in which strategic nuclear war could be limited, and for options that would hold down the levels of violence and allow leaders to terminate the war before it got totally out of hand. This idea was quite rational and was seen as a humane way of limiting the damage that all-out nuclear war would cause. As strategic planning based on the new concepts began to mature, however, implications for targeting and force sizing emerged quite plainly. Reportedly, in the year when Ford took office, 1974, the number of potential targets for

U.S. strategic forces amounted to 25,000; this number rose to 40,000 during the next few years.[13]

There actually was some debate within the Ford administration about the implications of acquiring all the capabilities for a nuclear war-fighting posture. Senator Edward Brooke (R-MA) had raised concerns about this. But it never became much of a public issue or a major internal administration squabble. Schlesinger referred to the debate in his posture statement to Congress of February 5, 1975.

One of the issues was whether "hard-target kill capability" implied a disarming first strike intention, that is, a strategy of building forces intended for a first strike against an opponent's strategic forces in the hope of minimizing the opponent's ability to strike back. Schlesinger responded that the administration "would prefer to see both sides avoid major counterforce capabilities" and that it did not appear that "the improvements we are proposing for it [the U.S. strategic posture] should raise the specter in the minds of the Soviets that their ICBM force is in jeopardy." Of course, there was every reason to expect that the Soviets would perceive such a threat. Probably this is why Schlesinger also said that U.S. counterforce programs "will depend on how far the Soviets go in developing a counterforce capability of their own." In the end, both sides went as far as they could. The Secretary also emphasized that the U.S. objective in developing limited strike options was deterrence, "but modern deterrence across the spectrum of the nuclear threat."[14] He refuted any idea that the availability of limited nuclear options would encourage first use of nuclear weapons by the United States except in extraordinary circumstances.

By 1975–1976, Rumsfeld had concluded that strategic nuclear restraint was of little benefit to the United States. He, like others, thought that the Soviet Union was building a nuclear strike force with which it could fight a lengthy nuclear war and emerge with advantages tantamount to winning the war. In speaking of limited nuclear options, Schlesinger had advised the Congress that "the flexibility we are developing does not require any major change in the strategic capability that we now deploy."[15] In contrast, Secretary of Defense Donald Rumsfeld, in his first report to Congress in January 1976, also argued the case for small-scale strategic strike options but said that "forces, command-control, and plans should be modified accordingly."[16] By that time, the requirements and implications of limited nuclear options had become better understood. Rumsfeld summed it up this way:

> the need for flexibility places certain requirements on our strategic forces over and above those generated by the mission of assured retaliation. Not only must

we have a substantial number of additional warheads and survivable delivery systems, we must also acquire the yields and accuracies necessary to attack targets with discrimination. In addition, we need survivable command and control and retargeting capabilities to permit the execution of preplanned options and to respond in a controlled and deliberate fashion to unforeseen events.[17]

A year later, in his Posture Statement of January 17, 1977, Rumsfeld added: "It should be evident that once the possibility of some options is admitted, the range of targets becomes wide."[18]

By the end of the Ford administration, Rumsfeld had concluded that the Soviet Union's objective was not just mutual nuclear deterrence but building a capacity to wage and to win nuclear war. He doubted whether the Soviets had accepted mutual limitations on ballistic missile defense with the Nixon administration to underwrite a condition of mutual vulnerability. Limited resources or fear of U.S. technology were equally plausible reasons he thought. Rumsfeld's 1977 Posture Statement to Congress bluntly concluded: "it should now be evident that the Soviets have taken the initiative in a wide range of programs, that restraint on our part (whatever its reason) has not been reciprocated—and is not likely to be—and that the behavior of the Soviets indicates an interest—not in the more abstract and simplistic theories of deterrence—but in developing their strategic nuclear posture into a serious war-fighting capability."[19]

Rumsfeld argued that it would be necessary for the United States to consider and plan for a nuclear war in which each side would be severely damaged but one side might be damaged less seriously than the other. Secretary Rumsfeld told Congress: "significant asymmetries in the outcome of a strategic nuclear exchange can be created, and these asymmetries could give—and would be seen to have given—a meaningful advantage to one side over the other."[20]

A rational mind was at work, one that reflected the atmosphere of the times. Writing at about the same time in *Foreign Affairs*, Paul Nitze spelled out even more clearly where these calculations were taking the United States.[21] Nitze postulated a situation in which the Soviet Union would first attack U.S. strategic forces, while holding in reserve sufficient additional strategic forces to destroy American cities. The question, he argued, was whether "a future U.S. president should be left with only the option of deciding within minutes, or at most within two or three hours, to retaliate after a counterforce attack in a manner certain to result not only in military defeat for the United States but in wholly disproportionate, and truly irremediable destruction to the American people."

Nitze's conclusion was that the United States should be able to respond to a Soviet counterforce attack with its own counterforce attack, with enough left over for a U.S. attack against Soviet cities. He thought there were 1,500 to 2,000 Soviet hard targets which a U.S. counterforce attack should be able to destroy, and he recommended a force of "3,000 deliverable megatons remaining in reserve after a counterforce exchange."

This U.S. capability could be acquired by deploying 550 MIRVed MX missiles, as well as highly accurate Trident II missiles in submarines, and B-1s equipped with cruise missiles. Nitze stressed that his objective "would not be to give the United States a war-fighting capability; it would be to deny to the Soviet Union the possibility of a successful war-fighting capability."

Nitze's article was very influential, and his vision of how to prevent a nuclear war came to dominate strategic thinking in Washington at the time. Deterrence based on a capacity for protracted large-scale strategic nuclear exchanges emerged as the topic du jour of strategic analysis. Ironically, Schlesinger, when unveiling his thinking about limited options, had suggested that nuclear strategy based on full-scale nuclear war might have reached a dead-end.[22] In reality, another age of nuclear excess was just beginning.

Notes

1. James R. Schlesinger, *Report of the Secretary of Defense to the Congress on the FY 1975 Defense Budget and FY 1975–1979 Defense Program*, March 4, 1974, 46.

2. *Public Papers of the Presidents*, Ford, 1976–1977, 548.

3. Richard M. Nixon, *RN: The Memoirs of Richard Nixon* (New York: Grosset and Dunlap, 1978), 1025.

4. *Public Papers of the Presidents*, Ford, 1975, vol. 1, 271.

5. Gerald R. Ford, *A Time to Heal* (New York: Harper and Row and Reader's Digest, 1979), 333.

6. *Public Papers of the Presidents*, Ford, 1976–1977, vol. 1, 890.

7. Joseph Pechman, *Setting National Priorities: The 1978 Budget* (Washington, D.C.: Brookings Institution Press, 1977), 7.

8. Ford, *A Time to Heal*, 323.

9. Ford, *A Time to Heal*, 320.

10. Donald R. Cotter, James H. Hansen, and Kirk McConnell, *The Nuclear "Balance" in Europe: Status, Trends, Implications* (Cambridge, Mass.: United States Strategic Institute, 1983), 26.

11. James R. Schlesinger, *The Theater Nuclear Force Posture in Europe*, Report to the United States Congress, in Compliance with Public Law 93-365, May 1975. The quotation is from the Preface.

12. The citations are from Schlesinger, *The Theater Nuclear Force Posture in Europe*.

13. Desmond Ball, "Counterforce Targeting: How New? How Viable?" *Arms Control Today*, February 1981; reprinted in *The Use of Force*, 2nd ed., ed. Robert J. Art and Kenneth N. Waltz (Lanham, Md.: University Press of America, 1983), 518.

14. Schlesinger, *Report to the Congress on the FY 1976 and Transition Budgets*, February 5, 1975, vol. 1, 13, 14, 15.

15. Schlesinger, *Report to the Congress on the FY 1976 and Transition Budgets*, vol. 2, 5.

16. Donald Rumsfeld, *Report to the Congress on the FY 1977 Budget*, January 27, 1976, 46.

17. Rumsfeld, *Report to the Congress on the FY 1977 Budget*, 48.

18. Donald Rumsfeld, *Report to the Congress on the FY 1978 Budget*, January 17, 1977, 70.

19. Rumsfeld, *Report to the Congress on the FY 1978 Budget*, 64.

20. Rumsfeld, *Report to the Congress on the FY 1978 Budget*, 72.

21. This summary of Nitze's views is based on Paul Nitze, "Deterring Our Deterrent," *Foreign Affairs* (Winter 1976–1977): 195–210.

22. James Schlesinger, *Report to the Congress on the FY 1976 and Transition Budget*, February 5, 1975, vol. 2, 4.

CHAPTER SEVEN

Jimmy Carter: The Limits of Presidential Power

During the Ford-Carter presidential campaign debate of October 6, 1976, Democratic candidate Jimmy Carter, former governor of Georgia, remarked: "as a nuclear engineer myself, I know the limitations and capabilities of atomic power." He spoke also of "a world of peace with the threat of atomic weapons eliminated."[1] A month later, the man who spoke these words was elected president of the United States. After political turmoil caused by Vietnam and Watergate, the United States had elected as its president a graduate of the U.S. Naval Academy and a real nuclear engineer. At his inauguration, Jimmy Carter promised the nation and the world that "we will move this year a step toward our ultimate goal—the elimination of all nuclear weapons from this Earth."[2]

The Democratic platform for 1976 had said "we believe we can reduce present defense spending by about $5 billion to $7 billion."[3] Carter's criticism of the Ford administration concerned a "gap" but it was not a security gap. It was a respect gap. Carter argued that the United States had lost respect in the world, but not because of a shortage of military power.

Except for the B-1 bomber, designed to modernize the Strategic Air Command's bomber fleet, there were not many clues to Carter's thinking on specific weapons systems. The B-1 had been one of Nixon's and Ford's key strategic modernization programs and the Republican platform had said "we will produce and deploy the B-1 bomber."[4] But Carter and the Democratic platform had called for a delay in the decision to produce the bomber. Carter had also said, however, that the United States must have a defense capability second to none. But the new president was in a position to make defense policy relatively free of campaign pledges or a campaign mandate. The public wanted to move beyond Watergate by cleaning house in Washington. Other issues were secondary.

In his first year in office, acting out of fiscal prudence and armed with valid analytical reasoning, Carter cancelled the B-1, the new Air Force strategic bomber. The next year, acting out of moral repugnance, he blocked a new nuclear weapon, the neutron bomb. Both systems had been endorsed by his predecessors and were supported by his political adversaries. However right those decisions may have been, President Carter lost irreplaceable political capital, and that loss left him with reduced room for maneuver. He was weakened further when American embassy personnel in Tehran were taken hostage. Finally, his hope for a strategic nuclear limitation treaty was denied when the Soviet Union invaded Afghanistan in December 1979. For all the great power given to American presidents, there are real limits to how much they can do.

The B-1 Bomber Decision

Carter was no dove. As president, he opted to spend at a lesser rate on defense than Ford had projected. His amendments to Ford's last proposed budget for fiscal year 1978 reduced total obligational authority for defense by $2.8 billion, but this still amounted to a considerable growth in the defense budget, since Ford had proposed an increase of $13 billion for fiscal year 1978.[5] Carter had inherited not only an already growing defense budget, but also growing public support for higher defense budgets. In 1976, Gallup polls showed that 28 percent of the American people favored higher levels of defense spending, whereas support had been only 9 percent in 1972 and 17 percent in 1974.[6]

On taking office, Carter and his secretary of defense, Harold Brown, a noted nuclear physicist, set up a Defense Department panel to review alternative ways of modernizing the strategic bomber force. What impressed Carter when he read the panel's report was the evidence that the long-term outlook for the B-1 bomber's ability to penetrate Soviet defenses was poor. His advisers began to focus on two alternatives to the B-1 program. Updating the air leg of the strategic triad, they thought, could be accomplished by equipping B-52s with cruise missiles or, since there were uncertainties about how effective Soviet air defenses really were, fewer B-1s might be acquired than the 244 that Ford had envisaged, perhaps no more than 70–75. The latter option could lead to a mixed force of B-1s and B-52s equipped with cruise missiles.

Brown, National Security Adviser Zbigniew Brzezinski, and Budget Director Bert Lance pressed the president to endorse the reduced B-1 option. The advantages they saw were that this would help with selling a new strategic arms limitation treaty in Congress, would add to the negotiating leverage with the Soviets, and would give the Air Force a new weapons system while a new intercontinental ballistic missile, the MX, was under review. There were elements of the "bargaining chip" approach in this recommendation.

This is the type of decision that can hurt presidents unless carefully managed. Eisenhower had been damaged politically when he trimmed the armed services' requests. Kennedy had to scramble to fix the Skybolt cancellation. Johnson had been whipsawed when he hesitated on the ballistic missile defense program. Now it was Carter's turn.

President Carter overruled his chief advisers and rejected the B-1 in favor of cruise missiles. He chose to announce the decision himself. At a press conference on June 30, 1977, the president said: "we should not continue with deployment of the B-1, and I am directing that we discontinue plans for production of this weapons system." Carter argued that the B-1 was not necessary because it was "a very expensive weapons system basically conceived in the absence of the cruise missile factor." The triad of land- and sea-based ballistic missiles and B-52 bombers armed with cruise missiles would be maintained. As Carter also explained: "if I had looked upon the B-1 as simply a bargaining chip for the Soviets, then my decision would have been to go ahead with the weapon." Asked if he was on a collision course with Congress on this issue, Carter said he thought not.[7]

Secretary of Defense Brown followed up with a press conference on July 1. He talked about the promising technology of the cruise missile. This, he suggested, played an even bigger part in the president's decision than had cost factors. But he added that the decision would save "many billions of dollars, because the alternative carriers, the B-52's and possibly others, will cost very much less than the $20 billion, $25 billion, $15 billion, depending upon what the B-1 would have cost, depending on whether we bought 240 or 150."[8]

Carter made his decision stick (although Ronald Reagan later reversed it in his administration). But Secretary of State Cyrus Vance described this decision as one of the most "politically costly defense decisions of his presidency." It was used, Vance wrote, "as evidence that the president was 'soft' on defense and was practicing 'unilateral' arms control."[9] Charles Mohr, writing in the *New York Times* of July 1, 1977, captured much of the essence of Carter's style at this point in his administration: "he is a pragmatist not bound by ideology and an atypical politician who seems to prefer the role of manager. There was widespread surprise in Washington over the decision, and one of the reasons was that a simple split-the-difference sort of 'solution' had been available."[10]

The Neutron Bomb Decision

The neutron bomb surfaced as an issue just as Carter was reaching his decision on the B-1. The neutron bomb, technically called the Enhanced Radiation Weapon (ERW), had existed as a concept as far back as the Eisenhower administration. It was designed to produce lethal doses of radiation beyond the zone affected by the blast effects of the explosion. The weapon was intended to be effective against an attack by tanks while minimizing damage to the civilian environment in which battles might have to take place in Europe. Approved for development by Secretary of Defense Schlesinger, it was ready for a production decision by the end of the Ford administration.

On June 6, 1977, the *Washington Post* printed the first of a series of articles about the neutron weapon, written by one of its reporters, Walter Pincus, based on his study of the defense budget. The stories emphasized that the warhead would kill people but leave buildings and property intact. The *Post* editorialized that this was akin to chemical weapons and that it might make more likely the early use of nuclear weapons. Others called it the "capitalist bomb" because it destroyed people but not property.

The Carter administration's dealings with Congress and the press on this issue were handled by its professional bureaucrats until July 12. They had been coping, fairly successfully, with congressional criticism of the neutron bomb. Facing his first press questions on the neutron weapon on July 12, Carter said, "I did not know what was in the bill." He added that "I have not yet decided whether to advocate deployment of the neutron bomb." The President said his "guess" was "that the first use of atomic weapons might very well quickly lead to a rapid and uncontrolled escalation in the use of even more powerful weapons with possibly a worldwide holocaust resulting."[11]

In Europe, where these weapons would be deployed, the Soviet Union began to contrast Carter's concern for human rights with his sponsorship of an immoral, inhumane weapon comparable with poison gas. German Chancellor Helmut Schmidt faced an open revolt in his Social Democratic Party, and Labor Prime Minister James Callaghan, in Britain, also had opposition within his own party. Religious and other citizens' groups across Western Europe took to the streets to protest the neutron bomb.

In an effort to pacify his followers, Chancellor Schmidt devised a tactical defense in which he sought to separate the production decision from the deployment decision. He argued that the former was an American decision and that the latter could be deferred. Schmidt later sought safety in numbers and negotiations by asserting that the Federal Republic could not be the only European NATO country where the weapon would be deployed and that any deployment should be linked to arms control negotiations. This concept also became the basis for NATO's decision to deploy new missiles in Europe.

Vance, Brown, and Brzezinski agreed that the neutron bomb project should continue. They discussed this with Carter on August 17. Brzezinski recorded Carter's reaction and the agreed course of action in his diary for that day: "he did not wish the world to think of him as an ogre and we agreed that we will press the Europeans to show greater interest in having the bomb and, therefore, willingness to absorb some of the political flak or we will use European disinterest as a basis for a negative decision."[12]

In light of subsequent events, the advisers heard the first part of the president's instructions while the president's heart was in the second part, that is, European disinterest as an exit from a morally uncomfortable position. A basic misjudgment occurred at this point. The president accepted the recommendations of his advisers to press America's allies for a positive decision on the neutron bomb, assuming that he could back away from the decision if they were unenthusiastic. His premise was incorrect. Once the United States presses an issue, a negative response is seen as a defeat.

Stepping up the Soviet attack on the bomb, Brezhnev, in an interview published in *Pravda* on December 24, 1977, denounced the neutron bomb and said that if the West developed such a weapon, the Soviet Union would answer the challenge. Carter was in Europe shortly after Brezhnev's remarks, and in a Warsaw press conference on December 30, he was asked what he thought about a mutual renunciation of the neutron bomb, an idea being floated by Brezhnev. His answer: "We would not deploy the neutron bomb or neutron shells unless it was an agreement by our NATO allies. That's where the decision will be made. But there are other new weapons, including the SS-20 [a Soviet intermediate-range MIRVed ballistic missile], much more threatening to the balance that presently exists."[13]

Meanwhile, at NATO headquarters in Brussels, a scenario was being devised that would endorse the deployment of the neutron bomb. This scenario was nailed down on Friday, March 17, and a meeting of the Permanent Representatives to the North Atlantic Council was set for Monday, March 20, when the proposal officially would be presented to the council. A second meeting on Wednesday, March 22, would ratify the decision through a summing-up by the secretary general of NATO. All NATO members had agreed to this procedure.

Therefore, it was primarily for information—rather than for decision—that on Saturday, March 18, Vance and Brown sent a memorandum to the president, to which Brzezinski added his own supporting memorandum, reporting on what was about to unfold at NATO headquarters. Carter, then weekending at St. Simon's Island, Georgia, responded very quickly in a way that "surprised" and "startled" his senior advisers. Brzezinski recalled: "To my surprise, they [the memoranda] came back with marginal notations that read: 'To Zbig, re: production, etc. Do not act until after consultation with me.' On the memo from Cy and Harold, the President wrote: 'Do not issue any statement re: ERW.' "[14]

Carter met with Vance, Brown, and Brzezinski for an hour and a half on the evening of Monday, March 20. The president described the discussion in his diary for that day as "fairly combative." He obviously thought that this issue could be deferred and he resented being pushed into a corner. Brzezinski wrote at the time: "I don't think that I have ever seen the President quite as troubled and pained by any decision item. At one point he said: 'I wish I had never heard of this weapon.' "[15]

According to Vance, Carter told Vance, Brown, and Brzezinski "that the burden and political liability for this weapon, which as far as he could see no ally really wanted, was being placed on his shoulders instead of being shared by the whole alliance."[16] Carter's diary for March 20 portrayed his advisers as trying to railroad him into a decision he was reluctant to make: "They had generated a lot of momentum. . . . My cautionary words to them since last summer have pretty well been ignored."[17]

Carter took a beating from the press as it became clear what had happened. On April 6, the New York Times reported reactions of "bewilderment and concern" in Washington and allied capitals. Vance, Brown, and Brzezinski were said to be "shocked." The New York Times lead editorial that day was headlined "The Mishandled Bomb." It said that "few episodes in the 15 months of the Carter Administration have been more disturbing than its handling of the 'neutron bomb.' "[18] Worse still, the Washington Post, which had started it all, ran a cartoon by the nation's premier cartoonist, Herblock, depicting Carter as an out-of-control missile. The caption read: "It's the Cartron bomb—it knocks down supporters without damaging opponents."[19]

The Euromissile Decision

The neutron bomb decision in the spring of 1978 led straight to the "Euromissile" debate and decisions in the late 1970s and early 1980s. Vance described the connection this way: "Brown, Brzezinski, and I, with our staffs, immediately began a series of intensive political and military studies on the-ater nuclear forces. U.S. and allied officials alike understood instinctively that after ERW it was especially important to NATO that the theater nuclear force issue be dealt with firmly, but with a united alliance and under visible American leadership."[20]

Despite the awesome powers of the presidency, American presidents sel-dom have a completely free hand in nuclear weapons decisions. President Carter was boxed in to a far greater degree in his handling of the Euromissile issue than he had been in the cases of the B-1 and the neutron bomb by his own decisions and by three external events. First, in October 1977, German Chancellor Schmidt delivered a speech in London which raised questions about the balance of nuclear forces on the European continent. This made the Soviet SS-20 and the American response to it a major public issue. The chancellor had not consulted with Carter in advance of his London speech. Second, with the help of American strategic experts, conservative defense circles in Western Europe began to worry publicly in 1977–1978 about whether Carter's strategic arms negotiations with the Soviet Union would close out the option of their having cruise missiles, either under their own or U.S. control. This forced the issue onto Washington's agenda, even though few in the administration saw much merit in it. Third, in the spring of 1978, under pressure from British and German representatives, NATO's "High Level Group," then studying the question of alternative nuclear force pos-tures for NATO, advised the NATO governments that longer-range missile systems should be deployed in Europe.

These factors were already affecting thinking in the alliance when Carter made his neutron bomb decision in April 1978. After that, as Vance sug-gested, it became inevitable that missiles for Europe would become a test of Carter's, and NATO's, ability to make hard decisions. An important back-ground issue was the administration's worry that strategic arms limitation ne-gotiations, being conducted by Arms Control and Disarmament Agency Di-rector Paul Warnke, would not receive the support of the Senate and of the Joint Chiefs of Staff if the administration showed weakness on the issue of Euromissiles. The Senate, in particular Senator "Scoop" Jackson, had sent that message by confirming Warnke as ACDA director by a fairly narrow margin.

All of this had happened even before Carter authorized an interagency re-view of "Long-Range Theater Nuclear Capabilities and Arms Control" (PRM-38) in June 1978. By fall the study had approved the idea of deploy-ing longer-range nuclear delivery systems in Europe. Carter's advisers were united in their opinions about what the president would have to do.

Many of the problems surrounding what became known as the "INF" (intermediate-range nuclear forces) decision already had come up in the discussions of the neutron bomb, particularly the linkage to an offer to negotiate with the Soviet Union. During 1979 the Allies worked overtime to develop a plan for the new missile deployments and an accompanying arms control offer. One of the final steps was to adopt a plan for a force of 572 Pershing intermediate-range ballistic missiles and ground-launched cruise missiles (GLCMs) in Europe. All of these systems could reach Moscow from Western Europe. For Soviet leaders, the planned deployment brought with it the threat of a "decapitating" threat, one that would make it difficult to exercise control over a nuclear response.

NATO decision-making was completed at a joint meeting of foreign and defense ministers in Brussels on December 12, 1979. I was one of the American participants, and while in Brussels I learned I was on a short list of candidates for the post of ambassador to Finland. (President Carter nominated me a few weeks later, and after being confirmed by the Senate, I left for Helsinki in March 1980.) My impression of the joint meeting was that the ministers were worried and uncomfortable. But, in the end, everybody rallied around. It was a good example of the difference between an alliance and a "coalition of the willing." The decision provided for deployment in Britain, Italy, Germany, the Netherlands, and Belgium of 464 cruise and 108 Pershing II ballistic missiles, to be fully under U.S. control. An offer was simultaneously extended to Moscow to negotiate on "certain U.S. and Soviet long-range theatre nuclear systems."

Carter gave a major speech on American defense policy to the Business Council on December 12. He spoke of reversing "a decade of relative decline in the military strength of the Atlantic Alliance." Then the president dramatically announced: "Just a few hours ago, I was informed that the NATO Alliance resolved to strengthen its theater nuclear weapons to offset actual Soviet deployments. The agreement reached this afternoon in Europe was a unanimous agreement very encouraging to all of us. Now, on the basis of strength, we can negotiate with the Warsaw Pact to reduce nuclear weapons."[21]

Early in his administration, following a familiar pattern for new administrations, Carter had proposed two NATO summit meetings aimed mainly at encouraging more spending on conventional defense. The first was held in London in May 1977; the second in Washington in May 1978. I helped President Carter plan for the London meeting and traveled with him to the meeting. I was the chief organizer of the Washington meeting the following year. The first of these meetings had been a time for hope. By the second summit, strains had set in. The neutron bomb decision damaged the sense of solidarity and shared commitments that the summit meetings were designed to reinforce.

The Euromissile decision helped to overcome doubts about Carter's ability to lead the alliance. The decision was seen as a victory for American diplomacy. Vance remarked in his memoirs that "we had a long, uphill struggle after the ERW (enhanced radiation weapon) episode to restore allied confidence in our leadership on security matters." By the end of 1979, Vance believed, the Alliance was "back on the track we had mapped in the summit of May 1977 and reaffirmed at the May 1978 summit in Washington."[22] The United States and the Soviet Union agreed to begin preliminary talks on the Euromissiles, and these began in Geneva on October 16, 1980. They were interrupted within a month by the change in the American presidency decided by the voters in November 1980.

The MX Decision

Carter wanted a strong defense posture, but he was a man of high principle and he loathed waste and inefficiency. This led to the cancellation of the B-1 bomber in 1977 and to the neutron bomb episode in 1978. These decisions, taken for quite valid reasons, created political firestorms for Carter and weakened his ability to follow his own instincts in other cases. Eventually, he approved defense programs that were virtually indistinguishable from those of Nixon and Ford. The accuracy of Minuteman III warheads was improved to enable them to destroy hardened targets. A similar capability was authorized for Trident submarine missiles. Command and control systems intended to endure a prolonged nuclear war were made a requirement for defense planning. The B-2 "stealth" bomber also was inaugurated in Carter's administration. Following his signing of the second strategic arms limitation treaty (SALT II) in 1979, and the Soviet invasion of Afghanistan in December of that year, Carter added still more funds to the defense budget.

One of his most important decisions was to produce the MX intercontinental missile, later called the Peacekeeper. At stake was the future of the American strategic triad. Whether there was a future for fixed, land-based missiles in an era of pinpoint accuracy was a complex question. They had become quite vulnerable. The Carter administration took over two and a half years to arrive at a decision. Some of Carter's advisers believed that the growing vulnerability of land-based missiles could not be repaired. Even the president himself wondered whether the land-based leg of the triad was essential under emerging conditions.

By early June 1979, administration studies had advanced to the point where the president was required to decide on the characteristics of a new intercontinental ballistic missile. An NSC meeting was set for June 4. How to base such a missile in order to minimize vulnerability was a key issue.

The president's mood that summer was influenced by his dissatisfaction with his cabinet. Perhaps a feeling of being let down by his advisers prompted his reaction to what he heard at the NSC meeting. He said that the group assembled there had created much of the perception that the Soviet Union was stronger than the United States.[23] Both the CIA director and the chairman of the Joint Chiefs of Staff weighed in to say there really was a problem. By the end of the meeting, Carter said he was leaning toward a favorable decision on the MX but was not yet ready for a decision on how to base it.

At a follow-on NSC meeting to decide on the general characteristics of the new missile, the president opted for the largest version of the MX and for deployment in a land-mobile mode. On June 8, 1979, in response to a question from a reporter, the deputy press secretary to the president announced that the president had decided to deploy a new ICBM that would be both survivable and verifiable. The deputy press secretary offered a few remarks on the president's thinking, and that was that.

The timing of the president's decision was dictated in part by an imminent summit meeting with Soviet General Secretary Brezhnev which had been scheduled for the purpose of signing the SALT II treaty on strategic offensive forces. The American position on a new ICBM had to be in hand by that time. The decision was related to the need to convince the Senate that the defenses of the nation would be kept in sound condition, so the SALT treaty could be safely ratified. On June 18, Carter and Brezhnev signed the SALT II treaty in the Hofberg Palace, Vienna. It was never ratified.

In addition to his dissatisfaction with his cabinet that summer, Carter's mood was influenced by what he saw as a "malaise" among the American people. Carter made that clear in a televised speech on July 15, 1979, in which he gave way to a pessimism that was rare for him or for any American president. "A crisis of confidence" was stalking the land, he said, and he called for "the restoration of American values." He quoted also from "the voices of Americans," one of which said: "some of your Cabinet members don't seem loyal."[24] Within days, several of them had obliged the president by tendering their resignations.

The NSC returned to the subject of how to base the new ICBM in August and September. Vance summed up the situation in his memoirs:

> The military planners had recommended a plan for moving 200 MX missiles on launcher vehicles randomly among 4,600 widely spaced concrete shelters in

valleys in Nevada and Utah. In August and early September, as we listened to the briefings on the proposed basing plan, it was apparent that neither the President nor most of his senior advisers felt comfortable. Tremendously expensive, politically controversial, and technically complex, it would be difficult to explain and defend. As one observer remarked, it would be the largest construction project in human history, dwarfing the pyramids of Egypt.[25]

A decision had to be made, since the president already had approved the missile. His spokesperson already had referred to the "summer months" as the time for decision, and the SALT ratification proceedings required a position. On September 7, despite his discomfort, Carter approved the basing mode which had been presented to him.

The Decision to Embrace "Protracted Nuclear War"

At the time Carter came to office, the transition to a nuclear war-fighting policy had not been completed. In his campaign, Carter had not advocated such a strategy. In fact, in the campaign and after taking office, he questioned whether limited nuclear war was possible. He spoke of a "holocaust" when he talked of nuclear war. Secretary of State Vance shared those sentiments and opposed measures that would lead the country into a nuclear war-fighting strategy. But Cyrus Vance resigned his position as secretary of state at the end of April 1980, having objected to the use of force to free the American hostages held by Iran. After that, the president moved step by step toward the protracted war doctrine advocated by Brzezinski. An account of the process by which Carter finally came to approve this doctrine is contained in Brzezinski's memoirs.

The national security adviser had worked for several months with Secretary of Defense Harold Brown on ideas for protracted nuclear war and thought he was in a position by mid-May 1980 to hand a proposed directive on the subject to Carter for his approval. Secretary Vance had opposed the idea and Vance's successor, Edmund Muskie, had not been brought into the discussions of the proposed presidential directive. Carter was preoccupied with Iran, with the Soviet invasion of Afghanistan, and with the political challenges to his presidency from Senator Edward Kennedy on his left and Governor Ronald Reagan on his right. These pressures probably affected Carter's thinking. There was no opportunity for debate or second thoughts. The president signed the directive, PD-59, on July 25, 1980.

Brown, in explaining PD-59 in a Naval War College speech, claimed that it was not a new strategic doctrine. In the sense that it was the logical conclusion of a development that began with the "Schlesinger doctrine," he was right. Brzezinski had a different opinion. Writing of one of a series of presidential directives which preceded PD-59, that dealing with command and control (PD-53), Brzezinski commented that "here we had a document in which for the first time the United States deliberately sought for itself the capability to manage a protracted nuclear conflict." Of PD-59, Brzezinski wrote:

> Till PD-59 was issued, American war planning postulated a brief, spasmic, and apocalyptic conflict. It was based on the presumption of a short war, lasting a few days at most. The new PDs that the President issued marked a departure from this earlier pattern, so reminiscent of allied planning prior to the outbreak of the war in 1914. The new directives were concerned with mobilization, defense, command, and control for a long conflict, and with flexible use of our forces, strategic and general-purpose, on behalf of war aims that we would select as we engaged in conflict.[26]

President Carter's impromptu remarks in a press conference on September 18, 1980, probably reflected his own instincts a little more closely: "it's not an inevitability but it's certainly a likelihood—that if an atomic exchange of any kind should ever erupt that it might lead to a more massive exchange of intercontinental and highly destructive weapons that would result in tens of millions of lost lives on both sides."[27]

The old question of "how much is enough" should have come up again when Carter considered his new strategic policy. Protracted nuclear war at the strategic level imposes large and exacting requirements for nuclear weapons systems. Years after Carter endorsed PD-59, the United States still lacked the forces and infrastructure to carry it out. The whole exercise was questionable in terms of enhancing deterrence and was certainly not a great public relations success for the Carter reelection campaign.

Even after the enunciation of Carter's protracted nuclear war-fighting doctrine, and after billions of dollars of investment in nuclear weapons systems, the essence of deterrence against nation-states remains what Robert McNamara said it was in his farewell report to Congress in January 1968: "it is the clear and present ability to destroy the attacker as a viable 20th Century nation and an unwavering will to use these forces in retaliation to a nuclear attack upon ourselves or our allies that provide the deterrent, and not the ability partially to limit damage to ourselves."[28]

The Negotiating Option

By 1980, arms control negotiations with the Soviet Union had been accepted as a necessary element in the strategic relationship. Carter was a strong exponent of arms control. He had hoped to reduce dependence on nuclear weapons, not increase it. Arms control was one of his prime means for achieving this goal. It was not to be. Carter's negotiation of the SALT II treaty was delayed by his decision in 1977 to abandon the Ford-Brezhnev Vladivostok Accords and try to persuade the Soviet Union to accept reductions in some of its more threatening missile systems.

This was good arms control policy but it only delayed the negotiation, since Brezhnev had spent his political capital in getting his colleagues to accept the Vladivostok Accords. By the time the SALT II treaty was negotiated in 1979, Carter had paid out some of his own political capital to secure the Panama Canal treaty and had forfeited some of his credibility in the B-1 and the neutron bomb episodes. A mini-dispute over Soviet troops in Cuba further delayed the Senate ratification proceedings. The Soviet invasion of Afghanistan in December 1979 finally led to the suspension of Carter's efforts to seek Senate consent to ratification of the treaty. Even so, the United States and the Soviet Union remained within the limits prescribed by SALT II until well into the Reagan administration, even though President Reagan had refused to submit the treaty to the Senate because he considered it "fatally flawed."

Perhaps it was just as well that events turned out that way. During much of the Cold War period, arms control agreements had been intended to provide the valuable function of reassurance. The negotiations were not aimed at arms reductions, but at creating the kind of stability that would make war less likely. So the central focus of U.S.-Soviet nuclear arms control was essentially to underwrite nuclear deterrence, not to eliminate it or transform it. The strategic arms limitation talks finally became a handmaiden to the idea that protracted nuclear war was the right way to think about nuclear weapons.

Comparisons to nineteenth-century conventional means of warfare are completely misplaced in the nuclear age. Nuclear weapons are orders of magnitude more powerful than any explosive that has gone before, not to mention the effects of firestorms and radiation. In the 1970s, the implications of that fact, which were quite clear to Eisenhower, were set aside on the theory that deterrence could only be maintained if U.S. nuclear forces were designed to fight a war in stages, with the United States holding the advantage at the end of the war. "Escalation dominance" had been applied to strategic nuclear wars.

Like SALT I before it, the SALT II treaty set very high ceilings for strategic missile and bomber forces. There were no limits set on the total number of warheads that could be deployed. There were limits on how many warheads each type of missile could carry, but those limits would easily permit several thousand missile warheads on each side. The treaty imposed limits on the building of new *types* of missiles. The MX, for example, was permitted as the one new U.S. missile which could be tested and deployed. The Soviets were similarly limited. The treaty permitted modernization of *existing* types of missiles in a way that allowed quite new characteristics to be built into missiles so long as certain limits on size and throw weight were observed. Together with SALT I, the SALT II treaty required destruction of older systems as new systems entered the strategic forces.

Those constraints were modest, but they served to set some outer limits on the size of the strategic forces of the two countries and to make the composition of the forces more predictable, perhaps all that could be done in the adversarial conditions that then existed. Neither SALT I nor SALT II did much to affect the pace of building programs on either side. The Soviet Union continued its modernization program, developing and producing both new missiles and a new bomber. The United States was able to proceed for some time with President Reagan's large strategic force buildup while being completely in compliance with the treaty. The time had come for a new arms control paradigm. And that would come with new leadership in Moscow and in Washington.

Rolling Back Nuclear Proliferation

President Carter saw the proliferation of nuclear weapons as one of America's most important security problems. He took over from President Ford an active antiproliferation program, inspired by a nuclear test explosion conducted by India in 1974. Carter took action early in his administration to discourage American companies from selling materials and equipment that might provide a nascent nuclear weapons capability to non-nuclear-weapon states. With his support, Congress in 1978 passed the Nuclear Non-Proliferation Act, which required sanctions against countries, even friends, who tried to acquire nuclear weapons. Carter strongly supported the Nuclear Suppliers Group, which Assistant Secretary of State George Vest and a State Department colleague, Lou Nosenzo, had created during Ford's term. The Suppliers Group is a clearinghouse for nuclear-related exports and is still one of the most effective international antiproliferation tools.

Relations with the Federal Republic of Germany and Brazil went through a rough patch when the United States objected to Germany's intention to supply Brazil with equipment for a full fuel cycle. The president received complaints from the U.S. nuclear power industry, which accused him of imposing too many restrictions on U.S. nuclear energy programs. Carter was willing to take the heat. The president's actions set precedents for the future and contributed to later decisions by Argentina and Brazil to renounce their nuclear weapons programs. His attitude was that more nuclear weapons in more countries' hands, whether friend or foe, were dangerous. He fought hard to prevent it, and his successes lasted far beyond his own single term of office.

Notes

1. *Public Papers of the Presidents*, Ford, 1976–1977, vol. 3, 2425, 2435.

2. *Public Papers of the Presidents*, Carter, 1977, vol. 1, 3.

3. *Congressional Quarterly's Guide to U.S. Elections*, 2nd ed., 1985, 132.

4. *Congressional Quarterly's Guide to U.S. Elections*, 136.

5. Joseph Pechman, ed., *Setting National Priorities: The 1978 Budget* (Washington, D.C.: Brookings Institution Press, 1977), 83.

6. *Congressional Quarterly*, October 9, 1976, 2903.

7. *Public Papers of the Presidents*, Carter, 1977, vol. 2, 1197–1200.

8. Bernard Weintraub, "Defense Chief Sees a Saving of Billions by Dropping the B-1," *New York Times*, July 2, 1977, 1.

9. Cyrus Vance, *Hard Choices: Critical Years in American Foreign Policy* (New York: Simon and Schuster, 1983), 57.

10. Charles Mohr, "Carter in the Role of Manager," *New York Times*, July 1, 1977, A11.

11. *Public Papers of the Presidents*, Carter, 1977, vol. 2, 1231–1233.

12. Zbigniew Brzezinski, *Power and Principle: Memoirs of the National Security Adviser, 1977–1981* (New York: Farrar, Straus and Giroux, 1983), 302.

13. *Public Papers of the Presidents*, Carter, 1977, vol. 2, 2211.

14. Brzezinski, *Power and Principle*, 304.

15. Brzezinski, *Power and Principle*, 304.

16. Vance, *Hard Choices*, 94.

17. Jimmy Carter, *Keeping Faith: Memoirs of a President* (New York: Bantam Books, 1982), 227.

18. John Vinocur, "Bonn Says Allied Alarm Caused Carter Weapon Shift," *New York Times*, April 6, 1978, A5; editorial, "The Mishandled Bomb," *New York Times*, April 6, 1978, A20.

19. Reprinted in *Newsweek*, April 17, 1978, 39.

20. Vance, *Hard Choices*, 96–97.

21. *Public Papers of the Presidents*, Carter, vol. 2, 2234–2235.

22. Vance, *Hard Choices*, 98.

23. Brzezinski, *Power and Principle*, 336.

24. *Public Papers of the Presidents*, Carter, 1979, vol. 2, 1235–1247.

25. Vance, *Hard Choices*, 365.

26. Brzezinski, *Power and Principle*, 457, 459.

27. *Public Papers of the Presidents*, Carter, vol. 1, 1830.

28. Robert McNamara, *Report to the Congress*, January 1968, 47.

PART IV

A BREAK WITH THE PAST, 1981–1988

Ronald Reagan

Ronald Reagan was unlike any other president in his revulsion against the immorality of nuclear war, his willingness to do something about it, and his ability to act on his instincts. He said, "a nuclear war cannot be won and must never be fought." Turning away from classical arms control, he insisted on nuclear disarmament and succeeded to a remarkable degree. He was lucky, of course. His last negotiating partner was a Soviet radical, Mikhail Gorbachev, who shared Reagan's zeal for change. Reagan and Gorbachev together moved decisively toward the end of the Cold War. The Soviet Union was formally dissolved in December 1991. The world had changed.

Reagan and his second secretary of state, George Shultz, broke with arms control tradition. After signing a treaty that eliminated a whole class of Soviet and American intermediate-range nuclear weapons systems, they pushed ahead to reduce strategic nuclear weapons, or to eliminate them if they could. Reagan's genuine interest in eliminating all nuclear weapons has not been shared to the same extent by his successors—to the world's loss. The revolution that Reagan started has been interrupted.

129

CHAPTER EIGHT

~

The Reagan Revolution
in Nuclear Weaponry

The "Reagan revolution" applied to the world of nuclear weaponry just as much as it did to social and economic issues in the United States.[1] During President Ronald Reagan's two terms, his was the decisive voice in:

- Negotiating a treaty that would eliminate a whole class of the most modern U.S. and Soviet nuclear weapons systems.
- Nearly completing a treaty that would reduce very significantly the numbers of deployed long-range strategic nuclear warheads.
- Reviving the idea of defense against missile attacks and using it to argue for eliminating nuclear weapons.
- Beginning the process of ending the Cold War.

Arms control theory argued that procurement and deployment of nuclear weapons should be carried out with an eye to strategic stability. To the extent possible, leaders in Moscow and Washington should not come under pressure during a crisis to use nuclear weapons for fear of losing them to enemy action—that is, "crisis stability." This argued for reducing temptations for first strikes by deploying forces that were hardened against attack or not easily detected and targeted. The nonproliferation treaty was an asset in this because it simplified the task of identifying the source of an attack. Strategic stability also meant that decisions regarding acquisition of weapons should take into account the impact on the adversary's weapons procurement decisions. To the extent possible, deployments of U.S. weapons should not incite the Soviet Union to counter with deployments of its own, and vice versa—that is, "arms race stability." This was the most controversial and least successful aspect of arms control. Nixon's Antiballistic Missile (ABM) treaty of 1972 was an example of this idea and far and away the most effective use of it.

"Crisis stability" was an idea that was widely accepted throughout the U.S. defense establishment but not necessarily by the Soviet General Staff, for practical economic reasons among others. U.S. delegations at arms control negotiations repeatedly tried to get the Soviets to endorse less vulnerable basing modes and systems, like aircraft, that allowed more time for decision-makers to control events. The efforts were only partially successful. Through the deployment of rail- and road-mobile ballistic missiles, the Soviets made an effort at invulnerability, as they did with submarine-based ballistic missiles.

Since the failure of the Baruch Plan, and despite a brief flirtation with Khrushchev's "general and complete disarmament" after the Cuban Missile Crisis, the numbers of nuclear warheads had not been a central focus of arms control negotiations. Limiting missile launchers and bombers was aimed at predictability and stability. Eliminating strategic nuclear weapons was seen as irrelevant to the problem of making nuclear war less likely, according to "classical" (since 1960) arms control theory. Reagan thought otherwise. When I returned to Washington from my assignment as ambassador to Finland in the fall of 1981, I found that Reagan had made it known he wanted reductions in nuclear weapons, not just limitations. To underscore that point, the administration changed the old acronym for U.S.-Soviet nuclear negotiations from "SALT" to "START," the latter term being the invention of Harvard professor Richard Pipes, then serving with the National Security Council staff. Reagan preferred to think of strategic arms reduction talks (START) rather than strategic arms limitation talks (SALT), which had been Nixon's term.

Despite his hard-line reputation, Reagan became deeply involved in arms control negotiations as soon as he became president. His first arms control decision came within days of his taking office in January 1981. The question was whether the United States would accept a Conference on Disarmament in Europe if a suitable mandate for the conference could be negotiated. Reagan agreed to this. He had inherited from President Gerald Ford the Helsinki Final Act of 1975 and its operating structure, the Conference on Security and Cooperation in Europe (CSCE). A review meeting of the CSCE was being conducted in Madrid at the time Reagan took office. Max Kampelman, a longtime champion of human rights and a Democrat, was representing the United States. Reagan asked him to stay on.

President Ronald Reagan, meeting in the Oval Office with Secretary of State George Shultz, National Security Adviser John Poindexter, Sven Kraemer of the National Security Council, and the author (to Reagan's left), January 17, 1985. (Courtesy of the White House)

Much of the Madrid meeting was devoted to human rights, but some countries, America's European allies in particular, wanted to draft a mandate for negotiations about confidence-building measures and disarmament in Europe. The president of France, Valéry Giscard d'Estaing, had made the idea of conventional arms reductions in Europe his special cause. Reagan accepted the idea, on condition that the mandate would establish a basis for serious negotiations. After a lengthy negotiation in Madrid, the mandate for a Conference on Confidence- and Security-Building Measures and Disarmament in Europe was finally accepted by all thirty-five participants in the CSCE. When the preparatory phase of the conference finally began in Helsinki in November 1983, Reagan appointed me head of the U.S. delegation. The conference formally began in Stockholm in January 1984, with Secretary of State George Shultz leading the delegation and me as his co-chair.

Eliminating a Whole Class of Nuclear Weapons

Reagan's first shot at eliminating nuclear weapons, his main interest, came in the context of the intermediate-range nuclear forces (INF) that NATO had endorsed in December 1979, under the leadership of Jimmy Carter. Everyone understood at that time that deployment of these missiles would require three or four years, during which time Moscow could be counted on to make life difficult for the West European governments that had accepted INF deployment in their territories. This was exactly what Soviet leader Leonid Brezhnev and his successors did. Brezhnev died in November 1982 and was replaced by KGB (state security) chief Yuri Andropov. When deployment began in November 1983, despite all the Soviet bluster, General Secretary Andropov pulled his arms control delegations out of Geneva. It was one of his last decisive acts. He died in February 1984 and was succeeded by Konstantin Chernenko, who died in March 1985.

As Reagan said, with justification, the Soviet leaders kept dying on him, and it was not easy to conduct any kind of a sustained dialog with them. Even so, had the last of Reagan's four Soviet counterparts, Mikhail Gorbachev, not been a revolutionary on a par with Reagan himself, nothing much would have happened in the realm of nuclear weapons. Gorbachev, a convinced Communist, saw that the ideological struggle with the United States was not serving the Soviet Union's basic national interest, which was economic reform. "We are going to do a terrible thing to you," one of the leading Soviet spokespersons said, "we are going to take away your enemy." And in many respects, that is just what Gorbachev did. In this changed environment, many things became possible, even the end of the Cold War.

All of this was still in the future in 1981 as Reagan began his presidency. The outlook for arms control then was not promising. Reagan presided over a divided cabinet in which the secretary of state, Alexander Haig, was pitted against the secretary of defense, Caspar Weinberger. Haig had hoped for more autonomy in the conduct of foreign policy (he should be the vicar of foreign policy, he said), but he was hemmed in by Reagan's White House advisers and challenged on basic issues by Weinberger. The secretary of defense—advised by Richard Perle, who had been an aide to Senator Scoop Jackson—thought that talks on arms control with the Soviet Union were either useless or dangerous.

But during the Carter administration, the United States had endorsed the principle of negotiations with the Soviet Union on intermediate-range nuclear forces, and Haig insisted that to satisfy this commitment to the NATO allies, a U.S. policy was needed soon. Haig also understood that U.S.-Soviet negotiations on strategic nuclear forces were expected at some point by most Americans, even though Reagan had rejected the Carter administration's SALT II treaty. The question for Haig was what would replace the SALT II treaty. For Weinberger and Perle, the question was how to put off any resumption of strategic arms talks.

Because of pressure coming from close NATO allies, and because INF talks already had begun late in the Carter administration, the first nuclear decision Reagan had to make concerned intermediate-range nuclear forces. European governments usually have a good sense of the policy debates within any American administration. In 1981, the European governments understood the situation in Washington very well and began publicly, as well as privately, to press the administration to begin talks with the Soviet Union.

After heated debate within his own cabinet, Reagan reaffirmed the principle that talks would begin. The next question was, what should the United States propose in the talks? As was usual in the Reagan administration, the State and Defense Departments gave the president different advice. State believed that the Europeans wanted some Europe-based intermediate-range nuclear forces to counter the Soviet SS-20 and fill a missing step in the ladder of escalation. This perceived need, after all, was what had started the whole debate during the Carter administration. At that time, the Europeans, led by British and German defense specialists, said that NATO lacked any retaliatory capacity between short-range battlefield weapons and strategic, intercontinental weapons.

Reagan's national security adviser, Richard Allen, as well as Haig, believed that some U.S. INF deployment was better than none. But Secretary of Defense Weinberger decided to support an option that would eliminate all Soviet SS-20s in return for no U.S. INF deployments. The idea had come from Germany, where grassroots antinuclear sentiments were very strong. For German Social Democrats, zero U.S. deployments would be satisfactory if the Soviets would only reduce their SS-20 deployments. The Free Democratic Party, Schmidt's centrist liberal coalition partner, supported a zero-zero solution: no Soviet and no U.S. missiles.

Following his antinuclear instincts and his sense of the dramatic, on November 12, 1981, President Reagan decided in favor of Weinberger's option. Reagan revised that position during the course of the negotiations with the Soviet Union to permit deployments on both sides. But it was the zero-zero option that Mikhail Gorbachev gradually came to accept in the months following the famous Reykjavik meeting of the two leaders in October 1986.

Strategic Forces: Changing Course

The debate over INF policy was nearing its end when I arrived back in Washington in late September 1981. The debate over strategic nuclear forces, the long-range weapons that each of the nuclear superpowers targeted on each other, had yet to begin. On the recommendation of the State Department, Reagan had appointed me to be vice chair of the START I delegation; Ed

Rowny, retired Army lieutenant-general, had been appointed chair. We had known each other at NATO headquarters and got along quite well, although our arms control philosophies were very different. I found, on my return to Washington, that the experts had not made much progress in defining the strategic rationale for the reductions that Reagan wanted. The experts knew what to recommend to achieve strategic arms race stability and crisis stability, the mantra of classical arms control since 1960. They also knew that lower levels of strategic forces would not automatically enhance stability. Nor would reductions, unless to very low levels, make a noticeable difference in the death and destruction visited on the American and Soviet people and the rest of the world if a nuclear war broke out. But the basic problem was not intellectual. The real problem was that the Defense Department had been in no hurry to help the president develop a new position.

In the spring of 1982, pressures began to mount to take some kind of position. The SALT II treaty, negotiated by Paul Warnke during the Carter administration, still provided the only parameters for the U.S-Soviet nuclear arms competition. And it was a bit bizarre to be negotiating for limits on Soviet nuclear weapons facing Europe while ignoring the Soviet nuclear forces directly targeted on the United States. Perhaps most importantly, a movement for a "nuclear build-down" had acquired real momentum in the United States. Very large demonstrations were taking place in major U.S. cities. The public's displeasure with the failure to deal with pressing nuclear problems was becoming too obvious and too heated for politicians to ignore.

One of the most difficult issues to resolve in the interagency debate within the government was how to deal with "throw weight." Throw weight is a measure of the payload a missile can deliver to its targets. Soviet superiority in this metric of comparison conferred an advantage on Soviet strategic forces, many experts feared, and the disparity must be eliminated. The disparity existed, of course, and it stemmed from choices the two countries had made during the Eisenhower administration. The principal missile threat on the Soviet side, many specialists thought, was a giant missile capable of carrying at least ten reentry vehicles, called by U.S. intelligence the SS-18. The United States had no missiles as large as that, but it did have advantages in other metrics: highly capable long-range bombers, a superb fleet of invulnerable missile-carrying submarines, and highly efficient warheads carried on missiles that could deliver them with great accuracy. It also had a vibrant new program, launched with the help of Henry Kissinger and Donald Rumsfeld, to build long-range air- and sea-launched cruise missiles.

I favored limiting warhead deployment and an approach to throw weight that would cut into the Soviet advantage. Richard Burt, a former *New York*

Times reporter, whom I had known for years, had become assistant secretary of state for politico-military affairs. He was a rational man who supported Reagan's hopes to reduce U.S. and Soviet nuclear forces. He was much closer to the leading members of the Republican administration than I was, and a better policy entrepreneur as well. We made a good team. I could build bureaucratic alliances which he could then parlay into policy decisions by the Reagan administration.

The key break occurred when the Joint Staff of the Joint Chiefs of Staff decided that the State Department's thinking on warhead limits more closely matched their own than the throw weight ideas of the Office of the Secretary of Defense. To begin the process of forming a State-JCS alliance, Rear Admiral Bill Williams, the JCS representative-designate in the talks on strategic arms reduction, brought me a proposal that the Joint Staff thought would satisfy the military needs of the joint chiefs. It contained the elements that I thought could form the basis for a U.S. proposal. I recommended it to Burt, and we soon secured Secretary Haig's blessing for the plan. The proposal was not an arms controller's dream in the sense of eliminating all disparities that might tempt a first strike. But it was a practical answer to President Reagan's challenge to the bureaucracy and it would be a responsible thing to do. To succumb completely to paranoia about what the Soviet Union—or we—might do in the face of asymmetries in strategic forces would lead to paralysis and irrational decisions. It already had, in my opinion, when the policy of protracted nuclear war became U.S. doctrine.

The JCS proposal, and ideas for encouraging retention of what Reagan called "slow-fliers"—cruise missiles—while reducing what he called "fast-fliers"—ballistic missiles—enabled the president to turn away from the old policies of limits, or caps, and toward new policies of reductions. The logic of his thinking about slow and fast fliers was impeccable in arms control terms. Ballistic missiles allow very little time for decision-makers to react; false warning signals could potentially have catastrophic consequences. Aircraft and cruise missiles, particularly before the days of "stealth" technology, allowed more time for considered judgments. The fly in the ointment was that the United States enjoyed a marked superiority in "slow fliers" while the Soviet margin of advantage was in land-based ballistic missiles, precisely the category of "fast fliers" equipped with multiple warheads that Reagan's proposal was aimed at.

The Office of the Secretary of Defense was not pleased to see the joint chiefs collaborating with the State Department, especially since Reagan did not give equal throw weight ideas the priority the secretary of defense preferred. The more ambitious proposals were relegated to a second phase of reductions. In his book *Deadly Gambits*, Strobe Talbott describes in detail the maneuvering that Haig and Burt had to engage in to give President Reagan a proposal that demanded a great deal from the Soviet Union but also offered some potential for future negotiations. I will not repeat that, but one detail bears more discussion. I was asked by Burt to draft a paragraph for a speech that the president would ultimately give at his alma mater, Eureka College, where he planned to unveil his proposals. In writing the summary of what President Reagan wanted to achieve, I thought about a speech that had been given on May 19, 1981, by the great American diplomat George Kennan. He had appealed to the president to propose an across-the-board reduction by 50 percent of the nuclear arsenals of the two superpowers. Now, with President Reagan's support for the State-JCS plan, it became possible to propose something like what Kennan had advocated. The key sentence in the Eureka speech was: "At the end of the first phase of START, I expect ballistic missile warheads, the most serious threat we face, to be reduced to equal levels, equal ceilings, at least a third below the current levels." Kennan had proposed reciprocal reductions with no negotiations, and Reagan's proposal certainly was not that. But, at last, the United States government had started to think seriously about nuclear disarmament again after a lapse of over twenty years.

Arms control, in its preoccupation with stability, was relatively indifferent to the consequences, moral and otherwise, of building ever more capable nuclear forces for large-scale use in war. But Reagan often said that "a nuclear war cannot be won and must never be fought." And he acted on that belief. Paul Nitze once told me that Ronald Reagan was more like Harry Truman than any other president he had known, in that they both meant exactly what they said. When Reagan made his proposal for reductions in nuclear weaponry, he succeeded in changing the paradigm that for two decades had governed the U.S. approach to U.S.-Soviet strategic arms negotiations.

In the Trenches

Armed with the Senate's confirmation of my appointment as ambassador, the rank attached to vice chair of the U.S. delegation, I left for Geneva in the summer of 1982. I left just after Secretary of State Haig had been relieved of his job by the president. Burt and I had briefed Haig on START the night before his fateful White House meeting. But the resignation issue concerned the authority that Haig thought he was entitled to have, not any particular policy issue.

Ed Rowny's philosophy, as he expressed it to the U.S. delegation, was that we had a good proposal and should stay with it. He hoped the Soviets would accept it but if, regrettably, they did not, the administration could use that as a justification for higher defense budgets. I thought that the president and the nation wanted us to see what we could do to reduce nuclear weapons. Since the delegation was on the front line of the negotiation, we would have a better sense of how to solve negotiating problems and bridge gaps between the two sides than anyone else. That put me in the same camp as Paul Nitze, who was once described by Richard Perle as "an inveterate problem-solver." The chief of the delegation and I had our differences, but to his credit, Rowny never interfered with my sending my own ideas back to the State Department, and I always kept him informed of what I was recommending.

The U.S.-Soviet negotiating process at that time was still in the pre-Gorbachev era, and before George Shultz gained ascendancy. It was quite formal and unproductive. Victor Karpov, the chief of the Soviet delegation, would read a statement and Ed Rowny would read his statement. Then the two men would adjourn to a private room to expound on the meaning of what they had just said. The other delegation members would do the same with their counterparts. There was very little exploration of issues in a problem-solving sense on either side. And so the talks droned on until the summer of 1983, uneventfully.

In the spring of that year Gene Rostow, director of the U.S. Arms Control and Disarmament Agency, had been fired by Reagan over an issue unrelated to arms control. Ken Adelman, an official at the U.S. Mission to the United Nations, had been named to succeed him. Rowny, who had hoped to become ACDA director himself at one point, thought that he should give Adelman his opinion of the ACDA staff. He therefore gave Adelman a memorandum containing his assessment of each of the senior people, adding his opinion of his own delegation. His comments were not very complimentary, especially about his delegation, and when the memorandum was leaked to the press, a firestorm broke out. The memo became known as the "hit list," and needless to say, it caused quite a bit of anguish in the delegation. I held it together while Rowny fought for his job and Adelman for his Senate confirmation. Both men weathered the storm.

It was clear to me that the time had come to move on, and I discussed this with Deputy Secretary of State Kenneth Dam at the end of that negotiating round. We agreed that I would return for another round, and during that time I suggested some ideas for breaking the impasse. That story is well told in Strobe Talbott's *Deadly Gambits*. Two events intervened to side-track the Geneva talks. One was the downing of a civilian Korean airliner by Soviet air defense. The other was Soviet General Secretary Yuri Andropov's decision to pull the Soviet delegations out of the INF and START negotiations when U.S. INF missiles were finally deployed in Western Europe in November 1983. By that time, I had been appointed head of the U.S. delegation to the Conference on Disarmament in Europe by President Reagan. The START and INF talks did not resume until early 1985 and then in a new format, with Max Kampelman in charge. Ed Rowny and Paul Nitze, who had headed the INF delegation, became senior advisers to the president and secretary of state.

Star Wars

Even before he became president, Reagan had mused about the contradiction between the magnificent American achievements in science and technology and the inability of the United States to defend itself against a missile attack. Edward Teller had encouraged him to think that a defense against ballistic missiles might be possible. His own "kitchen cabinet" of wealthy supporters from the private sector had encouraged the idea.

When Ronald Reagan became president, his reputation as a hard-line anticommunist hawk generated a public backlash in favor of nuclear disarmament. The American Catholic bishops issued a letter in 1983 that said the use of nuclear weapons was immoral. Reagan was being pilloried as a proponent of nuclear weapons. That stance did not conform to his own instincts about nuclear weapons and it was politically damaging. But he did preside over a very large increase in the defense budget to correct what he saw as a decade of neglect, especially in nuclear-related systems. And he had said that Carter's SALT II treaty was "fatally flawed."

A series of events orchestrated by Reagan's second national security adviser, Bud McFarlane, prompted the president to launch the "Strategic Defense Initiative" in March 1983. The first step was a meeting with the Joint Chiefs of Staffs on February 11, 1983. Army General John Vessey, the chairman, presented a proposal originally prepared by Admiral James Watkins, chief of naval operations, to proceed with ballistic missile defense. When he left the meeting, President Reagan, fortified by his own private advisers and by his own opinion, had decided that it was time to change the rules of the game.

For Reagan, the next step was a speech to announce his decision. This was typical of the way he liked to make policy—by inserting a statement of policy in a presidential speech. In this case, after his meeting with the Joint Chiefs of Staff, Reagan asked Bud McFarlane to develop ideas on defenses against ballistic missiles. McFarlane assigned Air Force officers attached to the National Security Council to prepare a draft for public announcement. By March 18, Reagan had decided to introduce the proposal in a defense speech he had already scheduled for March 23. The White House science adviser, George Keyworth, was brought in late in the day, but he loyally endorsed the idea and helped with the rationale. The secretaries of state and defense were brought into the picture only when the speech was almost set to go. They concurred, partly because they saw the proposal as the beginning of a long research program, partly because they knew that Reagan already had decided. Finally, on March 23, 1983, President Reagan announced that he was asking American scientists "to turn their great talents now to the cause of mankind and world peace, to give us the means of rendering these nuclear weapons impotent and obsolete."

The reaction from Moscow was predictable. Andropov was a reformer in the sense that he realized power was slipping away from Moscow because of corruption and an inability to match the economic and technical achievements of the West. His method of reform was to enforce greater discipline. He saw in Reagan's proposal a scheme that would force the Soviet Union to ever greater defense expenditures and end the period of relative stability that had marked Brezhnev's relations with Nixon, Ford, and Carter. This would complicate his ideas about reform. He was also worried about Reagan's intentions. Andropov denounced the Reagan speech and a period of bitter relations between the two countries ensued. The year 1983 was seen as an extremely tense time in Moscow.

The crisis was weathered, but not until Mikhail Gorbachev became general secretary in 1985 did the full import of what Reagan was proposing receive serious consideration in Moscow. Reagan, with the help of George Shultz and Paul Nitze, had added new ideas to the offense-defense equation that had not been seriously considered in previous administrations. What if it were possible to mutually and reciprocally reduce nuclear weapons while jointly and cooperatively building up a defensive system? In principle, there should be a cross-over point where defense would have dominance over offense. This had not been studied before in any detail. It was a conceptual innovation. But it required more mutual confidence between the Soviet Union and the United States than existed at the time. And at some point, other nuclear-weapon states would have to be included. Reagan had not thought through all of this before he made his speech on March 23. What he did know was that he hated nuclear weapons and that he could win political points by doing something about them.

Reagan and Gorbachev: Two Nuclear Abolitionists

Three and one-half years after this visionary initiative, Reagan took another leap into the unknown. It was in Reykjavik, Iceland, and it was taken together with another visionary, Mikhail Gorbachev, then general secretary of the Communist Party of the Soviet Union. The two men discussed the abolition of all nuclear weapons. Reagan made a proposal in writing to eliminate all ballistic missiles from the nuclear arsenals of the two nations. This breathtaking offer was derailed by what the American side saw as a Soviet effort to kill off the president's Strategic Defense Initiative.

President Ronald Reagan and Mikhail Gorbachev had met for the first time in November 1985, in Geneva, Switzerland. They established a surprising degree of rapport right away. Announcing that they shared common ground on the principle of 50 percent reductions in strategic nuclear forces and on the idea of an interim INF agreement, they agreed to meet again.

At the beginning of January 1986, Gorbachev sent Reagan a proposal for the elimination of all nuclear weapons in three stages by the year 2000. This led to a letter from Reagan sent on July 25, 1986, which intrigued Gorbachev, a fact Gorbachev publicly admitted not long after reading it. In a speech delivered in Vladivostok on July 28, Gorbachev said: "During my visit here, I received a reply from President Reagan. The reply sets one thinking. We have begun to study it. We shall treat it with responsibility and attention."[2]

Following up his private initiative to Gorbachev with another resort to public diplomacy, the president revealed the gist of his July 25 letter in an address to the United Nations General Assembly on September 22, 1986. It foreshadowed the discussions in Reykjavik and conveys a sense of the breadth of Reagan's ambitions:

> I wrote last summer to Mr. Gorbachev with new arms control proposals. . . . [W]e continue to seek a 50 percent reduction of American and Soviet arsenals with the central focus on the reduction of ballistic missile warheads. If the Soviet Union wants only a lesser reduction, however, we are prepared to consider it—but as an interim measure. . . .
>
> Similarly, in the area of intermediate-range nuclear forces, the United States seeks the total elimination of such missiles on a global basis. Again, if the Soviet Union insists on pursuing such a goal in stages, we are prepared to conclude an interim agreement without delay. . . .
>
> The United States continues to respect the ABM Treaty—in spite of clear evidence that the Soviets are violating it. We have told the Soviets that if they can agree—if we can both agree—on radical reductions in strategic offensive

weapons, we are prepared right now to sign an agreement with them on research, development, testing, and deployment of strategic defense based on the following:

First, both sides would agree to confine themselves through 1991 to research, development, and testing which is permitted by the ABM Treaty, to determine whether advanced systems of strategic defense are technically feasible.

Second, a new treaty, signed now, would provide that if, after 1991, either side should decide to deploy such a system, that side would be obliged to offer a plan for sharing the benefits of strategic defenses and for eliminating offensive ballistic missiles. And this plan would be negotiated over a two-year period.

Third, if the two sides can't agree after two years of negotiation, either side would be free to deploy an advanced strategic defensive system.[3]

In this brief space, Reagan raised the possibility of radical reductions in offensive ballistic missiles or the elimination of such missiles, a multiyear moratorium on deployment of ballistic missile defenses, an obligation to share the benefits of strategic defenses, and the total elimination of intermediate-range nuclear forces on a global basis. Quite an agenda.

Progress toward another Reagan-Gorbachev meeting was complicated by the arrest by the Federal Bureau of Investigation on August 22 of a Soviet U.N. employee named Gennadi Zakharov on spy charges; retaliation by the Soviet intelligence agency, the KGB, followed on August 30 with the arrest of U.S. journalist Nicholas Daniloff. Intense media coverage contributed to an atmosphere suddenly gone sour. The problem yielded to quiet diplomacy, and on September 12 both men were released to the custody of their respective ambassadors. Both were repatriated at the end of the month.

Tensions were still high when, on September 19, Soviet Foreign Minister Eduard Shevardnadze arrived in Washington, just before Reagan's U.N. speech, and delivered Gorbachev's reply to President Reagan's letter of July 25, 1986. In his letter, Gorbachev expressed uncertainty about the present U.S. position on arms control and suggested a meeting in Iceland or Britain to hear Reagan's thinking about arms issues firsthand. On September 30, 1986, Reagan announced that he had decided to accept Gorbachev's offer to meet in Iceland. The meeting would take place in less than two weeks, on October 11–12, at the suggestion of the United States.[4]

The Reagan administration thought that the Reykjavik meeting would be an informal exploratory session with a limited agenda. It would not be a "summit," but a preparatory meeting. The administration hoped for an agreement on INF in Europe, and some progress on a threshold nuclear test ban treaty. But Gorbachev came to Reykjavik with a lot more on his mind than he had let on. At the first session, on the morning of Saturday, October 11, Gorbachev unveiled proposals covering all aspects of the U.S.-Soviet nuclear arms negotiation. After a fifty-one-minute opening discussion during which Reagan explained and argued for his July 25 proposal, Gorbachev presented the following draft directive for the two foreign ministers to carry out:

1. Strategic Arms

Reduce by 50 percent strategic offensive armaments of the U.S.S.R. and U.S.A. taking into account the historical peculiarities of the structure of the strategic forces of both sides.

All types of strategic weapons including heavy missiles will be reduced in this framework. Also a solution of the problem of limitation of deployment of long-range SLCMs will be found.

The sides will negotiate all problems of strategic offensive arms taking into account the mutual interests, concerns and political will to reach an agreement.

2. Medium-Range Missiles

An agreement about complete elimination of medium-range missiles of the U.S.S.R. and U.S.A. in Europe. The nuclear potential of Great Britain and France are not touched upon or counted. Negotiations will begin on missiles that both sides have in Europe whose range is less than 1,000 kilometers. Separately, and as soon as possible, negotiations will begin on Soviet and U.S. medium-range weapons in Asia.

3. ABM Treaty—Comprehensive Test Ban

In order to strengthen the regime of the ABM Treaty of 1972, which has unlimited duration, the sides will agree that the USSR and USA commit themselves for 10 years not to use the right to withdraw from this treaty, and during this period strictly to follow all of its regulations.

All testing of space-based elements of a ballistic missile defense in outer space will be prohibited except research and testing in laboratories.

That will not require a ban on tests allowed by the ABM Treaty—of fixed land-based systems and their components.

The sides must find mutually acceptable solutions in this area during negotiations in the next several years. Both sides agree to make additional efforts to reach mutually acceptable agreements to ban ASATs [antisatellite weapons].

Bilateral negotiations on a comprehensive test ban [CTB] will be resumed as soon as possible. During these negotiations the USSR and USA should also deal with the question of control, limitations on the threshold and number of explosions and about the treaties of 1974 and 1976 [threshold test ban treaty and peaceful nuclear explosions treaty].

Beginning of negotiations on CTB is a precondition for development of an agreement on strategic weapons.

4. Conclusion
The general secretary and the president agree that the above agreements have crucial importance for achieving the purposes announced by them at Geneva in November 1985: the limitation and reduction of nuclear weapons, prevention of an arms race in space and halting it on Earth, strengthening of strategic stability and common security.[5]

The two leaders met again on the morning of Sunday, October 12. Gorbachev expanded on his proposal by suggesting the elimination of all U.S. and Soviet INF in Europe and ceilings on INF of 100 in Soviet Asia and in the United States. This was a major advance toward an agreement. In discussions headed by Paul Nitze on the U.S. side and Sergei Akhromeyev, chief of the Soviet General Staff, for the Soviet side, key parameters for the START agreement also were accepted by both sides, paving the way for the START treaty.

When the discussion turned to the ABM treaty and restrictions on ballistic missile defense, Gorbachev proposed that an extra, unscheduled session be held to discuss the issue. Reagan agreed, and the two delegations met in a session chaired by the foreign ministers. Shevardnadze insisted that there must be a ten-year period when there would be no withdrawal from the ABM treaty. If this could be agreed, all other issues could be solved. Shultz presented a draft written on the spot by Richard Perle and an NSC staff member, Air Force Colonel Bob Linhard. It was a variant of Reagan's July 25 letter and U.N. speech.

Later in the afternoon of October 12, the two leaders met again with their foreign ministers to discuss the offense-defense link. Reagan authorized a written text to be presented:

> The U.S.S.R. and the United States undertake for ten years not to exercise their existing right of withdrawal from the ABM treaty, which is of unlimited duration, and during that period strictly to observe all its provisions while continuing research, development and testing, which are permitted by the ABM treaty. Within the first five years of the ten-year period (and thus through 1991), the strategic offensive arms of the two sides shall be reduced by 50 percent. During the following five years of that period, all remaining offensive ballistic missiles of the two sides shall be reduced. Thus, by the end of 1996, all offensive ballistic missiles of the U.S.S.R. and the United States will have been totally eliminated. At the end of the ten-year period, either side could deploy defenses if it so chose unless the parties agree otherwise.[6]

The final session of the Reykjavik meeting rose to the heights and then sank to the depths. Gorbachev reiterated his desire to eliminate all nuclear weapons, not just ballistic missiles. Reagan agreed to the goal of nuclear disarmament. A White House official who was questioned on this point was reduced to saying that nothing was "fleshed out" along these lines.

The break-point began to appear when Gorbachev, following the script laid out in his initial presentation, insisted that all research and testing of space-based ballistic missile systems be restricted to the laboratory. Shultz reports in his memoirs that Gorbachev said, "the testing in space of all space components of antiballistic missile defense is prohibited, except research and testing conducted in laboratories."[7]

Some of the background to this extraordinary episode will help explain what happened next. In the spring of 1985, Nitze recalls, "the Soviet delegation in Geneva [in the resumed negotiations] had proposed banning testing and development of space-based missile defenses," adding that "at the time, the U.S. Government considered this already banned by the ABM treaty."[8] So did the U.S. negotiators of the ABM treaty, and most importantly, that is what the Senate thought when it consented to ratification. The treaty commitments included a provision "not to develop, test, or deploy ABM systems or components which are sea-based, air-based, space-based, or mobile land-based."

But pressure was mounting to begin testing exotic new technologies and, in response, lawyers were convened to consider how far the treaty could be stretched. Some of them argued that there was no ban on testing new technologies; others argued that deployment of systems based on new technologies, as well as testing, was permissible. The president, of course, was known to have his heart set on doing whatever was necessary to create strategic defenses. Even before the formalities of interagency decision-making were completed, the president's national security adviser went on television, on October 6, 1985, to announce that the ABM treaty imposed no limits on testing. The secretary of state had to clean up the mess this caused as best he could.

Shultz finally persuaded Reagan to agree that ballistic missile defense research would be conducted in accordance with the traditional, more restrictive interpretation of the treaty, while simultaneously asserting that a broad interpretation of the treaty was still justified. In other words, legally, testing in space of new technologies was permitted, and it was only through the grace of a U.S. policy decision that it was not, for the moment, being carried out. The Soviets, of course, disputed this new U.S. policy. Raising this convoluted issue first at Geneva and later at Reykjavik gave the Soviets an answer they had not wanted or expected. Surprises were one of the many charms of the Reagan administration.

In the final minutes at Reykjavik, Reagan, as reported by Shultz, reread the key clause to Gorbachev: "Listen once again to what I have proposed: during that ten-year period [of nonwithdrawal from the ABM treaty], while continuing research, testing, and development which is permitted by that treaty. It is a question of one word."[9] Reagan did not want to enter into a negotiation which might end up amending the treaty, as he understood it. Gorbachev refused to drop the word "laboratory," and it was clear that he was referring to space-based systems, although the terminology he used in discussions was not always precise. Over this one word, the negotiations broke off. The Americans read Gorbachev's proposal as an attack on the Strategic Defense Initiative broadly. That one word "laboratory" obviously rang alarm bells in the minds of those who had been operating under tense conditions for three days.

One Word and a World of Difference

Gorbachev's acceptance of President Reagan's language would not have solved the difference between them on the interpretation of the ABM treaty, as later events showed. But it is unfortunate that Gorbachev refused to refer the matter to the U.S.-Soviet negotiators in Geneva as Reagan proposed at one point at Reykjavik. A compromise might have been found, and Nitze tried very hard to find one later on. The two leaders never engaged on what the ABM treaty said and what it meant. In summit meetings there is too little time to explore complex issues and the leaders cannot be expected to be familiar with every detail. And so ended "the highest stakes poker game ever played," as Shultz described it.[10] In the president's words, "We proposed the most sweeping and generous arms control proposal in history. We offered the complete elimination of all ballistic missiles—Soviet and American—from the face of the Earth by 1996. While we parted company with this American offer still on the table, we are closer than ever before to agreements that could lead to a safer world without nuclear weapons."[11]

Reykjavik was not the last time the two sides discussed this issue of testing in space. Paul Nitze's account of trying to resolve essentially the same issue a few months later proves how hard it would have been to resolve it at Reykjavik.[12] Nitze reports that in the spring of 1987 he proposed a negotiation with the Soviet Union to develop criteria for what could be tested in space. The idea originated with Yevgeny Velikov and Roald Sagdeyev, two prominent Soviet scientists and administrators of major Soviet research programs. Nitze recognized that there were problems with inventing criteria. One was whether any agreed criteria would allow a vigorous ballistic missile defense testing program. The other problem was more political. As Nitze wrote, "if we agreed to definitions and thresholds of capability, then we might be heading toward constraints that did not appear in the treaty, an outcome that the President already had firmly opposed." Nothing much happened to his proposal. Soviet Foreign Minister Shevardnadze raised the matter himself in April 1987. He proposed a meeting of the U.S. and Soviet defense ministers to discuss, among other things, the question of permissible and prohibited testing in space. Weinberger and the president's new national security adviser, Frank Carlucci, vigorously opposed it and the matter was dropped.

Finally, in December 1987, Reagan and Gorbachev held their long-awaited Washington summit meeting. The main feature of it was the signing of the recently concluded treaty on the banning of U.S. and Soviet intermediate-range ballistic missiles, a formidable achievement. The signing took place at the White House on December 8. By that time, Carlucci had moved to the Pentagon to replace Weinberger, who had resigned, and General Colin Powell had become the president's national security adviser.

Nitze, his Reykjavik counterpart Akhromeyev, and other dignitaries met in the White House during the early afternoon of December 10 to finish an agreed statement that the two leaders were supposed to issue that day. One of the issues they discussed related to testing permitted under the 1972 ABM treaty. "Intense discussions" ensued in which Shultz, Powell, and Carlucci joined for the American side and Shevardnadze and Karpov for the Soviets. Akhromeyev gets the credit, in Nitze's report, for proposing the key sentence which Shultz accepted on the spot and which Reagan and Gorbachev endorsed: "the leaders of the two countries also instructed their delegations in Geneva to work out an agreement that would commit the sides to observe the ABM Treaty, as signed in 1972, while conducting their research, development, and testing as required, which are permitted by the ABM Treaty, and not to withdraw from the ABM Treaty, for a specified period of time."

This had become a charade by this time, but what happened next is almost certainly what would have happened in Reykjavik. Reagan was asked at a question-and-answer session the next day whether the Soviets had agreed to drop their objections to U.S. testing under the broad interpretation of the ABM treaty and whether the communique language resolved the issue. The president said "it resolves it . . . we have agreed that we are going forward with whatever is necessary in the research and development without any regard to an interpretation of ABM."[13] The Soviets retorted that there was no such agreement on what kinds of tests would be permissible under the treaty.

The Reagan administration had not allowed Nitze to pursue the criteria approach (what Nitze called "the list and threshold approach") to define what could be tested in space but, ever the problem-solver, Nitze tried one more time. This time his counterpart at meetings in Washington on September 22–23, 1988, was not his fellow problem-solver, Akhromeyev, but a Soviet diplomat, Alexei Obukhov, who had been my counterpart in Geneva. Nitze advanced two ideas: sensors in space would be permitted and each side would be allowed to have a small number of test platforms in space. As Nitze put it, his ideas "were not well received by our Soviet counterparts." That was Nitze's last effort to solve the problem that had brought the Reykjavik meeting to a bitter end.

In Retrospect

The most remarkable summit meeting ever held between American and Soviet leaders was that conducted between Mikhail Gorbachev and Ronald Reagan in Reykjavik. They came close to agreeing to eliminate all ballistic missiles held by their two countries and discussed the possibility of eliminating all nuclear weapons. Within a year, Gorbachev seems to have been convinced by his scientific advisers that the United States would not be able to overcome the technical difficulties of ballistic missile defense for a long time. In fact, two decades after Reykjavik, there is still no ballistic missile defense in the United States capable of blocking the kind of attack that Russia could launch, and that is not for the lack of trying.

What would have happened if Gorbachev had dropped the one word and his objections to testing in space? He would have been attacked in Moscow, as Reagan was attacked in Washington for having the temerity to talk about eliminating ballistic missiles. The timing of deployment of an effective ballistic missile defense system would not have been affected. Perhaps their "agreement" could not have stood the criticism. But Reagan and Gorbachev achieved a great deal at Reykjavik. It was a breakthrough in its own way: they had stretched the envelope of thinking about reducing the nuclear danger. They had clearly distinguished between nuclear weapons and all others, and had stigmatized nuclear weapons as immoral, their use unacceptable in conflicts among nations. And despite the famous one word—laboratories—the Reykjavik meeting led to the signing of the U.S.-Soviet treaty on banning intermediate-range nuclear forces and to a draft treaty on reducing strategic-range nuclear forces that was almost complete by the time Reagan left office. His successor, George H. W. Bush, signed the treaty soon after taking office.

Reagan told his administration from the beginning of his presidency that he wanted reductions in nuclear warheads. In saying this, he saw no contradiction with his policy of a U.S. nuclear buildup to close the lead that he believed the Soviet Union had opened up over the United States. In fact, had his administration ended in 1985 instead of 1989, it would have been remembered mainly for an enormous increase in defense spending and for arms control proposals that seemed designed to fail. Reagan's second term changed all that. The end of the Cold War was within sight by the time he left office.

Reagan's Strategic Defense Initiative had not been realized when he left office, nor has it been in all the years since. It is usually overlooked that by insisting that ballistic missile defenses should protect all of the American people and not just missile sites, Reagan maintained control over the deployment of the defensive missiles. Such a defense never materialized, and unlike Lyndon Johnson, Reagan was never forced by Congress to deploy a ballistic missile defense system to deflect political pressures.

Reagan wanted to abolish nuclear weapons and he saw two ways of doing that. One was by eliminating nuclear weapons; the other was to build a defense that would make them impotent and obsolete. Linking the two methods offered a way forward. Robert Kennedy was fond of saying: "some see things as they are and ask why. I see things that never were, and ask why not?" Reagan's approach to nuclear weapons was exactly that.

Ronald Reagan and Mikhail Gorbachev brought two great nations close to the end of the era of the Cold War. Two revolutionaries, each in his own way, became history's odd couple. Gorbachev realized that the Soviet Union needed radical economic reform, and that to do it, he had to end the ideological confrontation with the West. Reagan was prepared to believe that genuine change had come to the Soviet Union and to accept that the "evil empire" had vanished. Asked about that during his summit meeting with Gorbachev in Moscow in the summer of 1988, Reagan said: "I was talking about another time, another era."

Notes

1. In writing this chapter I have drawn on three case studies I wrote with Frederick Donovan at Georgetown University. The case studies became part of the "Pew Case Studies in International Affairs" managed by the Institute for the Study of Diplomacy, School of Foreign Service, Georgetown University. The three studies are as follows: "Changing the Rules: President Ronald Reagan's Strategic Defense Initiative (SDI) Decision," Case 320; "High Stakes, High Risks: The Reykjavik Base Camp," Case 317; "Choosing Zero: Origins of the INF Treaty," Case 319. I thank the Institute for the Study of Diplomacy for its willingness to let me draw on these case studies in this book. I especially want to thank my Georgetown colleague Fred Donovan, whose research provided the basis for our case studies.

2. "Excerpts from Gorbachev's Speech," *New York Times*, July 29, 1986, A6.

3. "Documentation: Summit Meeting in Reykjavik (1986)," *Survival* (March/April 1987): 167–168.

4. Michael Gordon, "Soviet Called Unsure on U.S. Arms Aim," *New York Times*, October 3, 1986, A3.

5. Text of Gorbachev's proposals in Don Oberdorfer, "At Reykjavik, Soviets Were Prepared and U.S. Improvised," *Washington Post*, February 16, 1987, A28. Another translation of this may be found in Don Oberdorfer, *The Turn* (New York: Poseidon Press, 1991), appendix, 445.

6. "Text of U.S. Offer in Iceland," *New York Times*, October 18, 1986. Also in George P. Shultz, *Turmoil and Triumph: My Years as Secretary of State* (New York: Charles Scribner's Sons, 1993), 770–771.

7. Shultz, *Turmoil and Triumph*, 769.

8. Paul Nitze, *From Hiroshima to Glasnost* (New York: Grove Weidenfeld, 1989), 412–413.

9. Shultz, *Turmoil and Triumph*, 772.

10. David Hoffman, "Iceland Talks: One Word Chills Hope," *Washington Post*, October 19, 1986, 1, A37.

11. "Report on Reykjavik," *Department of State Bulletin*, December 1986, 17.

12. The story is told in detail in Nitze, *From Hiroshima to Glasnost*, 443–457.

13. See www.reagan.utexas.edu/archives/speeches.

PART V

ONCE MORE INTO THE UNKNOWN, 1989–2006

George H. W. Bush, Bill Clinton, and George W. Bush

The Cold War was ending when George H. W. Bush took office. One question he faced was what would happen to thousands of nuclear weapons in a collapsing superpower. Another major concern was how the division of Europe could be overcome in a way that would avoid war and future recriminations. Bush signed two major strategic arms reductions treaties, of which only the first, largely completed in Reagan's administration, remains valid today. He took the unprecedented step of unilaterally removing short-range nuclear weapons from forward positions. Gorbachev followed suit, which meant that when the fifteen republics of the Soviet Union became independent, only four still had nuclear weapons on their territories.

Bill Clinton took office at a time of increasingly polarized national politics. He was highly successful, despite that, in helping Russia, Ukraine, Belarus, and Kazakhstan expedite nuclear reductions required under START I, and improving controls over nuclear materials to prevent nuclear smuggling. Clinton tried to preserve the essence of the 1972 ABM treaty and move on to START III. In this, he failed. He began a policy shift toward regional nuclear weapons issues by focusing on North Korea and Iran.

George W. Bush saw a new world and hoped to create a new international order to replace the outmoded Cold War order. His vision involved a new relationship with Russia and other large nations, fewer restrictions on the use of American power, and correspondingly, less reliance on international agreements. But he soon faced unprecedented problems of violent Islamic extremism which complicated normal state-to-state relationships and required him to deal with substate entities. His security policies focused on rogue states and their relations with terrorist movements. Bush saw military force as a prime means of dealing with what he called "gathering threats." In Iraq, he exercised the military option, asserting that this was required to stop Saddam Hussein from acquiring nuclear, chemical, and biological weapons. In the cases of Iran and North Korea, both nascent nuclear-weapon states, Bush exercised diplomacy, relying on other governments to provide the carrots while he provided the sticks.

CHAPTER NINE

George H. W. Bush: Managing the Soviet Succession

In the summer of 1988, President Reagan called me to say he wanted to appoint me as ambassador to Greece. I was delighted at the prospect and told him so. But when the nomination later went to the Senate for confirmation, the Foreign Relations Committee declined to give me a hearing because of the upcoming presidential election. Reagan offered me a recess appointment to the position, but that would expire fairly early in the next administration, and I had no wish to uproot my family for such a short period. I declined the offer.

When Reagan's former vice president, George H. W. Bush, took office, I waited long enough to understand that I would not be offered Greece or anything else. I then retired from the Foreign Service in June 1989. Thus, my perspective on U.S. nuclear policies during the administration of the first President Bush was that of an outsider, for the first time in thirty-five years.

For some time after Gorbachev took power, George H. W. Bush was more skeptical than Reagan had been that real change had come to the Soviet Union. But after becoming president, Bush became convinced that Gorbachev was a real reformer. He worried about Soviet backsliding, and he was deeply concerned by a coup attempt against Gorbachev in August 1991. Russian President Boris Yeltsin's decision to pull Russia out of the Soviet Union in December 1991 and to form the Commonwealth of Independent States created a wholly new geopolitical situation. But the Bush-Yeltsin partnership continued in the tradition of the Cold War. Bush was cautious about dropping the Cold War paradigm, so policy-making stayed within that conceptual framework, although he added very important innovations. His policies yielded two major agreements on strategic nuclear arms, START I and START II. These were the last US-Soviet/Russian agreements of that type, and the second was never ratified. It was the end of an era.

President Bush's best-known achievements in foreign policy concern the reunification of Germany and ejecting Saddam Hussein from Kuwait. But his achievements in disarmament also were very substantial. Bush and his secretary of state, James Baker, were worried about turmoil in the Soviet Union because of the potential for loss of central control over the tens of thousands of nuclear weapons scattered throughout the country. This was a problem that was unprecedented in human history. Baker conjured up the image of "a Yugoslavia with nukes," Yugoslavia being then in the throes of ethnic conflicts. The president counseled caution about breaking ties with Moscow in a speech in the Ukraine, which soon became known to wags as the "Chicken Kiev" speech.

Considering that Bush and his Soviet, then Russian, counterparts were collaborating in the midst of a major geopolitical transition, what they accomplished was a tour de force. Bush faced at least seven interlocking problems that had to be solved in order to protect nuclear weapons during the collapse of a nuclear-armed superpower:

- Remove short-range (tactical) nuclear weapons from areas of political instability in the Soviet Union.
- Work for centralized control of Soviet nuclear weapons.
- Associate Belarus, Kazakhstan, and Ukraine—where Soviet strategic nuclear weapons were located—with the legal requirements of the START I treaty and with the nuclear nonproliferation treaty as non-nuclear-weapon states.
- Prevent theft or illicit trade in nuclear weapons and fissile material.
- Facilitate the process of destroying or removing long-range (strategic) nuclear weapons systems from Belarus, Kazakhstan, and Ukraine.
- Scale back Reagan's Strategic Defense Initiative to a defense against small-scale missile attacks while seeking Russia's cooperation in that program.
- Foster a security environment that would be supportive of all the above actions (recognizing that there also were alliance considerations which affected specific policies in this area).

The solutions to these problems, worked out by Bush, his national security adviser, Brent Scowcroft, and his secretary of state, James Baker, made it possible for the Soviet Union to break up into fifteen independent republics without any nuclear incidents, a real miracle under the circumstances. New precedents and nascent international rules of behavior were put in place. One of the most important was that how a nation protects its nuclear materials is a matter of international concern. Of course, it was possible to do all this because of serious and highly responsible people in the former Soviet Union who, sometimes grudgingly, realized the dangers.

Tactical Nuclear Weapons

The Soviet military had stored short-range nuclear delivery systems and their associated nuclear warheads in all of the fifteen republics of the Soviet Union. The U.S. military also had deployed tactical nuclear weapons at forward bases overseas and on ships. Some in the U.S. Army, Colin Powell in particular, had come to the conclusion that these weapons were more of a nuisance than an advantage, since their use under late Cold War conditions was highly unlikely.

In his memoirs, Colin Powell recounts that, as chairman of the Joint Chiefs of Staff, he proposed to Defense Secretary Cheney that the Army should get rid of artillery-fired nuclear weapons. The idea was rejected by the armed services and by Cheney and his staff.[1] But after the 1991 Persian Gulf War, at a meeting on September 5, 1991, President Bush asked for new ideas on nuclear disarmament. Bush's request produced the nuclear initiatives that he announced on September 27, 1991.

On that date, President Bush ordered U.S. forward-based tactical nuclear systems withdrawn to secure storage and many destroyed. He also ordered the Strategic Air Command to reduce its alert status. He hoped that the Soviet Union would reciprocate, but it was not a requirement. There was good reason to think that Gorbachev would do so, and Bush's expectations were not misplaced. Gorbachev gladly responded on October 5, 1991, by withdrawing all tactical nuclear weapons from bases outside of Russia, promising to destroy many of them.

These actions by Bush and Gorbachev prevented a disaster. The breakup of the Soviet Union could have led to fifteen nuclear-armed states, and that could have resulted in a loss of centralized control over nuclear weapons. Nuclear weapons would then have been in the hands of several states, or even terrorist groups who certainly would be willing to pay well for nuclear weapons. All that was avoided in one of the great acts of nuclear diplomacy.

Centralized Control

Yeltsin had created the Commonwealth of Independent States (CIS) in December 1991 to link the Slavic states of the former Soviet Union: Russia, Ukraine, and Belarus. Kazakhstan's president, Nursultan Nazarbayev had to ask to be included, but Kazakhstan was readily admitted, as were other former republics of the Soviet Union. A centralized command for the armed forces of the CIS was established on December 8, 1991. The chain of command for the strategic rocket forces was unclear.

The Bush administration reacted quickly to this problem. Speaking at Princeton University on December 12, 1991, Secretary Baker gave a detailed explanation of the position of the Bush administration:

> We do not want to see new nuclear weapons states emerge as a result of the transformation of the Soviet Union. Of course, we want to see the START treaty ratified and implemented. But we also want to see Soviet nuclear weapons remain under safe, responsible, and reliable control with a single unified authority. The precise nature of that authority is for Russia, Ukraine, Kazakhstan, Belarus, and any common entity to determine. A single authority could, of course, be based on collective decision-making on the use of nuclear weapons. We are, however, opposed to the proliferation of any additional independent command authority or control over nuclear weapons.
>
> For those republics who seek complete independence, we expect them to adhere to the non-proliferation treaty as non-nuclear weapons states, to agree to full-scope I.A.E.A. [International Atomic Energy Agency] safeguards, and to implement effective export controls on nuclear materials and related technologies. As long as any such independent states retain nuclear weapons on their territory, those states should take part in unified command arrangements that exclude the possibility of independent control. In this connection, we strongly welcome Ukraine's determination to become nuclear-free by eliminating all nuclear weapons from its soil and its commitment, pending such elimination, to remain part of a single, unified command authority.[2]

This statement amounted to a reaffirmation of the nuclear nonproliferation treaty at a turbulent time when old Cold War premises might have been questioned or dismissed. Despite the adversarial relationship that still existed between Moscow and Washington, Bush had decided that Russia should be the sole nuclear power among the states succeeding the former Soviet Union.

The Lisbon Protocol

The language of the START I treaty had already been negotiated between the United States and the Soviet Union by the time the Soviet Union collapsed. It was signed by Bush and Gorbachev on July 31, 1991. The main provisions called for reductions to 1,600 deployed delivery vehicles and 6,000 associated warheads. The end of the Soviet Union was signaled by a coup mounted against Gorbachev in August 1991. It quickly collapsed when the military failed to back it. Boris Yeltsin pulled Russia out of the Soviet Union and that state officially expired on December 25, 1991. The question then became how to deal, legally, with Soviet strategic nuclear weapons located in Belarus, Kazakhstan, and Ukraine. The U.S. secretary of state, supported by President Bush, produced a remarkable outcome. He persuaded the three newly independent states where strategic nuclear weapons were located to become parties, with Russia and the United States, to the START I treaty and also to become parties, as non-nuclear-weapon states, to the nuclear nonproliferation treaty. This deal was codified in the Protocol to the START I treaty which was signed at Lisbon, Portugal, on May 23, 1992. This meant that Russia, Ukraine, Kazakhstan, and Belarus were successor states to the former Soviet Union for purposes of the START I treaty but also that Belarus, Kazakhstan, and Ukraine would give up all their nuclear weapons deployed on their territories. Russia would carry out the reductions required under the START I treaty. It was a diplomatic victory that salvaged the nuclear restraint regime painstakingly built up over decades. START I and the Lisbon Protocol entered into force on December 5, 1994.

Preventing Loss of Control of Fissile Material and Nuclear Weapons

In 1991 the U.S. Congress adopted legislation sponsored by Senators Sam Nunn (D-GA) and Richard Lugar (R-IN) which offered assistance to the states of the former Soviet Union in expediting implementation of the START I treaty and preventing the proliferation of nuclear weapons. Defense Secretary Cheney was not entirely pleased by this legislation, since the funds were to be derived from the budget of his department, but he went along. Retired Major General William Burns negotiated the first Nunn-Lugar agreements with Russia in 1992.

Burns negotiated several agreements with Russia, including a broad umbrella agreement that outlined the scope of cooperation, and several implementing agreements that provided details about the cooperation that would occur. It was apparent that Belarus, which had been severely damaged by radioactive fallout from the Chernobyl reactor explosion, would surrender its nuclear weapons systems as the Lisbon Protocol required, but time ran out before the Bush administration could work out a Nunn-Lugar assistance program. Ukraine and Kazakhstan were more difficult. Their governments thought they were entitled to retain the thousands of nuclear weapons on their soil. It was not at all clear at that stage, despite the Lisbon Protocol, that an increase in the numbers of nuclear-weapon states could be prevented. Ukraine, in particular, was demanding a high price for surrendering nuclear weapons on its territory.

But by the time Bush left office, the essential elements of an offer to Ukraine were on the table. The offer included assistance in dismantling nuclear systems on Ukraine's territory, compensation for nuclear materials shipped to Russia, plus security assurances. The status of Kazakhstan was still uncertain, but the Bush administration had begun to lay the groundwork for what eventually happened, which was a removal of all nuclear weapons from Belarus, Kazakhstan, and Ukraine to Russian territory for dismantling.

The Bush administration, in one of its last acts of preventive diplomacy late in 1992, announced that it would buy 500 metric tons of highly enriched uranium derived from dismantled Soviet warheads. The deal would cover warheads removed to Russia from Belarus, Kazakhstan, and Ukraine, as well as those already in Russia. The material would be converted into fuel for civilian nuclear power plants. This idea was suggested by a member of the MIT faculty, Tom Neff. It was a brilliant success, providing additional incentives to Belarus, Kazakhstan, and Ukraine to return warheads on their territories to Russia for dismantling. The history of this episode and its aftermath has been described in detail by one of its prime movers, James Timbie of the State Department.[3]

Ballistic Missile Defense

When George H. W. Bush took office, he inherited a research program that had run into political difficulties and had not yet shown that ballistic missile defense was workable. Reagan's Strategic Defense Initiative program, which was a defense of the American population, was technically impossible to do at that point. President Bush postponed it and instead opted for a more limited program. His program offered a way of developing ballistic missile defenses on a cooperative basis with other countries, especially Russia. It meant that a less than perfect defense might be fielded, an idea that Reagan had resisted. But with the collapse of America's main nuclear-armed adversary, the case for a defense system on the scale that Reagan had envisaged became less persuasive.

With the encouragement of Senator Sam Nunn and others, Bush proposed that a ballistic missile defense system be developed that would deal with accidental launches and deliberate small-scale attacks. It was dubbed Global Protection against Limited Strikes (GPALS). When Bush discussed the idea with Boris Yeltsin, the idea appealed to the Russian president because it was not an adversarial program but one that could be mutually taken—in theory.

GPALS really could have been a method of overcoming the deficiencies of all previous ballistic missile defense plans, not technologically, but in terms of political cooperation among nations. The problem always has been that a competitive approach to building these systems means that other advanced countries, like Russia, can easily offset defenses with less expensive offensive weapons and decoys. The genius of Bush's plan was that it was portrayed as a global system, not directed at a particular country, and was open to the participation of countries that could contribute advanced technology.

The administration did not assign much priority to this plan. It became more of a place-holder for a ballistic missile defense policy that never really gelled in the one term of President George H. W. Bush. It became a dead letter even before the end of his administration and was dropped by his successor.

The Security Environment

Actions taken by President Bush to accommodate changes in Europe were directed at facilitating the peaceful reunification of Germany, the nonviolent breakup of the Soviet Union, and membership of a united Germany in NATO. Bush had to do this while creating as nonthreatening an environment as circumstances would permit. This was not easy. A nuclear-armed superpower had never before dissolved into its constituent parts. It was vital to minimize any possibilities that Soviet/Russian nuclear weapons, many on high alert, would be launched because of a misinterpretation of warning indicators at that uncertain time. Imagine a threatening, provocative U.S. administration combined with a military coup in Moscow designed to restore the Soviet Union. The Bush administration created, with the European allies, a structure to cushion the shocks that Russia was receiving. That, plus the caution displayed by the administration, provided a nonthreatening background for a very dangerous transition.

Much credit should go to the two Soviet/Russian leaders—Gorbachev and Yeltsin—who governed as best they could through a turbulent time. And never forget, either, the Russian "cadres," the bureaucrats and specialists, who kept their heads through all the difficulties.

An Illusory Success

Presidents Bush and Yeltsin agreed in June 1992 to negotiate further reductions in strategic weapons, beyond those in START I. Yeltsin at this stage was still hopeful that substantial U.S. economic assistance and other support for his struggling government would be forthcoming. The nuclear negotiation proceeded rather rapidly to produce a treaty that became known as START II. It was signed by Presidents Bush and Yeltsin on January 3, 1993, just before Bush left office. The treaty required that land-based missiles could not be loaded with multiple, independently targetable, reentry vehicles (MIRVs). Fixed, land-based, MIRVed ballistic missiles had been the target of U.S. arms control initiatives for years. Finally, in START II, this goal was attained, including the elimination of the heaviest missile in the Soviet/Russian inventory, the SS-18, and the U.S. Peacekeeper, the famous MX. The other MIRVed land-based missiles were "down-loaded," that is, they were allowed to carry only one warhead. Submarine-launched ballistic missiles were allowed to be MIRVed.

The treaty was not well received by Russian defense experts. They believed that the United States had gained an advantage with its superiority in MIRVed missiles at sea and in long-range bombers equipped with cruise missiles. The treaty, in retrospect, turned out to represent the last "successful" U.S.-Russian strategic arms control negotiation. No additional treaty was negotiated during the two Clinton terms. When George W. Bush took office, he junked START II in favor of another treaty quite unlike those negotiated by his Republican predecessors, Nixon, Reagan, and George H. W. Bush.

The epitaph for that era of negotiations was expressed to me in a meeting with Secretary of State James Baker shortly before he left that office in the summer of 1992 to become George H. W. Bush's campaign manager. I had gone to see him in the capacity of a State Department senior inspector to ask him what he thought about the future of the U.S. Arms Control and Disarmament Agency. His comment to me was this: "We have negotiated the greatest disarmament program in history and it isn't even on the radar screen of the American people."

An Unrealized Antiproliferation Program

In January 1992 the U.N. Security Council decided that nuclear proliferation constituted a threat to international peace and security. In his General Assembly speech in September 1992, President Bush launched several important initiatives. The Security Council "should become a key forum for nonproliferation enforcement." The Security Council should take immediate action to provide assistance to any non-nuclear-weapon state party to the nonproliferation treaty that should become a victim of aggression involving nuclear weapons. The nonproliferation treaty should be extended for an indefinite period. And a global protection system was needed against limited strikes.

In the new world following the Cold War, it was a forward-looking set of proposals that could be supported even today by the United States and its friends. Bush himself was not able to follow through. Bill Clinton won the election in November.

Notes

1. Colin Powell, with Joseph E. Persico, My American Journey (New York: Ballantine Books, 1995), 525.

2. U.S. Department of State Dispatch, December 16, 1991.

3. James Timbie, "Energy from Bombs: Problems and Solutions in the Implementation of a High-Priority Nonproliferation Project," Science and Global Security, 12, no. 3 (2004): 165–192.

CHAPTER TEN

Bill Clinton: Facing New Threats

Soon after Bill Clinton took office in January 1993, I was approached by two emissaries from the State Department who asked if I would handle the negotiation of Nunn-Lugar agreements with the states that had emerged from the collapse of the Soviet Union. Many of the nuclear-related facilities in those countries were not well protected. Belarus, Kazakhstan, Russia, and Ukraine needed help in dismantling their nuclear weapons expeditiously in a safe and secure manner as required by the START I treaty and the Lisbon Protocol. Nunn and Lugar had had the foresight to get legislation passed allowing the United States to intervene in a very dangerous situation to help the new states get through the transition. Their idea was like the Marshall Plan in its boldness and in its practical way of dealing with very real problems. I was delighted to become the chief negotiator for Nunn-Lugar agreements.

Cooperative Threat Reduction

I succeeded William Burns, a retired Army major general and a friend of some years, who had had the unenviable task of conducting negotiations during a presidential election year and with Secretary of Defense Dick Cheney not entirely pleased about having Defense Department funds diverted to something he saw as less than central to his mission. Bill Burns had presided over the conclusion of a truly landmark agreement that enabled the United States to purchase 500 metric tons of highly enriched uranium from dismantled warheads. He had also negotiated a Nunn-Lugar umbrella agreement and a few implementing agreements with the Russian Federation. But otherwise, Nunn-Lugar was a book yet to be written. In the next year, my interagency team negotiated over thirty umbrella and implementing agreements with Russia, Ukraine, Kazakhstan, and Belarus. Between March 1993 and March 1994, the financial commitments made to the recipient countries showed an almost vertical climb on the Pentagon's briefing charts.

These agreements described the main goals of the parties, defined the specific programs, and laid down the legal basis for cooperation. The Pentagon's Cooperative Threat Reduction Office, under the able leadership of retired Major General Roland Lajoie, another good friend, was responsible for converting these agreements into the nuts and bolts of providing assistance. I had two superlative deputies: Gloria Duffy from the Defense Department and Jim Turner from the Department of Energy. Mike Stafford, from State, was our chief of staff. The system worked very well. At the end of a frenetic year of travel and negotiation, I returned to private life at the U.S. Institute of Peace, where I had been appointed a distinguished fellow.

Neither President Clinton nor Secretary of State Warren Christopher followed the details of these negotiations very closely, although both became di-

President Bill Clinton, meeting in the president's private office with (from left to right) Nancy Gallagher, the author, and General John Shalikashvili, January 5, 2001. (Courtesy of the Clinton Presidential Library)

rectly engaged at times in the work my delegation was doing with Ukraine and Kazakhstan. Each of these countries had been reluctant to surrender the nuclear weapons left on their territories after the collapse of the Soviet Union. In the case of Kazakhstan, President Nazarbayev thought that he could use the presence of the weapons to extract some benefits from Russia and the United States. In the end, he gave them up in return for Nunn-Lugar assistance and a summit meeting with President Clinton.

Ukraine was a tougher nut to crack. A faction in the Supreme Rada, the Ukrainian parliament, believed that Ukraine should not return the nuclear weapons on its territory to Russia for dismantlement. This group exercised considerable influence over Ukraine's president, Leonid Kravchuk. They also had the backing of some officials in the Ukrainian Foreign Ministry, including some who were thinking mainly of benefits to be achieved through bargaining.

The turning point in Ukraine came in October 1993. Secretary Christopher had been rebuffed by Nazarbayev in Almaty when he arrived there, ready to sign a Nunn-Lugar umbrella agreement and some implementing agreements that I had negotiated with the Kazakhstanis. Nazarbayev insisted on a meeting with President Clinton in Washington and delayed the signing ceremony. When Christopher arrived in Kiev, after a frustrating meeting in Almaty, he was quite anxious for a success in the Nunn-Lugar enterprise with the Ukrainians.

At first, he pursued an idea for "early deactivation," under which Ukraine would disable its missiles and bombers or, alternatively, remove nuclear warheads from weapons systems. The Ukrainians were not entirely comfortable with that scheme because they were interested in compensation for their warheads and had been talking with the Russians about this. They soon made it clear to Christopher that as a first step, Ukraine wanted to proceed without further delay with the negotiation of the Nunn-Lugar umbrella agreement. That, of course, threw the negotiating ball to me.

By that time, I had authorized my Defense Department legal adviser, Jack Beard, to return to Washington via Frankfurt for pressing business in the Pentagon. My two deputies had other business to attend to, so Mike Stafford and I began the talks with the Ukrainians on the second floor of the Ukrainian president's house, while Christopher and his party held a working dinner downstairs with President Kravchuk and other senior Ukrainian officials. At the end of the dinner, all the senior Americans and Ukrainians came to the room where the negotiations were taking place. We were still in a wary circling phase, with many issues not yet addressed. They made it very clear that they expected us to produce an agreement by morning. To emphasize the point, Christopher and his Ukrainian counterpart, Foreign Minister Ana-toliy Zlenko, initialed the umbrella agreement, which by that time was more a concept than a reality.

We negotiators then repaired to the Ukrainian Foreign Ministry, giving Kravchuk the privacy of his own house for the rest of the night. Despite the evident desire of the two foreign ministers to conclude the umbrella agree-ment, none of the negotiators on either side was ready to concede points eas-ily. On several occasions, I called Beard in Frankfurt to seek his concurrence in language Stafford and I had worked out. Jack was tough but sensible, and he concurred in the points where his concurrence was necessary or gave us ideas for other solutions. The discussions continued until we finally reached full agreement at 6:30 a.m. Boris Tarasiuk, then a deputy foreign minister, later Ukraine's foreign minister, had remained in the ministry all night with us. When we reported success to him, he broke open a fine bottle of Scotch whisky and we all toasted the results. I then went straight to Secretary Christopher's hotel and delivered the final agreement.

The next turning point with Ukraine came when I returned to Kiev in December to conclude the key implementing agreement, the one that would provide assistance for Ukraine's dismantlement of its nuclear-armed missiles. President Kravchuk had written to President Clinton about deactivating some of the most modern missiles, the SS-24s. Secretary of State Christopher had exchanged letters with Foreign Minister Zlenko, and I had already had some discussions with the Ukrainians. But until my visit, the Ukrainians had not told us specifically how and when they intended to deactivate the SS-24s. They provided the details about this during my December visit. They then proceeded to conclude the Nunn-Lugar agreement for assistance in dis-mantling their strategic forces. My Ukrainian defense ministry counterpart was General Lieutenant Olexiy Kryzhko. He had emerged as the key Ukrain-ian negotiator and proved to be a man of great integrity and vision. The ses-sion had shown clearly that Kravchuk's administration had finally decided to give up the nuclear weapons on its territory and dismantle its powerful mis-sile force. This, obviously, was a step of historic proportions, especially for a state that was still struggling to maintain its independence and establish its own identity apart from Russia. It showed great courage on the part of Pres-ident Kravchuk.

My next stop was Moscow, where I had scheduled a meeting at the De-fense Ministry. Accompanied by U.S. Ambassador Tom Pickering, I briefed Andrei Kokoshin, then the Russian deputy defense minister, about the Ukrainian decision. His military colleagues had received reports about activ-ity at some of the Ukrainian missile sites, but they ascribed this to routine maintenance. They were not convinced that the Ukrainians were doing what they claimed to be doing.

As events later unfolded, it became clear that Ukraine had indeed made a strategic decision to give up nuclear weapons. It had been facilitated by parallel discussions between Russia and Ukraine at Massandra, in Crimea. To pull the whole deal together, the United States, Russia, and Ukraine agreed to hold trilateral meetings, culminating in a summit meeting in Moscow on January 14, 1994. A combination of Nunn-Lugar assistance, security assurances, and compensation for nuclear materials sent back to Russia, including compensation for warheads from short-range systems already returned to Moscow's custody, brought about a successful conclusion to the effort to denuclearize Ukraine.

At the endgame of this negotiation, President Clinton acted to forestall any backsliding by going public with the impending news of the agreement. At an earlier stage, in the spring of 1993, he also had supported a change in policy toward Ukraine that broadened U.S. relations with Kiev. This was a crucial move, making it possible for Ukraine to conclude that it had something to gain from its relationship with the United States. This model remains one of the central lessons in how to deal with nuclear proliferation. Addressing the motivations for a government to seek nuclear weapons means addressing that government's own strategic concerns. Any solution that is limited to the narrow field of nuclear weapons development is not likely to stand for very long. The Clinton administration's policies in Ukraine, from mid-1993 onward, reflected this basic truth.

Strategic Nuclear Arms Control: A Missed Opportunity

In another area of nuclear weapons control, U.S.-Russian strategic forces, the administration missed opportunities to continue the reductions program that Ronald Reagan had started. The incoming Clinton team wanted outgoing President Bush to sign the START II treaty before he left office. Bush did so, with the Russian president, Boris Yeltsin, on January 3, 1993. Key senators at that time had no difficulties with START II, which was in fact highly favorable to the U.S. side of the strategic equation. But the Clinton administration and key senators agreed that undue haste in recommending ratification might send the wrong signal to Moscow, so the Senate delayed a vote on ratification for a year. On January 26, 1994, the Senate gave its advice and consent to START II by a vote of 84–7. The ratification process was delayed by Russia's State Duma, where the treaty was far more contentious than it had been in the U.S. Senate.

Meeting in Helsinki, Finland, on March 21, 1997, Clinton and Yeltsin agreed that the deadline for the elimination of strategic nuclear delivery vehicles under the START II treaty would be extended to December 31, 2007. That amendment gave the Russian government more time to complete its commitments, but it would require the U.S. Senate to revisit the treaty. Further complicating the process were two related agreements that the administration had negotiated with the Yeltsin government: an Anti-ballistic Missile (ABM) Demarcation Protocol and a Memorandum on ABM Treaty Succession. The first was designed to distinguish between permitted tests to support theater ballistic missile defense systems and tests that were not permitted, because they would support a national ballistic missile defense system, outlawed by the 1972 ABM treaty. The second agreement concerned the designation of Belarus, Kazakhstan, and Ukraine, together with Russia, as successor states of the former Soviet Union for purposes of conforming to the requirements of the 1972 ABM treaty.

The administration acquiesced in sending these two agreements to the Senate, although it believed that ratification was not required. What ensued was fairly typical of Clinton's relations with the Senate in those years. The chair of the Senate Foreign Relations Committee, Jesse Helms (R-NC), disliked the two new accords intensely and would not consider the modestly amended START II treaty so long as the two additional accords were on the table.

The Russian State Duma consented to ratification of the START II treaty in April 2000. The Duma attached conditions that made approval of the Demarcation Protocol and the ABM Treaty Succession a requirement for Russian ratification of START II and also required continued U.S. adherence to the 1972 ABM treaty. The stage was set for an impasse. This lasted until President George W. Bush scrapped the whole package and gave notice that the United States would withdraw from the ABM treaty.

Warhead Dismantlement: Another Missed Opportunity

As President Clinton's special representative for nuclear security and dismantlement, I was responsible for working out a program for U.S.-Russian nuclear warhead dismantlement. The device we used was a communique to be issued by a Clinton-Yeltsin summit meeting in May 1995. I traveled to Moscow with an interagency team and met with a Russian delegation to hammer out a joint statement. We succeeded and President Clinton approved the text, as did President Yeltsin.

That was not quite the high-water mark of the effort to build some degree of transparency and irreversibility into U.S.-Russian warhead dismantlement. Later, we almost clinched an agreement that would have permitted the exchange of sensitive information, a necessary part of the mutual transparency. An issue arose over the American desire to describe the possible scope of information exchange and the Russian insistence on limiting the scope to the most immediate problems. We also discussed the exchange of data that would help confirm numbers and types of warheads each side had. There, we overreached. The whole project was scrapped by the Russians within months after the two presidents agreed to it. To my regret, President Clinton chose not to make an issue of the Russian reversal.

But the president returned to the warhead dismantlement issue at the meeting with Yeltsin in Helsinki on March 21, 1997. Again, President Yeltsin agreed to cooperative arrangements in nuclear warhead dismantlement, and that agreement was recorded in the communique the two presidents issued. There were discussions between the two sides after that, which seemed promising, according to the participants, but nothing came of them. A real opportunity was missed in 1995–1996.

Comprehensive Test Ban Treaty

Negotiations related to a ban on all nuclear weapons tests had begun in 1958 under the leadership of President Dwight Eisenhower. The negotiations survived the breaking of the nuclear test moratorium in 1961 by the U.S.S.R., the Cuban Missile Crisis of 1962, and years of aimless discussion in various international fora. Ronald Reagan had not been a strong supporter of a test ban, despite his antinuclear instincts, because he believed that while nuclear weapons existed they should be tested. The U.S. Congress, however, began to press President George H. W. Bush to end underground testing, the only environment in which testing was allowed. He reluctantly agreed to do so in 1992 for those tests needed to develop new types of nuclear weapons. Thus began a moratorium on all U.S. underground nuclear testing that has lasted to this writing. The majority in Congress wanted more than a unilateral moratorium and adopted legislation (PL102-377, 1992) that asked the president to achieve a comprehensive test ban treaty by September 30, 1996.

President Clinton took office in January 1993, and a year later negotiations on a comprehensive test ban treaty got under way in a multilateral forum sponsored by the United Nations in Geneva. The U.S. representative in that forum, the Conference on Disarmament, was Ambassador Stephen Ledogar. He and I had worked together at NATO headquarters and in the European Bureau in the Department of State. He was a tenacious and meticulous negotiator who practiced multilateral diplomacy with consummate skill.

A comprehensive test ban treaty had always been seen as a bulwark against the spread of nuclear weapons technology. That was why President Kennedy had supported it. So it was a foregone conclusion that a conference scheduled to review the implementation of the nonproliferation treaty in 1995, as required by the treaty, should consider the test ban issue. As it turned out, extension of the treaty became critically dependent on the willingness of the nuclear-weapon states to accept a mandate to do their level best to negotiate a ban on all nuclear weapons tests.

President Clinton appointed Ambassador Thomas Graham, former general counsel of the U.S. Arms Control and Disarmament Agency, to lead the effort to extend indefinitely the terms of the nonproliferation treaty. Graham traveled throughout the world to convince governments that an indefinite extension of the treaty would be in their interest. He very ably succeeded in this. Clinton accepted the outcome, which included an understanding that the nuclear-weapon states would try to negotiate a comprehensive test ban treaty by the end of 1996. The indefinite extension of the nonproliferation treaty was one of the historic achievements of the Clinton administration.

Ambassador Ledogar worked in Geneva with other similarly disposed delegations in the Conference on Disarmament to complete a test ban negotiation by 1996, as requested by Congress. The delegations succeeded in this, although there were two critical holdouts, the Indians and the Pakistanis. The treaty was literally comprehensive: it prohibited any nuclear explosion that would generate fission yield and, hence, was called a zero-yield ban on testing.

Senator Helms was still chair of the Senate Foreign Relations Committee in 1996. As a longtime foe of arms control agreements and no fan of Clinton, Helms refused to hold hearings on the treaty. Lulled by the apparent impasse on the Hill, the White House failed to keep a close watch on what was happening. That was a fatal mistake. A small group of conservative Republican senators began to coalesce in opposition to the test ban treaty. They received briefing papers from opponents of the treaty outside the government and eventually recruited a substantial bloc of Republicans to their camp. Within a year or two, they were ready to take on the administration but they bided their time. In the meantime, the administration had done little or nothing to campaign for the treaty or to counter the arguments that were quietly winning most Republican senators to the opposition side.

The showdown came in 1999 when Senate Majority Leader Trent Lott (R-MS), after being goaded by Democratic supporters of the treaty, brought the treaty to the floor of the Senate, allowing three days for testimony and debate. In that short time, the unprepared administration failed to convince most Republican senators of three key arguments: that the treaty could be verified, that the safety and security of the U.S. nuclear stockpile could be maintained indefinitely without explosive testing, and that a test ban would have a decisive effect on preventing the proliferation of nuclear weapons.

Recognizing, to its dismay, that the Senate would almost certainly refuse to give its consent to ratification, the administration asked that the treaty be withdrawn from active consideration. That procedure, which is traditional in such cases, meant that a vote would not be taken and the treaty would be held in a kind of limbo. Many senators joined in support of this appeal, including Republicans, but the Senate leadership, very unusually, refused to grant President Clinton his request. The vote went ahead and the treaty went down by a vote of 51–48, with one abstention. Since a two-thirds majority is required to ratify treaties, the vote was a stinging defeat for the administration and for nuclear nonproliferation.

Hoping to keep the treaty alive, Secretary of State Madeleine Albright, with White House support, decided to create a mechanism for consultation with senators. The idea was to talk with individual senators to determine whether there was a way to address their concerns and ultimately reverse the negative vote. Retired General John Shalikashvili, former chairman of the Joint Chiefs of Staff, agreed to accept the position of special adviser to the president and the secretary of state for the comprehensive test ban treaty. I became his deputy. Shalikashvili was courageous in civil affairs as well as military. I admired him greatly for his common sense and dedication to the nation's best interests. Together, we met with about a third of the Senate, both supporters and opponents of the treaty. With the able assistance of Nancy Gallagher and Damien LaVera, we put together a formula that we thought would meet the concerns of all but the most committed opponents. The key was Senate participation in a review of the treaty's effectiveness after a period of years. Although the separation of powers was bent somewhat by this proposal, the administration was prepared to accept it, as were many senators.

With the indispensable help of John Parmentola of the Defense Department, we asked for and received reports from defense consulting firms on various aspects of the treaty. These reports plus Shalikashvili's own previous evaluations as chairman of the Joint Chiefs of Staff and his conclusions after reviewing the issues in detail all pointed to a judgment that U.S. interests would be well served if the treaty came into force.

Shalikashvili and I, together with Gallagher and LaVera, presented a report to the Secretary of State on January 4, 2001. With her endorsement, we then presented our findings to President Clinton in the White House on January 5, 2001. The president discussed the report with us in detail and I came away impressed by his command of the stakes involved. His hope, he said, was that the president-elect, George W. Bush, would reconsider the treaty that as candidate he had clearly opposed. President Clinton remarked that presidents, himself included, often found on entering the office that positions they had taken in the campaign had to be revised. He said he would raise the matter with the president-elect, since he regarded the ratification of the treaty as a matter of major importance for the United States.

Whether that conversation ever took place I do not know. If it did, it encountered the same reaction that President Bush displayed to nearly all of the works of his predecessor. The administration declared that it would not seek ratification of the treaty. Zealots within the administration even looked for legal ways to "de-sign" the treaty. It remains still today with the U.S. Senate, ready for a president and a Senate that wants to put it into force. In the meantime, there has been a moratorium on testing U.S. nuclear weapons since 1992.

Ballistic Missile Defense

The Clinton administration was under strong pressure from Congress to endorse an active ballistic missile defense program. Clinton signed legislation when it was presented to him that made it U.S. national policy to develop and deploy a ballistic missile defense system when certain conditions were met. The administration made a serious effort to work out some arrangement with the Russian government that would preserve the 1972 ABM treaty, allow deep cuts in warhead levels, and permit some kind of ballistic missile defense on an agreed basis. U.S. and Russian negotiators made progress in the area of "theater missile defense," but this was not enough to satisfy the American proponents of a national ballistic missile defense. The Russians were highly suspicious of any changes in the ABM regime, but they did show considerable interest in collaborating on theater missile defense; Clinton and Yeltsin agreed to an "integrated cooperative defense" effort at Helsinki in 1997. Nothing much came of it, although this was a promising approach to a new strategic paradigm.

Clinton's efforts to satisfy critics in Congress while saving the core of the ABM treaty failed and nothing was put forward to replace the offense-defense construct developed in 1972. That made it almost inevitable that Richard Nixon's 1972 antiballistic missile defense treaty would be scrapped, as indeed it was by President Bush in 2001. That treaty stood for almost three decades as a barrier to a runaway arms race between the United States and the Soviet Union. Despite billions of dollars spent on ballistic missile defense, there is still no system in sight that can deal with a sophisticated nuclear attack.

Pivoting to a New Strategic Problem

The focus on the U.S.-Russian nuclear relationship began to change almost as soon as the Cold War ended. Regional problems loomed larger, and first among them in the Clinton administration was Korea. In 1992, North Korea signed a safeguards agreement with the International Atomic Energy Agency (IAEA) to monitor the obligations it had accepted when, under Soviet pressure, it signed the nonproliferation treaty in 1985. President Bush had removed all U.S. nuclear weapons from South Korea in 1991 and North and South Korea had signed two seemingly transformational agreements: the "Basic Agreement," a framework for peaceful cooperation, and a second agreement declaring all of the Korean peninsula free of nuclear weapons. But the IAEA discovered in its inspection of North Korea's nuclear facilities in 1992 that plutonium most likely had already been separated from spent fuel rods from a reactor at Yongbyon, raising ominous questions. This, and other confrontations, led to a war-threatening crisis. North Korea began unloading irradiated fuel rods from its 5 megawatt reactor, making it impossible to verify what had happened to the plutonium in question. Its government stated that it would withdraw from the nonproliferation treaty.

President Clinton saw these actions as a violation of a "red line": North Korea appeared to be moving toward building nuclear weapons. His secretary of defense, William Perry, began making plans for military action against North Korea. Kim Il Sung, the leader of North Korea since 1945, had his spokespersons announce that even a blockade of his country would be considered an "act of war."

At this point, June 1994, Jimmy Carter intervened. In a meeting with Kim Il Sung in Pyongyang, the former president persuaded the North Korean leader to freeze plutonium production. A month later, in July 1994, Kim Il Sung suddenly died and his son, Kim Jong Il, assumed the leadership of North Korea. He followed Confucian tradition in mourning his father and in not assuming all his father's powers immediately. He also followed his father's wishes, presumably, in allowing an "Agreed Framework" to be signed with the Americans in October 1994 that froze the operations of the reactors and separation facilities at Yongbyon that produced plutonium. The negotiations that led to the Agreed Framework were conducted on the U.S. side by Ambassador Robert Gallucci. That accord meant that North Korea did not build the many plutonium-based nuclear weapons that it might otherwise have done.

In 1998, North Korea flight-tested a three-stage ballistic missile that flew over Japan, causing a strong adverse reaction there. In addition, the Agreed

Framework was lagging in the building of light-water reactors that had been promised North Korea under the Agreed Framework. Tensions were rising once again. At this point President Clinton appointed William Perry, who had left the position of secretary of defense, to recommend a plan for dealing with North Korea.

Perry recommended a two-track process. The idea was to offer North Korea incentives to stop its nuclear and missile programs, failing which the United States would impose all the sanctions it could against that country. The Perry process seemed to pay real dividends. There was progress toward freezing North Korea's missile program. The results seemed so promising that in 2000 the top North Korean army general visited Washington and Secretary of State Albright visited Kim Jong Il in Pyongyang. Events were moving favorably in North-South Korean relations also. South Korea's president, Kim Dae Jung, traveled to Pyongyang to meet with Kim Jong Il in 2000. The Clinton administration ended with a seemingly very promising diplomatic negotiation in store with North Korea. But unbeknownst to any of the Americans and South Koreans, Pakistani scientist A. Q. Khan had made a deal with North Korea to supply centrifuge machines capable of enriching uranium for nuclear bombs.

Plusses and Minuses

President Clinton managed arms control during a time of rapid transition from the U.S-Soviet rivalry of the Cold War to an altogether different relationship with a much reduced Russian Federation. His Russian partner, Boris Yeltsin, was not fully in control of his own governmental apparatus. In Washington, Clinton endured the unremitting hostility of right-wing Republicans who made it difficult for him to accomplish anything in the field of arms control. Jesse Helms, chair of the Senate Foreign Relations Committee during Clinton's administrations, blocked any U.S.-Russian agreement. The Senator's actions deprived the United States of major assets in the antiproliferation campaign. Playing from a weak hand, the Clinton administration missed opportunities to reshape the arms control paradigm.

Clinton's unwillingness to push harder for an agreement on warhead dismantlement was a missed opportunity. That might have been achieved. It would have been Clinton's signature contribution to nuclear arms control. A new U.S.-Russian relationship required a new framework, and that framework could have included not only warhead dismantlement but also an active program of early warning and ballistic missile defense cooperation. The administration accepted these ideas in principle, but these programs enjoyed no priority or any high-level support, and they were never seen as the building blocks of a new strategic relationship. U.S.-Russian collaborative programs in these areas could have reframed the strategic relationship to reflect changed circumstances.

But Clinton accomplished a great deal in the area that counted most at that time. Faced with the collapse of a nuclear-armed superpower, he took decisive action, building on his predecessor's work, and with the support of Congress, to prevent loss of control of the nuclear weapons, materials, and technology in Russia, Ukraine, Belarus, and Kazakhstan. It was the most important victory over nuclear proliferation in the post–Cold War period.

The Clinton administration's chief successes were:

- Indefinite extension of the nonproliferation treaty.
- The denuclearization of Belarus, Kazakhstan, and Ukraine.
- The use of the Nunn-Lugar legislation to help Russia meet its obligations to reduce nuclear weapons under the START I treaty.
- Tightening the security of nuclear facilities in the former Soviet Union.
- An Agreed Framework with North Korea that froze plutonium production in that country for several years.

Like his predecessor, President George H. W. Bush, Clinton faced an enormously dangerous situation and steered a course that enabled the United States to influence very substantially the course of events. This was arms control reinvented to meet a new danger, and it succeeded.

~

CHAPTER ELEVEN

George W. Bush: Overthrowing the Old Order

George W. Bush lost the popular vote in the presidential election of 2000, but won in the Electoral College because of a disputed vote count in Florida which the Supreme Court decided in his favor. The new president lost no time in signaling his determination to change the way the United States had been conducting its affairs in every realm. George W. Bush was convinced that radical change in international relations was in order a decade after the end of the Cold War. His two immediate predecessors had preferred an evolutionary approach in changing times. The second President Bush thought the time had finally come to scrap the old order. He did that and forced "regime change" in Iraq as well. In the presidential election of 2004, Bush won a decisive victory.

A New Strategic Framework

The year 2001 would be devoted to changing the concept of nuclear deterrence as it had been practiced since the days of Harry Truman. On February 15, 2001, Vice President Dick Cheney told the Conservative Political Action Committee that President Bush had "big changes in mind." "At the earliest possible date," Cheney mentioned, "this administration will build and deploy a defense against ballistic missiles."[1]

On May 1, 2001, the president began to outline his thinking about a new strategic framework in a speech at the National Defense University:

- Against the likes of Saddam Hussein, old-style deterrence is not enough.

- Active defenses against weapons of terror will strengthen deterrence by reducing the incentive for proliferation.
- The thirty-year-old antiballistic missile treaty is not in the U.S. interest or the interest of world peace.
- The new strategic framework will include missile defenses and further cuts in nuclear weapons.

In this policy speech, Bush defined a new relationship that he hoped to create with Russia. The adversarial legacy of the Cold War would be replaced by a cooperative relationship. The president said: "I want to complete the work of changing our relationship from one based on a nuclear balance of terror, to one based on common responsibilities and common interests."

Not yet evident in this landmark speech was the Bush doctrine of preventive war against "gathering threats," but there were glimmerings of it. He mentioned "active nonproliferation" and the need to "work together with other like-minded nations to deny weapons of terror from those seeking to acquire them." That could have referred to more vigorous export control policies. But the real meaning was made clear in the national strategy that was even then in the making and which was unveiled at the end of the year.

That June, President Bush traveled to Europe for his first trip as president. In a press conference following his meeting with the NATO heads of state and government in Brussels on June 13, Bush reported that he had spoken about the need for a new framework for nuclear security. The balance of terror relationship and the antiballistic missile (ABM) treaty no longer made sense, the president remarked and, furthermore, "cooperative work on a new strategic framework could be a great task which brings NATO and Russia together."

President Bush discussed the new threats the NATO allies faced, stressing that uncertainty was the main characteristic. This required the nations to think differently, to cease being locked into a Cold War mentality. He promised consultation on ballistic missile defense deployments but warned that he was "intent upon doing what I think is the right thing." As to reductions in offensive arms, "we'll move by ourselves," the president declared, signaling an end to U.S.-Russian negotiations on that subject.

Bush continued his themes of a new strategic framework and a new relationship with Russia as he traveled eastward in Europe. In a speech in Warsaw on June 15, 2001, the president spoke of "growing threats from weapons of mass destruction and missiles in the hands of states for whom terror and blackmail are a way of life." He repeated his ideas about the four components of a new strategic framework:

- Active nonproliferation.
- Counterproliferation.
- Deterrence that includes defenses.
- Reductions in nuclear weapons.

Overhauling the U.S.-Russian Relationship

Bush met with Russia's President Vladimir Putin in Slovenia on June 16, 2001. In a joint press conference after their two-hour meeting, Bush told the world that he took much the same position as in his previous meetings elsewhere in Europe: "we need a new approach for a new era, an approach that protects both our peoples and strengthens deterrence by exploring and developing our new attitudes towards defenses and missile defenses."

Putin chose to emphasize the positive, but he said that "the 1972 ABM treaty is the cornerstone of the modern architecture of international security." And he warned that states on the threshold of acquiring a nuclear weapons capability would welcome the end of the ABM treaty. To react to their rudimentary programs by deploying ballistic missile defenses would be to recognize their status as nuclear-weapon states. He also thought that the Americans and Russians could solve their differences by working together, citing the protocols to the ABM treaty that had been worked out with the Clinton administration. Putin was expecting—or hoping—for a dialogue about the ABM treaty. He was to be disappointed. On July 13, Bush's national security adviser, Condoleezza Rice, spoke at the National Press Club in Washington. She characterized the Bush-Putin meeting as "warm, positive, but very frank" and declared that the old paradigm was obsolete and that "we cannot cling to the old order." Putin, in the meantime, was doing just that.

Shortly after his meeting with Bush, on June 18, Putin gave a three-hour interview to several news organizations. He said he had not reached a common position with Bush on a new strategic framework, and he spoke of revising but not terminating the ABM treaty. He was skeptical about the need for ballistic missile defenses to counter rogue states, such as North Korea. He emphasized the need for America and Russia to work together, including cooperation in developing ballistic missile defense. To show that he had options to defeat missile defense, he mentioned the possibility of uploading Russian missiles to carry more than one warhead. Hardly a ringing endorsement of Bush's vision, Putin's comments made it very clear that he wanted restraints on ballistic missile defense, and if ballistic missile defense went forward, he wanted Russia to benefit from it in tangible ways.

Bush traveled to Europe again in July for a meeting of the Group of Eight in Genoa. Again he and President Putin discussed nuclear matters. At a joint press conference on July 22, Putin said he agreed with Bush's position that there should be further cuts in offensive nuclear forces. He expressed the hope that looking at offensive and defensive systems together—as a set—might make it unnecessary to look at the option of MIRVing single-warhead missiles in the event of a unilateral (read U.S.) withdrawal from the ABM treaty.

The third Bush-Putin meeting of 2001 took place in Shanghai on October 21. The world had changed by then. Three thousand people had lost their lives in the attacks on the World Trade Center and the Pentagon on September 11, 2001. The United States had gone to war against al Qaeda forces and the Taliban government in Afghanistan on October 7. Moreover, President Bush had declared a global war on terror. The Bush-Putin meeting resulted in a joint statement on counterterrorism. The conflict in Chechnya was no longer an issue that Bush would raise with Putin, as he had earlier in the year.

The two presidents discussed their meeting at a press conference. Putin spoke eloquently of U.S.-Russian cooperation, describing it as "a partnership which is based upon common values of one civilization." He announced that the two presidents had reaffirmed their mutual intention to reduce strategic offensive weapons. But differences between the two presidents regarding the ABM treaty had not been bridged. President Bush made his view crystal clear: "The events of September the 11th make it clearer than ever that a Cold War ABM treaty that prevents us from defending our people is outdated, and I believe dangerous." President Putin, when asked if he agreed with this assessment, said that the ABM treaty "is an important element of stability in the world." He was prepared to agree that future threats should be analyzed and adequate responses to them discussed between the two sides, but that would require the United States to provide the parameters for the analysis.

Bush and Putin then exchanged thoughts about the nature of the threat that Bush saw, and whether it justified scrapping the ABM treaty. Bush argued that a defense was needed against "terrorists who might acquire weapons of mass destruction to be delivered by ballistic missiles." Putin was not convinced. "But it would be difficult for me," he said, "to agree that some terrorists will be able to capture intercontinental missiles and will be able to use them." No agreement was reached in the third Bush-Putin meeting of 2001 about fundamental issues: how to codify the deeper offensive force reductions that both sides wanted, what was the new threat that would justify "moving beyond the ABM treaty," as Bush liked to put it, and what to do about the treaty. It was probably becoming ever clearer to Putin, however, that Bush was prepared to move with him or, if necessary, without him. With few cards to play, Putin really had no choice in the matter.

Condoleezza Rice made that abundantly clear in a press briefing on November 1. She was asked about a report that "the Russians had indicated to us that there's a lot more that we can do in terms of testing within the framework of the ABM treaty than we think we can do." Her response was that the Russians had been told precisely the kinds of things the United States was thinking of doing, that they should know what the United States was doing as it moved toward limited defenses. She was then bluntly asked whether the Bush administration was willing to accept amending the ABM treaty or whether the administration was determined to scrap it entirely. Rice gave an unambiguous answer: "we need to find a way to achieve two goals. One is to give ourselves maximum flexibility for exploring the technologies that might give us the chance of an effective limit to defense [sic]. The ABM treaty is constraining. The President also made clear that he does not believe that this treaty is appropriate to this period of time, and that we need a new strategic framework with the Russians that is appropriate to this time. This was a treaty with the Soviet Union, signed in 1972."

The questioner persisted in asking whether the question of amending or scrapping the treaty was still under negotiation. Rice said that this was not a matter of negotiation, but of principle. The ABM treaty was problematic not just because of the testing constraints, but also because of the nature of the U.S.-Russia relationship.

Rice also took the occasion to emphasize that the Bush administration had broken with the practice of negotiating strategic nuclear arms control treaties with Moscow. She said that President Bush "believes the restructuring of American nuclear forces and numbers that are consistent with the deterrent mission is a matter of military planning; it's not a matter of negotiation." As she explained it, "the old arms control agreements in which you had to match warhead for warhead, system for system, ignoring geography, ignoring history, ignoring the threats around you, was the old way of thinking about this."

Rice, in these remarks, not only rejected ideas that Putin had publicly endorsed, but that previous American presidents had endorsed since the late 1960s. It was perhaps an overdue response to the end of the Cold War, but it was taken without serious public debate. It was predicated on an assumption that U.S. military planning should exclusively govern how many and what type of nuclear weapons the United States would build and deploy, without reference to the views or interests of other nations. It was a demand for complete autonomy in nuclear affairs, not surprisingly, since Rice had earlier written in a *Foreign Affairs* article that such a thing as an international community was "illusory."

Putin saw advantages in legally binding commitments when the two sides were just emerging from forty years of hostility. But Bush and Rice made it clear that a negotiation about such matters was not on. Putin talked about the value of the ABM treaty in promoting stability. Bush and Rice announced that the treaty was a Cold War relic, a treaty with a country that no longer existed.

Putin's hopes for what might come out of talks with his American counterpart were rapidly fading. The next nail in the coffin of his vision was driven in at the fourth meeting of 2001 between the two presidents. This one took place in Washington and at the president's ranch in Texas. Speaking together at a joint press conference on November 13, the two men explained how the nuclear question was being "resolved" by an agreement to disagree. First, President Bush announced that he had informed Putin that the United States "will reduce our operationally deployed strategic nuclear warheads to a level between 1,700 and 2,200 over the next decade." Second, Bush acknowledged that he and Putin "have different points of view about the ABM treaty, and we will continue dialogue and discussions about the ABM treaty." Putin continued to talk about "a reliable and verifiable agreement on further reductions of the U.S. and Russian weapons," not at all the approach that Bush had in mind. As to the ABM treaty, Bush reiterated that the two nations should move beyond it. He said, in language heard before: "it is a piece of paper that's codified a relationship that no longer exists."

Putin accepted that the U.S.-Russia relationship was not like the U.S.-Soviet relationship. As he stressed in the November 13 press conference: "we intend to dismantle conclusively the vestiges of the Cold War and to develop an entirely new partnership for the long term." But Putin saw the ABM treaty as an element of stability as that long-term partnership developed. It was not, for him, a vestige or relic of the Cold War, and certainly not just a scrap of paper.

The joint declaration issued by the two leaders at the end of their meeting contained language with very far-reaching implications: "The United States and Russia have overcome the legacy of the Cold War. Neither country regards the other as an enemy or threat." This raises the question of why the United States needed 1,700–2,200 operationally deployed nuclear warheads if Russia was not a threat. A nondeployed reserve force of U.S. nuclear weapons should suffice as insurance against a change in the Russian government. The two countries could deal with the other contingencies they face with just a few hundred operationally deployed warheads.

With this optimistic declaration but with deep disagreements set out for the public record, Bush and Putin moved their discussions to the president's ranch near Crawford, Texas. An invitation to the ranch was Bush's way of signaling that the guest was highly regarded by the president and a person of great importance to the United States. Bush said repeatedly that Putin was the first world leader to call him after 9/11, a fact that he genuinely appreciated. Putin was quoted several times by Rice, in a press briefing on November 15, as having said that whatever happened on the missile defense issue, it would be in the context of a substantially changed U.S.-Russian relationship.

Rice had to point out, of course, that Putin still believed the ABM treaty had a certain importance even in the post–Cold War era and that actions taken by the Bush administration to address new ballistic missile threats should be done within the context of the ABM treaty. Despite that, Bush believed he had to move forward with a robust testing program and so would have to abandon the constraints of the ABM treaty. A mood of inevitability began to set in. Putin understood that Bush would denounce the treaty, but he was not willing to acquiesce. Bush had hoped that Putin would accommodate him by agreeing to kill off the treaty in a joint withdrawal, but he was disappointed in this.

Secretary of State Colin Powell traveled to Moscow in early December to follow up on the question of codifying offensive nuclear reductions and to deliver the bad news about the ABM treaty. On the first issue, the idea was to have some kind of an agreement ready for Bush and Putin when they met in Moscow in mid-2002. Powell acknowledged that a treaty was a possibility. But it was apparent by now that the first President Bush's START II treaty was being jettisoned. Subsequent mythology has it that the Russians walked away from the START II treaty. Not so. The thinking of George W. Bush's administration was incompatible with the START II treaty. Rice underscored in her Crawford press briefing that any new U.S.-Russian agreement would not look like the SALT and START treaties.

In Moscow, the Russians reiterated that they were unwilling to abrogate the ABM treaty even though the Americans wanted a joint withdrawal. Bush would have to do that on his own. Foreign Minister Igor Ivanov said that the treaty needed to be preserved because it was "the key element of the entire treaty system of providing or assuring strategic stability in the world." But, said Ivanov, Russia had heard the message and Russian planning would take that into account.

Russia was worried about what China might do to offset a U.S. ballistic missile defense system, since a Chinese offensive buildup would affect Russian defenses. American officials briefed the Chinese government on its planned missile defense program and advised it to maintain the nuclear test moratorium. The Russian military, nonetheless, remained worried. The chief of the Russian General Staff, General Anatoly Kvashnin, said on December 13 that U.S. withdrawal from the ABM treaty "will untie the hands of a series of states and could lead to a new round of the arms race." A closer Russian-Chinese military relationship has been one of the results of this concern.

On December 11, 2001, Bush delivered a speech on national security at the Citadel in South Carolina. He said the 9/11 attacks on the United States showed that America needed to build limited and effective defenses against a missile attack. America, he said, must not be bound to the past, to a treaty written in a different era, for a different enemy. Two days later, on December 13, 2001, in the White House Rose Garden, Bush announced he had, on that day, given formal notice to Russia that the United States of America was withdrawing from the 1972 ABM treaty. He used the familiar arguments in justifying this unilateral action:

- The treaty constrained testing and development programs.
- Russia and the United States were no longer locked in a hostile relationship.
- The greatest threats came from terrorists and rogue states.
- Terrorists and those who support them were seeking a ballistic missile capability.

The president hinted that a treaty on strategic offensive forces might be concluded when he visited Moscow and said that Putin had agreed his decision to withdraw from the ABM treaty would not undermine the new U.S.-Russian relationship or Russian security.

The diplomatic note transmitted by the State Department to Russia, Belarus, Kazakhstan, and Ukraine on December 13 stated: "the United States has decided that extraordinary events related to the subject matter of the Treaty have jeopardized its supreme interests." As provided in Article XV of the treaty, withdrawal would be effective six months from the date of the notice.

Putin responded on the same day with a televised statement to the Russian people. He said that Bush's decision was a mistake. But the decision would not pose a threat to the national security of Russia because Russia possessed an effective system to overcome antimissile defense. "Our country," said Putin, "elected not to accept the insistent proposals on the part of the U.S. to jointly withdraw from the ABM treaty and did everything it could to preserve the treaty." He spoke of the international legal foundation for disarmament and nonproliferation and argued that a legal vacuum should not be allowed in this field. He believed that a legal basis should be given to radical, irreversible, and verifiable cuts in strategic nuclear weapons. He proposed a level of 1,500–2,200 nuclear warheads for each side. And he gave Bush what the president needed by saying: "the present level of bilateral relations between the Russian Federation and the U.S. should not only be preserved but should be used for working out a new framework of strategic relations as soon as possible."

Secretary of State Colin Powell, called upon to defend U.S. abrogation of the treaty in a press briefing on December 13, said that the Russians understood the ballistic missile defense program that the United States was planning would not affect Russian national security. The size and quality of their strategic nuclear offensive capability precluded that. This comment, reflecting Putin's televised comments, showed that a stake has not yet been driven through the heart of the action-reaction mindset in U.S. and Russian relations.

As further evidence of Russian acquiescence in Bush's decision, Powell noted that Putin was still willing to reduce Russian offensive forces to 1,500–2,200 nuclear warheads. For some time it had been evident that Russia could not sustain a strategic offensive force at the level permitted by START II because of obsolescence and the lack of resources to deploy new single-warhead systems rapidly or to build new missile submarines at a rapid rate. The lower numbers were more consistent with Russia's economic realities. The new arrangements would permit Russia to maintain MIRVed missiles and to build new MIRVed systems and so maintain a rough parity with U.S. strategic forces.

President Bush lost no time in telling the American people that he was ready to proceed with the construction of a ballistic missile defense, tested or not. In a public statement on December 17, 2001, Bush said: "I have directed the Secretary of Defense to proceed with fielding an initial set of missile defense capabilities. We plan to begin operating these initial capabilities in 2004 and 2005, and they will include ground-based interceptors, sea-based interceptors, additional Patriot (PAC-3) units, and sensors based on land, at sea, and in space."

The president added an important point, designed to secure international support for his decision. He said that missile defenses would be developed and deployed to be capable of protecting U.S. friends and allies, as well as the United States and its deployed military forces. And, as a clincher, he said that the United States would structure its missile defense program in a manner that would encourage industrial participation by other nations. The latter point was especially interesting to the Russians, and to others. The Russian Foreign Ministry issued a statement on December 18 which, after complaining about the U.S. unilateral withdrawal from the ABM treaty, urged the United States to enhance missile defense cooperation. Progress in that area, however, has been slow in coming during the developmental state. A reluctance to share U.S. technology will have to be overcome if this promise is to be kept.

George W. Bush focused intently during his first year in office on discrediting the idea of U.S.-Russian nuclear weapons agreements, especially the 1972 ABM treaty. He achieved that objective without the need for compromises and with minimal adverse repercussions, either domestically or abroad. The idea that the United States and Russia might accept mutual limitations on their nuclear offensive forces was seen as an unnecessary encumbrance by Bush, who thought that U.S. nuclear weapons forces should be structured entirely independently of international agreements. To all intents and purposes, he had succeeded in this, too, by May 2002. A one-page treaty codifying the operational warhead levels that the United States intended to have by 2012 was quickly negotiated in the spring of 2002. The Treaty of Moscow was signed on May 24, 2002.

New Threats, New Doctrines

In a speech at West Point on June 1, 2002, President Bush said: "America has, and intends to keep, military strengths beyond challenge—thereby making the destabilizing arms races of other eras pointless, and limiting rivalries to trade and other pursuits of peace." These words foreshadowed a key point in his "National Security Strategy of the United States," issued on September 19, 2002: "We must build and maintain our defenses beyond challenge . . . our forces will be strong enough to dissuade potential adversaries from pursuing a military buildup in hopes of surpassing or equaling the power of the United States."

The National Security Strategy is essential for understanding Bush's nuclear weapons policies. It also codified Bush's preventive war thinking. It spoke of "taking anticipatory action to defend ourselves, even if uncertainty remains as to the time and place of the enemy's attack." Recognizing the dangers that lurked in these words, the authors of the National Security Strategy also spoke about integrated intelligence capabilities and working with allies to form a common assessment of the most dangerous threats.

Simply put, at the heart of the Bush strategic doctrine was this: unchallenged military supremacy over any other nation in the world, and anticipatory military action against perceived gathering threats.

Another policy document of 2002 was the "National Strategy to Combat Weapons of Mass Destruction" released in December. It identified some important implementing policies, which included "targeted strategies against hostile states and terrorists" and the right to respond with "overwhelming force—including through resort to all our options—to the use of WMD" (weapons of mass destruction). It became known that "all our options" included nuclear weapons.

Nuclear Nonproliferation

Also essential to understanding President Bush's approach to nuclear weapons are three basic premises that have permeated his administration's nonproliferation policy:

- Nuclear weapons are not the fundamental problem; they become a major security problem when they get into the hands of rogue states or terrorist groups.
- Global norms have their place, but the most effective means of countering proliferation are through coalitions of democracies, using military force if necessary.
- Restraints on the ability of the United States and other democratic nations to maintain nuclear forces that they alone deem necessary for their security should be avoided.

This thinking has freed the administration to focus intensely on certain key countries which pose a proliferation threat. This is an advantage, provided incentives are included as well as coercive measures. The disadvantage is that the possession of nuclear weapons may be seen as quite normal and acceptable, unless they happen to belong to an irresponsible foe.

Selectivity in the application of nonproliferation norms and policies actually encourages proliferation. It drives potential proliferators to acquire nuclear weapons, either to deter the United States, like North Korea, or because there are no sanctions against proliferation, in the case of friends of the United States, like India. And there is also no presumption that the nuclear-weapon states have obligations to scale back their nuclear weapons to levels lower than they have unilaterally determined they need. A debate at the United Nations in New York in the spring of 2004 in the committee preparing for the 2005 review conference of the nonproliferation treaty essentially broke down over the issue of reciprocal obligations between the nuclear-weapon and non-nuclear-weapon states. The May 2005 review conference of the nonproliferation treaty also ran into a dead-end over the same issue. And it proved impossible, for essentially the same reason, to include anything on arms control and nonproliferation in the September 2005 summit declaration on new challenges for the United Nations. The U.N. secretary general called this a "disgrace."

Remnants of the older antiproliferation structure, including the START I treaty and the nonproliferation treaty itself, with all its supporting arrangements, remain in place. President Bush can be credited with having added several new methods of dealing with nuclear weapons proliferation. The newer parts of the regime include an emphasis on preventive war, now seen as quite circumscribed in its utility as a nonproliferation tool. The main elements of the Bush system are as follows:

- A gentlemen's agreement—the Treaty of Moscow—which provides that by 2012 the United States and Russia will reduce to 1,700–2,200 deployed warheads. That number is the same as the number President Bush had previously declared the United States planned to deploy. The number does not have to be reached until the year the treaty expires—2012—and there is no schedule for reductions. Nuclear warheads and missiles do not have to be eliminated. The United States will retain a few thousand additional warheads as a hedge against renewed competition with the Soviet Union. The treaty can be revoked on ninety days notice. The impact of this treaty on nuclear proliferation has been minimal.
- A strategic doctrine that calls for anticipatory actions against "gathering threats," which include the potential acquisition of weapons of mass destruction by hostile states. The model for the implementation of this doctrine is, of course, Iraq but President Bush has said that the military option remains on the table in other cases, too.
- A rudimentary ballistic missile defense system being deployed in Alaska.
- A "Proliferation Security Initiative" consisting of cooperation with a number of countries in interdicting shipments of materials related to proliferation of weapons of mass destruction. This initiative enjoyed its greatest success in preventing a shipment of centrifuge parts from reaching Libya.
- A Global Partnership against Proliferation that has committed a group of countries to providing assistance to Russia and others for the purposes of tightening control over nuclear materials.

- Multilateral efforts in North Korea and Iran to pressure those governments to roll back their nuclear weapons programs.
- A diplomatic campaign announced by the president on February 11, 2004, the centerpiece of which seeks to block countries from possessing all the capabilities they need to build nuclear weapons. The key element is a moratorium on new uranium enrichment facilities and plutonium separation plants. This would plug a loophole in the nonproliferation treaty.
- A U.N. Security Council Resolution adopted in May 2004 (UNSC 1540) designed to criminalize certain transactions in weapons of mass destruction and to assist nations in controlling nuclear materials.
- A continuing moratorium on nuclear weapons testing, in place, in the case of the United States, since 1992.
- A Global Threat Reduction Initiative, designed to remove highly enriched uranium from research facilities in several countries.

Targeted strategies were developed against Iraq, Iran, Libya, and North Korea. Of these, Iraq was the weakest example of a "gathering threat." In the other cases the Bush administration opted for diplomacy and international cooperation. China was a major player in negotiations with North Korea. Britain, France, and Germany took the lead in dealing with Iran. The Iraq and North Korea cases will be discussed later in this chapter. At this writing, Iran still is positioning itself to become a nuclear-weapon state, under the guise of a peaceful nuclear energy program. But Libya was a great success for the administration. Hoping to bring economic benefits to his country, Muammar Qadaffi quietly negotiated with British and American intelligence officials to terminate all his programs for developing weapons of mass destruction.

The framework for post–Cold War nuclear arms restraint was overhauled by President Bush, with some older elements dropped and new elements added. Unilateralism is not an accurate description of the changes in U.S. nonproliferation policy. Some important new elements are multilateral: the Proliferation Security Initiative, a program for intercepting illicit shipments of weapons materials, and U.N. Security Council Resolution 1540, a cooperative program to strengthen the legal regime governing handling of nuclear materials and improve controls. The end of the Cold War and the collapse of the Soviet Union required changes in American nuclear policies and in those of other nations. New forms of constraints on nuclear weapons became necessary to meet changing circumstances. A clear focus on specific regional proliferation problems was very much needed. President Bush wrote a new set of rules. Only time can answer whether his approach will succeed in blocking a rapid expansion in the number of nuclear-weapon states.

A New Threat Paradigm

Two important shifts in U.S. thinking about nuclear threats and how to deal with them took place in the Bush administration. First, the focus of presidential decision-making moved from the superpower relationship to the acquisition of nuclear weapons by rogue states and terrorists. Second, preventive war resurfaced as a plausible means of dealing with gathering nuclear threats. The first of these two shifts in emphasis is likely to remain a top priority for future presidents. In the 2004 presidential campaign, Bush and his Democratic opponent Senator John Kerry agreed on this much. Some of these changes had started in the presidencies of George H. W. Bush and Bill Clinton in response to the end of the Cold War and new threats of nuclear proliferation. Clinton, for example, focused quite a lot of attention on North Korea, and his biggest accomplishment in the Russian relationship was preventing nuclear proliferation, not the traditional strategic arms agreements. But the definitive change in emphasis was made by George W. Bush. The changed paradigm was most vividly illustrated in the administration's treatment of an alleged nuclear weapons program in Iraq as a *casus belli.*

The attacks on the World Trade Center and the Pentagon on September 11, 2001, redefined the Bush presidency. From that point forward, the president would be preoccupied with a global war on terror. The White House and Pentagon shifted their policy focus to Iraq, a nation that senior administration officials saw as a potential source of weapons of mass destruction for terrorist organizations. Vladimir Putin was Bush's reluctant partner in demolishing the old order in nuclear affairs. British prime minister Tony Blair became Bush's more than willing partner in demolishing the regime of Saddam Hussein.

This story begins with a meeting between President Bush and Prime Minister Blair in April 2002. In a joint news conference in Crawford, Texas, on April 6, Bush talked about Saddam Hussein's use of chemical weapons against his own people. He then bluntly said he had told the prime minister that "the policy of my government is the removal of Saddam and all the options are on the table." Asked whether Bush had convinced him of the need for military action against Iraq, Blair finessed the question. But he said that the threat of weapons of mass destruction was real: "the threat exists and we have to deal with it, that seems to me a matter of plain common sense." He added: "we know he has been developing these weapons." And so, by the spring of 2002, Bush had committed to removing Saddam Hussein, by force if necessary, and he had an essential ally, lending credibility to the claim that Saddam Hussein had or was developing weapons of mass destruction. That assumption became a part of the public dialogue and was rarely questioned.

During the summer of 2002, debate raged within the administration over whether congressional and U.N. approval should be sought to disarm Saddam Hussein. Speaking at the Veterans of Foreign Wars Convention on August 26, Vice President Cheney suggested that dictators might obtain weapons of mass destruction and share them with terrorists, a scenario think tanks had worried about for years. He said that Saddam Hussein was continuing to pursue the nuclear program he had started years before. "But we now know," he stated, "that Saddam has resumed his efforts to acquire nuclear weapons." He cited Iraqi defectors as sources for this charge, including Saddam Hussein's son-in-law. Cheney's bottom line was this: "Many of us are convinced that Saddam will acquire nuclear weapons fairly soon." Cheney said that Americans would be greeted with joy in the streets of Iraqi cities and Arab extremists would have to rethink their strategy of jihad. He also raised the classic dilemma of preventive war. If it is not certain that an adversary has a nuclear weapon is an attack justified? But can an attack be made after it is clear the adversary does possess nuclear weapons? Cheney put it this way: "many of those who now argue that we should act only if he gets a nuclear weapon, would then turn around and say that we cannot act because he has a nuclear weapon." The Bush-Cheney public campaign in 2002 was an effort, largely successful, to provide an answer to this dilemma.

On September 7, Blair and Bush talked briefly with the press after meeting at Camp David. Blair implied that Saddam Hussein's government was reactivating nuclear weapons sites in Iraq: "we know that they were trying to develop nuclear weapons capability . . . the one thing that no one can deny is that Saddam Hussein is in breach of the United Nations resolutions on weapons of mass destruction—that is, chemical, biological, nuclear weapons."

When asked if he would seek a U.N. resolution prior to any action against Iraq, Bush replied that he would give a speech in a few days. The speech was delivered to the General Assembly of the United Nations in New York on September 12, 2002. Bush said that Iraq retained the physical infrastructure to build a nuclear weapon and alleged that Iraq had made several attempts to buy high-strength aluminum tubes used to enrich uranium. Given Saddam Hussein's record of deception, the president suggested that the first time the world might be completely certain that he had a nuclear weapon would be when he used one. Bush indicated he would work with the U.N. Security

Council for the necessary resolutions to hold Iraq to account, but he made clear at a press opportunity the next morning that he expected the U.S. Congress to endorse military action in Iraq without waiting for a U.N. resolution.

The president continued his steady drumbeat of suggestions that Saddam Hussein was close to acquiring nuclear weapons. In his radio address to the nation on September 14, he said: "today Saddam Hussein has the scientists and infrastructure for a nuclear weapons program, and has illicitly sought to purchase the equipment needed to enrich uranium for a nuclear weapon. Should his regime acquire fissile material, it would be able to build a nuclear weapon within a year."

Bush sent to the Congress on September 19 proposed language for a congressional resolution on Iraq. He billed it as a resolution that would help him keep the peace. In a press opportunity with Secretary of State Colin Powell that morning, he said that the leadership in Congress had recognized that Congress should act before the 2002 midterm elections. Asked if the resolution would give him the authorization to use force, he said it would. But, he repeated: "It's a chance for Congress to say, we support the administration's ability to keep the peace. That's what this is all about." And he went on to say that regime change was the policy of the U.S. government.

Bush continued to pressure Congress with arguments that Iraq was in the process of acquiring nuclear weapons and had links to terrorist organizations. It was a powerful argument for a nation that had gone through the traumatic experience of a major terrorist attack only a year earlier. The argument that a radical regime armed with nuclear weapons could pass one to al Qaeda was very persuasive, even though Saddam Hussein and Osama bin Laden had very few common interests.

Congressional leaders met with Bush in the White House on the morning of September 26, having made substantial progress toward a resolution authorizing force against Iraq. In Rose Garden remarks after the meeting, Bush said: "The [Iraqi] regime has long-standing and continuing ties to terrorist organizations. And there are al Qaeda terrorists inside Iraq. The regime is seeking a nuclear bomb, and with fissile material, could build one within a year. . . . Each passing day could be the one on which the Iraqi regime gives anthrax or VX-nerve gas—or some day a nuclear weapon to a terrorist ally."

President Bush continued his public campaign to prepare Americans for war while the Congress debated the Iraq resolutions. In a closely reasoned speech on October 7, in Cincinnati, linking Saddam Hussein to al Qaeda and speaking in detail of Hussein's programs for building weapons of mass destruction, Bush said: "the evidence indicates that Iraq is reconstituting its nuclear weapons program." To support that claim, he stated: "Satellite photographs reveal that Iraq is rebuilding facilities at sites that have been part of its nuclear program in the past. Iraq has attempted to purchase high-strength aluminum tubes and other equipment needed for gas centrifuges, which are used to enrich uranium for nuclear weapons."

He said that the U.N. inspections approach had not worked in the past and that Saddam Hussein "is moving ever closer to developing a nuclear weapon." But he expressed the hope—though not the expectation—that Saddam Hussein might finally cooperate with the United Nations. And he said again that congressional approval of the Iraq resolution "does not mean that military action is imminent or unavoidable." On October 16, 2002, President Bush signed that resolution, passed the day before by substantial votes in both houses of Congress.

Also in October 2002, the CIA released to the public an unclassified National Intelligence Estimate that had helped to shape opinions in Congress. It said that "most analysts assess Iraq is reconstituting its nuclear weapons program." It added that "how quickly Iraq will obtain its first nuclear weapon depends on when it acquires sufficient weapons-grade fissile material." The latter was a statement of the obvious, but it conveyed the sense that events were moving in the direction of a nuclear-armed Iraq. It was a warning that most politicians would find hard to dismiss. Extrapolating from a disputed estimate about the purpose of Iraq's attempt to acquire aluminum tubes, the estimate theorized that "based on tubes of the size Iraq is trying to acquire, a few tens of thousands of centrifuges would be capable of producing enough highly enriched uranium for a couple of weapons per year." The estimate also stated that "Baghdad may have acquired uranium enrichment capabilities that could shorten substantially the amount of time necessary to make a nuclear weapon." It was learned later that Pakistani scientist A. Q. Khan had tried to sell centrifuge components to Iraq but that the deal had never materialized.

The Department of State, as well as the Department of Energy, disagreed with the estimate on key points, but it became Colin Powell's task to persuade the U.N. Security Council to adopt a resolution requiring Iraq to disarm or, as Bush put it, to be disarmed by the United States and others. Powell was highly successful in this. There was a great deal of debate regarding the use of force and whether this resolution should authorize the use of force if Saddam Hussein failed to comply with its requirements. The Bush administration, worried about delays and obfuscation, hoped for one resolution. But in the end, it was agreed that there was no automaticity in the resolution. The view of most Security Council members was that if force were to be authorized, a second resolution would be required.

The Bush administration insisted on extensive rights of access for U.N. inspectors. The U.N. Monitoring, Verification, and Inspection Commission (UNMOVIC) and the International Atomic Energy Agency (IAEA) should be able to go anywhere, any time. Members of the Security Council agreed. The draft resolution required an unprecedented degree of privilege and access for the inspectors. The key finding in the resolution was that "Iraq has been and remains in material breach of its obligations under relevant resolutions, including resolution 687 (1991), in particular through Iraq's failure to cooperate with United Nations inspectors and the IAEA, and to complete the actions required under paragraphs 8 to 13 of resolution 687 (1991)."

Paragraphs 8–13 of UNSC resolution 687 (1991) referred to Iraq's obligation to eliminate all weapons of mass destruction and long-range missiles. Included in the list were nuclear weapons and nuclear-weapons-usable materials. The Security Council was prepared to accept the Bush administration's repeated charges about Iraqi weapons of mass destruction.

The Security Council adopted a very tough resolution, 1441 (2002), on November 8, 2002. All members voted for it, a remarkable achievement. It was a triumph for the diplomacy of the Bush administration. The resolution required a comprehensive report from the Iraq government on its weapons programs in thirty days. It also required the return of U.N. inspectors to Iraq. Two different teams were set up: UNMOVIC was to search for chemical and biological weapons programs, and the IAEA was to look for nuclear weapons programs. Now Hans Blix, director of UNMOVIC, and Mohamed ElBaradei, director general of the IAEA, had enormous authority in their hands to search for evidence of weapons of mass destruction throughout Iraq.

Immediately after the vote, President Bush appeared in the White House Rose Garden to applaud the action and underscore what he expected to happen next. He made it clear that he would not need a second U.N. resolution to justify an attack on Iraq if Saddam Hussein failed to comply with the resolution just passed: "The United States has agreed to discuss any material breach with the Security Council, but without jeopardizing our freedom of action to defend our country. If Iraq fails to fully comply, the United States and other nations will disarm Saddam Hussein." Again, Bush suggested that Iraq was moving toward a nuclear weapons capability: "If Iraq's dictator is permitted to acquire nuclear weapons, he could resume his pattern of intimidation and conquest and dictate the future of a vital region."

The president told Blix and ElBaradei that the United States would support them fully, and the inspectors entered Iraq in November 2002 after an absence of four years. In their subsequent interim reports to the Security Council, Blix and ElBaradei reported that Iraq had not given full cooperation but the inspection teams had visited many sites and so far had found no evidence of stockpiles of weapons of mass destruction. There was no "smoking gun," as Blix put it, although he seemed to think there was more to be found. As the Bush administration saw it, the U.N. inspectors had not been successful in penetrating Saddam Hussein's massive campaign of deception. Another concern was that allowing the inspectors to carry on indefinitely would undercut the sense of urgency which the administration thought the circumstances warranted.

The Iraqi government's report was submitted in December and was promptly denounced by the Bush administration. It appeared to be a pastiche of previous reports and failed to clear up any questions about missing items. Writing in the *New York Times* on January 23, 2003, the national security adviser, Condoleezza Rice, branded Iraq's report to the U.N., which denied that it had weapons of mass destruction, "a 12,200-page lie." She complained that "the declaration fails to account for or explain Iraq's efforts to get uranium from abroad," a reference to the later discredited story about Iraq's dealings with Niger. Rice concluded that Iraq had an obligation to provide answers to many questions about its nuclear, chemical, and biological weapons programs and arsenals and "it is failing in spectacular fashion."

On January 28, 2003, President Bush delivered his State of the Union Address and made his case for war against Iraq. The most famous sixteen words, later disavowed by the administration, were these: "The British government has learned that Saddam Hussein recently sought significant quantities of uranium from Africa." Bush also said: "from three Iraqi defectors we know that Iraq, in the late 1990s, had several mobile biological weapons labs." This had been a disputed estimate within the intelligence community and was later discredited.

A week later, Prime Minister Blair visited Bush in Washington to sort out their Iraq policies. An issue before them was whether to seek a second U.N. resolution, reflecting Saddam Hussein's failure to cooperate. Bush thought that the earlier U.N. resolution, 1441, provided all the authority needed, but he ultimately agreed to try for a second one. In a joint press conference on January 31, 2003, Bush mentioned "al Qaeda links, links that really do portend a danger for America and for Great Britain." He added: "Saddam Hussein would like nothing more than to use a terrorist network to attack and to kill and leave no fingerprints behind."

"The strategic view of America changed after September the 11th," Bush declared, and "we must deal with threats before they hurt the American people again." But when asked if he thought there was a direct link between Saddam Hussein and the September 11 attacks, Bush said: "I can't make that claim."

After the IAEA and UNMOVIC inspectors had submitted their report to the U.N. Security Council, Saddam Hussein invited the U.N. inspectors to return to Baghdad for consultations. Both Bush and Blair saw this as nothing more than playing for time. In the January 31 press conference, Blair said: "they want to play the same games as they've been playing all the way through" but "they have to disarm." Blair was clear: "if they don't do it through the U.N. route, then they will have to be disarmed by force."

In an effort to rally support for a second Security Council resolution authorizing the use of force against Iraq, Secretary Powell delivered a massive indictment of Saddam Hussein's violations of previous U.N. resolutions. Speaking on February 5, 2003, he marshaled the evidence to show that Saddam Hussein was engaged in programs to develop and make weapons of mass destruction, including a nuclear weapons program. He said: "every statement I make today is backed by sources, solid sources. These are not assertions. What we are giving you are facts and conclusions based on solid intelligence."

It was a masterful presentation and was greeted with praise by the American media. One of Powell's central points was that Iraq was trying to buy aluminum tubes for use in centrifuges to enrich uranium. "There is no doubt in my mind," said Powell, "these illicit procurement efforts show that Saddam Hussein is very much focused on putting in place the key missing pieces from his nuclear weapons program, the ability to produce fissile material." Experts concluded later that the aluminum tubes were for another purpose, accepting the estimate that Powell's own Bureau of Intelligence and Research had made throughout the debate.

Bush's agreement to try for a second U.N. resolution was based on Tony Blair's judgment that such authorization was politically necessary in Britain. The majority of the Security Council, however, wanted to give the inspectors more time. The votes were not there for a resolution authorizing force. Even close friends of the United States, including Canada and Mexico, were opposed. The moral support which a U.N. Security Council resolution would have provided was not available to the "coalition of the willing" that was preparing to go to war.

Speaking from the White House on March 17, 2003, Bush demanded that Saddam Hussein and his sons leave Iraq within forty-eight hours or face military action. The president justified this decision by saying that "intelligence gathered by this and other governments leaves no doubt that the Iraq regime continues to possess and conceal some of the most lethal weapons ever devised."

The war began on March 19, 2003. That evening, President Bush spoke to the nation from the Oval Office. His message was one that Americans, and especially American troops and their families, accepted whole-heartedly:

"The people of the United States and our friends and allies will not live at the mercy of an outlaw regime that threatens the peace with weapons of mass murder. We will meet that threat now, with our Army, Air Force, Navy, Coast Guard and Marines, so that we do not have to meet it later with armies of fire fighters and police and doctors on the streets of our cities."

Bush and Blair met again and gave the world their assessment of the campaign in Iraq in a joint "press availability" on March 27. The leaders stressed that Iraqi generals who launched any weapons of mass destruction would be tried as war criminals. It was left to Blair to make the case that Saddam Hussein had weapons of mass destruction. "The dominant security threat of our time," he said, "is the combination of weapons of mass destruction in the hands of unstable, repressive states and terrorist groups." Blair said that the brutality of the regime was not the reason for initiating the war against Iraq, although Bush already had said it was. "That," he said, "is in relation to weapons of mass destruction."

The military triumph of American and allied forces—mainly British, but also Dutch, Australians, and others—was complete. On May 1, Bush celebrated the conquest by flying to the carrier *Abraham Lincoln* where a banner proclaimed "Mission Accomplished." But by July, the Iraqi insurgency had begun to flex its muscles. American troops went on the offensive against these "dead-enders," as Defense Secretary Rumsfeld called them. Questions were beginning to be asked, especially in Britain, about why weapons of mass destruction had not yet been found.

Blair visited Washington again and spoke to a joint session of Congress on July 17. In a joint press conference afterward, Bush remarked: "Saddam Hussein produced and possessed chemical and biological weapons and was trying to reconstitute his nuclear weapons program." Blair repeated his warning about the dangers posed by terrorism and weapons of mass destruction. The first question from the press was about Bush's State of the Union message in which he had cited British intelligence as reporting that Iraq was trying to buy uranium from an African country. Bush did not answer that question but said once again that Saddam Hussein possessed chemical and biological weapons. "I strongly believe," Bush said, "he was trying to reconstitute his nuclear weapons program."

Blair stood behind the British report: "The British intelligence that we had we believe is genuine." He mentioned that Iraq, in the 1980s, had purchased 270 tons of uranium from Niger. Both Blair and Bush defended the intelligence they were given about Iraq's weapons of mass destruction. Blair said that "the proposition that actually he [Saddam Hussein] was not developing such weapons and such programs rests on this rather extraordinary proposition that . . . [he] voluntarily destroyed them but just didn't tell any-one." That, in fact, appears to be exactly what happened.

On July 31, Condoleezza Rice appeared on Jim Lehrer's *News Hour*, where she had to deal with charges that President Bush made a serious misstate-ment in his State of the Union message. The issue had been boiling for weeks and Rice's deputy, Stephen Hadley, admitted that the CIA had warned the White House twice not to include a reference to Iraq's purchase of uranium from an African nation in presidential speeches. CIA Director George Tenet took the blame for not pressing the case forcefully enough.

In the *News Hour* interview, Rice said that "five of the six intelligence agencies believed that he [Saddam Hussein] had an active program of recon-stitution of his nuclear weapons program." It happened that the dissenting intelligence agency was the State Department. Pointing to all of the evi-dence presented in the National Intelligence Estimate which suggested that Iraq had an active nuclear weapons program, Rice said: "left unchecked he might be able to have a nuclear weapon by the end of the decade." She con-cluded: "that is the judgment on which the president was going."

Rice drew on the authority and reputation of the U.S. intelligence com-munity to support her argument: "the intelligence case against Saddam Hus-sein and his weapons of mass destruction is a broad and deep case from mul-tiple sources over twelve years." She added: "we are now in Iraq in a way that we will be able to find out precisely what the case was here with his weapons of mass destruction program." She praised David Kay, the American official who was now in charge of finding Iraqi weapons of mass destruction. Her bot-tom line was: "we will know precisely what happened to Saddam Hussein's weapons of mass destruction." Asked if the idea that Saddam Hussein was on the verge of reconstituting a nuclear weapons program was supportable in retrospect, Rice answered: "It's absolutely supportable."

On that same day, July 31, Condoleezza Rice spoke with ZDF German tel-evision and reiterated that, in twenty years of experience, some of the strongest cases she had seen confirmed that Saddam Hussein was trying to re-constitute his nuclear program. She said: "nobody doubted that he had weapons of mass destruction." This was not just a question of American cred-ibility: "everyone shared the view that this was a country that had weapons of mass destruction."

Rice spoke in the same vein several weeks later when weapons of mass de-struction had not yet been found in Iraq. Briefing the press on September 22, she reiterated that David Kay had an orderly process under way. "Let me be very clear," she said, "what we find there will establish precisely what was go-ing on with Iraq's programs." Defending the administration's decision to invade Iraq, she said: "there was nobody who knew anything about Iraq who believed that Saddam Hussein had destroyed all of his weapons of mass destruction, that he simply didn't have any."

The president was about to begin a state visit to Britain when David Frost of BBC-TV interviewed him on November 17. Frost asked the president if he thought that he had been the victim of an intelligence failure. "Not at all," said Bush, and repeated that David Kay had found evidence which meant that Saddam Hussein was in material breach of Resolution 1441. In his Whitehall Palace speech in London on November 19, Bush said: "The greatest threat of our age is nuclear, chemical, or biological weapons in the hands of terrorists, and the dictators who aid them." This statement of the drastically altered threat perception in the United States since Cold War days is likely to dominate strategic thinking for a long time to come.

President Bush had a good December. American troops captured Saddam Hussein and the president's favorable ratings in public opinion polls shot up. Optimism about Iraq was at its height. He had some domestic legislative victories as well. In a press conference on December 15, 2003, Bush remarked: "Had David Kay been the lead inspector, and had done the work that he did prior to our removal of Saddam, he would have reported back to the U.N. Security Council that Saddam was, in fact, in breach of the Council resolutions that were passed."

Not long after the president voiced that opinion, David Kay resigned his post. In an interview to Reuters on January 23, 2004, he dropped a political bombshell. "I don't think they existed," Kay said, referring to the weapons of mass destruction that Iraq was supposed to have. Testifying before the Senate Armed Services Committee on January 28, 2004, Kay said: "we were almost all wrong, and I certainly include myself here." But he also said that "Iraq was in clear violation of the terms of Resolution 1441."

A few days later, CIA Director Tenet responded to the growing criticism of the intelligence on which the Bush administration said it had depended. At Georgetown University, on February 5, 2004, Tenet said that the analysts had never spoken of an "imminent" threat. As regards nuclear weapons, Tenet said, "We do not know if any reconstitution efforts had begun, but we may have overestimated the progress Saddam was making."

The American survey team in Iraq never found any evidence that Saddam Hussein had been "reconstituting" Iraq's nuclear weapons program. In an interview broadcast on September 9, 2005, General Powell was asked if his presentation to the U.N. would tarnish his reputation. "Of course it will," he said, "it's a blot . . . it was painful. It's painful now." According to President Bush in a speech on December 18, 2005, "we found some capacity to restart programs to produce weapons of mass destruction, but we did not find those weapons." Bush stated that "much of the intelligence turned out to be wrong. And as your president, I am responsible for the decision to go into Iraq."

The North Korea Case

North Korea is a case where the Bush administration has been directly involved in negotiations through a multilateral mechanism—the Six-party Talks. Hosted by China, the other participants are Japan, Russia, North and South Korea, and the United States. When the Clinton administration left office, its legacy was a 1994 Agreed Framework that froze North Korea's plutonium-producing programs. Talks had begun about halting North Korean long-range missile programs. Secretary of State Albright had visited the North Korean leader, Kim Jong Il, in Pyongyang, and Clinton himself had briefly considered a visit.

Secretary of State Colin Powell had expected to resume negotiations with North Korea during the first year of the Bush administration. That was not to be. He was publicly overruled by the White House. A subsequent policy review dragged on well into 2002. Not until October of that year did Assistant Secretary of State Jim Kelly meet with North Korean representatives to discuss Washington's thinking. The talks broke down immediately when Kelly told the North Koreans that there was evidence that North Korea was building a uranium enrichment facility. After seemingly admitting this, the North Korean government then denied it.

At this point, the 1994 Agreed Framework was renounced by both sides. North Korea ejected the IAEA inspectors who had been monitoring the plutonium freeze and declared that the 8,000 fuel rods under their supervision would be reprocessed to extract plutonium. North Korea also declared that it had a nuclear deterrent. Intelligence is quite uncertain about what this means, but it is likely North Korea has enough plutonium for a handful of nuclear weapons.

In August 2003, the Six-Party Talks began in Beijing. The United States and North Koreans were far apart in their initial negotiating positions. The Americans asked for a commitment to complete, verifiable, and irreversible dismantlement of the North Korean nuclear weapons program before any concessions could be given. The North Koreans insisted on simultaneity: word for word, action for action. The U.S. position was modified in June 2004 to allow for other participants in the talks to provide energy assistance to North Korea during a short preparatory period while plans were being drawn up to begin the dismantlement process.

At that point North Korea's leader, Kim Jong Il, decided to suspend the talks until after the U.S. elections. They were resumed a year later. During the recess, harsh comments were made on both sides about each other's character and intentions. But when the talks resumed in July 2005, Condoleezza Rice, now the secretary of state, gave her chief negotiator more tactical leeway than Colin Powell had been able to give his negotiator.

A series of well-publicized bilateral U.S.-North Korean discussions took place within the framework of the Six-Party Talks. Furthermore, South Korea announced that it would supply North Korea with energy from an electrical grid built in South Korea and connected with the North. The negotiators reached an agreement on a set of principles, including denuclearization of the Korean peninsula, on September 19, 2005. These principles, if implemented, could lead to a comprehensive settlement, but no progress had been made at this writing.

The North Korea experience offers several lessons. The most important is that the preventive war doctrine has very limited application. A military attack on North Korea could result in hundreds of thousands, possibly millions, of fatalities. A limited, pinpoint attack on North Korea's nuclear facilities would not be likely to succeed, since the locations of all North Korean nuclear facilities are not known.

A second lesson is that nuclear proliferation issues have to be dealt with in a broad political and economic context. The North Korean weapons program is likely to be definitively solved only when the Korean War, which was halted with an armistice in 1953, is brought to a final conclusion. This would mean some kind of broad political settlement and normal economic relations between North and South Korea.

A third lesson is that "regime change" is not the best approach to preventing proliferation. This was thought to be necessary in Iraq but proved not to be so. It has not worked in North Korea, where Kim Jong Il still holds power. A corollary of this lesson is that any administration will have difficulties in securing its nonproliferation goals if it cannot bring itself to decide between the opposed methods of regime change or engagement. American negotiators were hobbled for the first five years of the Bush presidency because the administration was deeply divided on this issue. And in the meantime, North Korea steadily moved toward the status of a full-fledged nuclear power.

Reflections

International solidarity was never more in evidence than in the reaction of ordinary people all over the world to the September 11, 2001, terrorist attacks on New York and Washington. It was an unprecedented display of unity and sympathy. For the first time, NATO invoked Article V of the North Atlantic Treaty, declaring that the attack on the United States was an attack on all members of the alliance.

That mood of "all for one and one for all" quickly dissipated because the Bush administration's foreign policy is based on a conviction that the defense of American interests is best served by retaining the freedom to act, unfettered by other obligations. Limited, temporary coalitions, rather than entangling alliances, are seen as the best way to achieve American aims in the external realm. America's friends see in this a departure from the America they knew, a nation that pursued a foreign policy based on norms and rules, and steadiness in commitments.

In its second term, the Bush administration appeared to give more weight to older values recognizing, perhaps, that efforts to alter the American style in foreign affairs will not ring true, at home or abroad, and will ultimately fail. The current struggle with terrorism pits all legitimate governments against shadowy conspiracies. The international community is facing a new medievalism in the form of privately directed, large-scale violence coupled with a fealty to a movement that transcends frontiers. This struggle is a fundamental clash between competing principles, between states and transnational militancy. If the states fail to act together to uphold the constraints imposed by international law and custom, the terrorists will win.

Note

1. All quotations attributed to the president and the vice president are from the White House website. Others' quotations are available from the various news and government information sources on the Internet.

~

Afterword

During most of the Cold War years, nuclear weapons dominated international relations. They were central to the bipolar structure at the heart of the global order of that era. The United States and the Soviet Union were usually called the "nuclear armed" superpowers. In their hands, quite literally, rested the fate of civilization, and this was perceived to be the case by the public around the world. The impact that nuclear weapons had on American life from the late 1940s to the mid-1960s, and even into the early 1980s, is hard to overstate.

The impact of nuclear weapons on political thought and cultural life is minimal today in the United States except in historical terms. The play *Copenhagen*, a portrayal of Werner von Heisenberg and Niels Bohr, is a fascinating psychodrama but has no policy meaning for modern times. Its impact is far different from that of *On the Beach* and *Dr. Strangelove*, films of an altogether different epoch. Nuclear weapons still matter, in ways that defy the imagination. But American thinking about them has changed.

This change carries serious consequences for the United States, and for other countries, if the collective memory fails to retain the lessons of the past. Nuclear weapons impelled the United States and the Soviet Union to work out rules of behavior, both formal and tacit, to guide their conduct and required their governments to establish a special relationship between them. If one theme runs through this history of how American presidents managed their responsibilities, it is their search for norms and rules of the road in the nuclear age.

Franklin Roosevelt believed that international cooperation was as necessary in the field of nuclear weaponry as in any other issue of war and peace. He accepted limits on U.S. unilateral behavior in the agreements with Winston Churchill. He was intrigued by the idea brought to him by Niels Bohr that the Soviet Union should be approached sooner rather than later to head off a nuclear arms race. His most senior advisers, especially the scientists, were concerned about postwar control of atomic energy and told him so. He finally decided that close cooperation with a country that shared common values, Great Britain, was the correct policy. Roosevelt did not live to see the Manhattan Project come to fruition with the world's first nuclear explosion in the New Mexico desert sixty years ago. How he would have reacted to the effects of the two American nuclear weapons dropped on Japan in August 1945—or even whether he would have agreed to their use in this way—is unknowable.

We do know how the U.S. government under Harry Truman's leadership behaved in the years immediately following the wartime use of two atomic bombs. Congress insisted on civilian control of atomic energy and cut off all weapons cooperation with the British, in the hope of maintaining an American monopoly. Truman decided to begin negotiations with the Soviet Union to bring all atomic enterprises under international control. The plan his administration brought to the table was so far-reaching that its negotiability was always in doubt. But they gave it a try. The Korean War, McCarthyism, crises in Europe, and Stalin himself made negotiations impossible.

Within two years of Stalin's death in 1953, Eisenhower was probing for ways to begin disarmament negotiations with Moscow. Eisenhower did not begin the tradition of trying to negotiate with America's most powerful and ideologically hostile adversary, but his enormous reputation gave it legitimacy. He provided the impetus for the first nuclear agreements with the Soviet Union: the creation of the International Atomic Energy Agency and the limited nuclear test ban treaty. He did these things because he saw the atomic bomb as a weapon that had made war unthinkable as a way of pursuing national goals. He also expected that the confrontation with the Soviet Union would go on for a very long time, and he knew that ways must be found to permit Russians and Americans, whatever their differences, to go on living together in the same world.

Kennedy followed this tradition by concluding, in 1963, a limited test ban treaty along lines first proposed by Eisenhower. His handling of the Cuban Missile Crisis served to reinforce the notion that nuclear weapons were too dangerous to use or to trifle with in futile attempts to gain an advantage.

Johnson laid the groundwork for strategic nuclear arms agreements with the Soviet Union. He concluded the nuclear nonproliferation treaty that has been a bulwark against the spread of nuclear weapons capabilities ever since.

Nixon signed the antiballistic missile (ABM) treaty and SALT I interim agreement in 1972, the first agreements to limit U.S. and Soviet strategic nuclear arms. Ford and Soviet leader Brezhnev agreed on the outlines of a new strategic arms treaty. The attempt failed, as did its successor treaty in the Carter administration. Indeed the time *had* come for a fresh approach. Nuclear strategy had gone off into flights of fancy about fighting and winning a protracted nuclear war.

Reagan, a nuclear abolitionist, provided that new approach. He declared that a nuclear war could not be won and must never be fought. He reached an agreement with the Soviet Union to abolish a whole class of nuclear armed ballistic missiles. He started the first negotiations—START I—to reduce and eliminate nuclear weapons systems. It was well on the way to completion when Reagan left office. Together, Reagan and Gorbachev began to dismantle the Cold War.

George H. W. Bush built a remarkable record in regulating nuclear weapons with the newly independent states after the collapse of the Soviet Union. He initiated a set of reciprocal actions with the last president of the Soviet Union which removed tactical nuclear weapons from potentially vulnerable forward deployments as the Soviet Union collapsed. He completed the START I treaty, and added to it the Lisbon Protocol, which brought Ukraine, Kazakhstan, and Belarus into the treaty's obligations as non-nuclear-weapon states, and ultimately as members of the nonproliferation treaty. He negotiated a START II treaty with the first president of the Russian Federation, Boris Yeltsin, that would have eliminated land-based MIRVed missiles. Bush also launched the executive branch's implementation of the Nunn-Lugar cooperative threat reduction program in 1992.

Clinton advanced the Nunn-Lugar program, building on concepts that the Senate and the first Bush administration had provided. Cooperative threat reduction, in the Clinton administration, helped Russia to implement its START I obligations on schedule. It was a key factor in denuclearizing Ukraine, Kazakhstan, and Belarus. Clinton succeeded in signing a comprehensive nuclear test ban treaty in 1996, a goal that had eluded every president since Eisenhower. The Senate refused to give its consent to ratification. His administration negotiated the Agreed Framework with North Korea that prevented a buildup of nuclear weapons by North Korea. It signaled the beginning of a more regional approach to nuclear weapons issues.

In the presidency of George W. Bush, more emphasis was placed on military force and unilateral actions to deal with nuclear threats, now seen as emanating from rogue states aligned with terrorists. Agreements with Russia were seen as unnecessary because Russia and the United States were now friends. The administration's policy was to dissuade nuclear proliferation through unchallengeable military might, to prevent it through anticipatory military actions, and answer it through defensive systems. But in the second term, this was modified to place more emphasis on diplomacy, focusing on states, like North Korea and Iran, that were close to or had already achieved a capacity for making nuclear weapons.

There is reason for considerable pride in what American diplomacy accomplished in the first sixty years of the nuclear era: nuclear weapons were never used in anger after 1945. And much can be learned, even now, from a study of the prudential statecraft that nuclear weapons imposed on political leaders during the Cold War. There was little margin for error during those times. Disregarding the rules of the game developed during the Cold War, even though some are no longer operationally relevant, would be dangerous. The tradition of nonuse of nuclear weapons is the prime example.

After each great historic turning point in world affairs, mistakes have planted the seeds of future catastrophe. This can happen again. Many of the issues the United States will face as it confronts the challenge of nuclear weapons in the twenty-first century involve the basic terms on which the nation chooses to be involved in the world. Does it see itself as part of a community of nations or as essentially alone—free of foreign entanglements and their obligations? The United States in the early twenty-first century has become so powerful that it is in a position to act with few constraints, except those imposed by the American people.

Will the United States accommodate itself to the conventions, rules, and norms of the international community, with all the constraints that entails, or will it act as though its interests and needs require freedom to accomplish its purposes—even if this results, as it has, in declining support for the United States abroad? Only a judicious balance between the ideas represented by the two poles of independence and interdependence provides the basis for sound U.S. policy. Indeed, the genius of American diplomacy in the period following World War II and until very recently was that it struck this balance in a way that made other nations want to be on America's side. This was as true in the effort to control the atomic bomb as in other areas.

President Ronald Reagan and Secretary of State George Shultz were largely responsible, with Mikhail Gorbachev, for ending the Cold War. They did a great deal to make the world a safer place, including giant steps toward ending the nuclear arms race of the Cold War. I met with President Reagan and Secretary Shultz in the Oval Office several times. On one occasion President Reagan turned to me with a steely look and said: "You tell people that I'm willing to go as far as anyone else in getting rid of nuclear weapons." Reagan showed me that tough-minded people who put America's interests first also can take the view that nuclear weapons in anybody's hands are a dangerous liability for the United States, and for others. America's leaders have lost this perspective in the last few years. The country is less safe because of it.

Index

ABM Treaty (1972): Belarus, 170;
Bush, George W., withdrawal from,
170, 174, 180–86; Democratic Party
and, 78; Kazakhstan, 170; Nixon,
Richard M., achievement of, 86,
93–94, 132, 207; Putin, Vladimir,
and, 181–87; Republican Party and,
79; Reykjavik meeting, issue at,
142–48; Rice, Condoleezza,
opposition to, 181, 183, 185; Russia,
170; Ukraine, 170. *See also* ballistic
missile defense
Acheson, Dean, 14, 50
AEC. *See* United States Atomic Energy
Commission
Afghanistan, xii, 114, 123, 182
Albright, Madeleine, 173, 176, 202
Andropov, Yuri, 134, 139–40, 141
antiballistic missile treaty of 1972. *See*
ABM Treaty (1972)
atomic energy: international control of,
8, 14, 206

Baker, James, 156, 158, 159, 162
ballistic missile defense: Bush, George

H. W., and, 79, 160–61; Bush,
George W., support for, 79, 179, 180,
185, 186, 187–88, 190; Chinese
nuclear threat, response to, 79–80,
89, 91, 186; Clinton, Bill, and, 79,
153, 174, 176; Congress and, 34, 77,
78, 79, 82, 90, 91, 93, 150;
Eisenhower, Dwight, resistance to,
34, 77; feasibility of, 48, 149, 174;
Global Protection against Limited
Strikes (GPALS), 160–61;
Gorbachev, Mikhail, 146, 147;
Johnson, Lyndon, views of, 19, 75,
77, 78–79, 80, 89, 90, 115, 150;
Joint Chiefs of Staff, 77, 78, 140;
Kennedy, John F., and, 48–49, 77;
McNamara, Robert, and, 48, 77, 78,
79, 80, 89, 90, 92; MIRVs as
response to, 74–75; Nixon, Richard
M., views on, 89–90, 91, 92, 93;
public opinion and, 90; Reagan,
Ronald, support for, 140, 141, 143;
Russia, 176; Sentinel system, 80, 89;
Soviet Union, 48, 75, 76, 77, 89, 93,
94; Strategic Defense Initiative (Star

About the Author

Ambassador James E. Goodby is a nonresident senior fellow at the Brookings Institution and a research affiliate at the Massachusetts Institute of Technology. He has held several senior government positions dedicated to arms control and nonproliferation, including deputy to the special adviser to the president and secretary of state on the Comprehensive Test Ban Treaty (CTBT), 2000–2001; special representative of President Clinton for the security and dismantlement of nuclear weapons, 1995–1996; chief negotiator for nuclear threat reduction agreements, 1993–1994, and vice chair of the U.S. delegation to the Strategic Arms Reduction Treaty talks, 1982–1983. He served as U.S. ambassador to Finland in 1980–1981.